IT Certification Success

Third Edition

Ed Tittel

D1472510

IT Certification Success Exam Cram, Third Edition

Limits of Liability and Disclaimer of Warranty

The author and publisher of this book have used their best efforts in preparing the book and the programs contained in it. These efforts include the development, research, and testing of the theories and programs to determine their effectiveness. The author and publisher make no warranty of any kind, expressed or implied, with regard to these programs or the documentation contained in this book.

The author and publisher shall not be liable in the event of incidental or consequential damages in connection with, or arising out of, the furnishing, performance, or use of the programs, associated instructions, and/or claims of productivity gains.

Trademarks

Trademarked names appear throughout this book. Rather than list the names and entities that own the trademarks or insert a trademark symbol with each mention of the trademarked name, the publisher states that it is using the names for editorial purposes only and to the benefit of the trademark owner, with no intention of infringing upon that trademark.

The Coriolis Group, LLC
14455 N. Hayden Road
Suite 220
Scottsdale, Arizona 85260

(480)483-0192
FAX (480)483-0193
www.coriolis.com

Library of Congress Cataloging-in-Publication Data
Tittel, Ed
  IT certification success exam cram /by Ed Tittel.--3rd ed.
    p. cm.
  Includes index.
  ISBN 1-57610-792-2
  1. Electronic data processing personnel--Certification. 2. Application software--Examinations--Study guides. I. Title.
QA76.3.T573655 2000
004--dc21   00-055461
                                          CIP

President and CEO
Keith Weiskamp

Publisher
Steve Sayre

Acquisitions Editor
Shari Jo Hehr

Marketing Specialist
Cynthia Caldwell

Project Editor
Hilary Long

Technical Reviewer
Shawn McNutt

Production Coordinator
Wendy Littley

Cover Designer
Jesse Dunn

Layout Designer
April Nielsen

Printed in the United States of America
10 9 8 7 6 5 4

The Coriolis Group, LLC • 14455 North Hayden Road, Suite 220 • Scottsdale, Arizona 85260

ExamCram.com *Connects You to the Ultimate Study Center!*

Our goal has always been to provide you with the best study tools on the planet to help you achieve your certification in record time. Time is so valuable these days that none of us can afford to waste a second of it, especially when it comes to exam preparation.

Over the past few years, we've created an extensive line of *Exam Cram* and *Exam Prep* study guides, practice exams, audio training, and interactive training. To help you study even better, we have now created an e-learning and certification destination called **ExamCram.com**. (You can access the site at **www.examcram.com**.) Now, with every study product you purchase from us, you'll be connected to a large community of people like yourself who are actively studying for their certifications, developing their careers, seeking advice, and sharing their insights and stories.

I believe that the future is all about collaborative learning. Our **ExamCram.com** destination is our approach to creating a highly interactive, easily accessible collaborative environment, where you can take practice exams and discuss your experiences with others, sign up for features like "Questions of the Day," plan your certifications using our interactive planners, create your own personal study pages, and keep up with all of the latest study tips and techniques.

I hope that whatever study products you purchase from us—*Exam Cram* or *Exam Prep* study guides, *Practice Tests, Flash Cards, Personal Trainers,* or one of our interactive Web courses—will make your studying fun and productive. Our commitment is to build the kind of learning tools that will allow you to study the way you want to, whenever you want to.

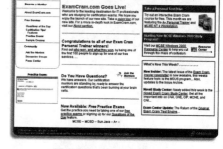

Visit ExamCram.com now to enhance your study program.

Help us continue to provide the very best certification study materials possible. Write us or email us at **learn@examcram.com** and let us know how our study products have helped you study. Tell us about new features that you'd like us to add. Send us a story about how we've helped you. We're listening!

Good luck with your certification exam and your career. Thank you for allowing us to help you achieve your goals.

Keith Weiskamp
President and CEO

Look for this other product from The Coriolis Group:

IT Career Guide Exam Cram
by Drew Bird and Mike Harwood

About the Author

Ed Tittel is the originator of the Exam Cram series concept for Certification Insider Press. He has contributed to over 30 titles in that series and to over 100 computer-related books in general.

Ed also teaches for NetWorld+Interop and at The Internet Security Conference (TISC), where he specializes in network operating systems, plus Internet technologies and security. In a past life, Ed worked for Novell, Inc., where his last job was Director of Technical Marketing. In that position, Ed oversaw technical content for trade shows and for the BrainShare developer's conference, prior to his departure in 1994.

In his spare time, Ed is an enthusiastic pool player, if not an overly expert one. He also likes to cook—especially homemade stock and all the good things that come from it. Ed and his trusty Labrador retriever, Blackie, make their home in Austin, Texas. You can reach Ed via email at **edtittel@examcram.com**.

Acknowledgments

To my good friend and colleague, Kurt L. Hudson, thanks for planting the seed that sprouted *Exam Cram*. I hope you're as happy with the results as I am! Your offhand remarks and initial steps down this path gave me the inspiration to create this series.

To the LANWrights gang—Dawn Rader, James Michael Stewart, Bill Brogden, Mary Burmeister, Chelsea Valentine, and Kim Lindros—thanks for helping me build such a valuable and successful organization. Special thanks to Louise Leahy and Kim Lindros for their work on this book.

To Keith Weiskamp, Shari Jo Hehr, Paula Kmetz, Cynthia Caldwell, and the rest of the Coriolis crowd, thanks for your invaluable help in turning *Exam Cram* into a raging monster. Thanks for believing in us, and for giving us a voice in the way things turned out. I appreciate your many efforts, ideas, programs, and your ability to deliver a quality product to the marketplace. Thanks also to Carole McClendon, and the rest of the folks at Waterside Productions, for their role in keeping everything on track. You guys are the greatest!

Finally, thanks to my family—especially my Mom and Dad, and my sister, Kat—for your insight and support over the years. You've always been there for me when I needed you!

To my friends, especially Robert Wiggins, and others too numerous to mention, thanks for letting me vent about work when that's what the doctor ordered and for reminding me that there's more to life than work when I needed a break. You people helped to keep me sane—or as sane as I get, anyway...

To my readers, thanks for all your feedback—good, bad, and indifferent. Thanks also for voting for our work and ideas with your hard-earned money. I can only hope you continue to find value in what we do from here on out!

—*Ed Tittel*
Austin, TX
May 2000

Table of Contents

. . . .

Introduction

Welcome to the third edition of *IT Certification Success Exam Cram!* This book is aimed squarely at people who are curious about the proliferation of computer-oriented vendor and industry certifications that keep popping up in today's marketplace. If you're intrigued by the occasional bits of alphabet soup you see in the magazines or in the classified ads for "Engineering/Technical" jobs, you've come to the right place.

By the time you're through with this book, you'll know the difference between an MCSE and a CCIE. In fact, you should even be able to understand what it takes to start stringing some of these letters behind your own name. You'll also get a pretty good idea about how much work and expense is involved in obtaining a certification and what steps you need to take to obtain one (or more) of these credentials.

In short, this book is intended to explain some of the most popular, if not most important, computer certifications that are available. Along the way, you should also get a pretty clear picture of what's involved in obtaining such certifications and how well these certifications might match your computing and professional proclivities and interests.

The Certification Game

Although the details vary widely from program to program, all certification programs have certain elements in common. Such common elements are covered in Chapter 1. The rest of this book takes these common elements and explains how certification programs sponsored by leading technology organizations fit this model.

Most certification programs covered in this book, in keeping with the current state of the computing industry, are vendor sponsored. In other words, companies such as Microsoft, Novell, Oracle, Cisco, and Sun create complex products or technologies. To make sure that they can sell these products or technologies to their customers, among other things, they must be able to guarantee a supply of knowledgeable, competent individuals who can use their stuff to get things done. In the simplest of terms, this explains why certification is important to vendors in particular—that's because it's an important part of the overall delivery system that's necessary to deliver complex products and technologies to the marketplace.

Some certification programs—such as the Computing Technology Industry Association's (CompTIA's) A+, Network+, i-Net+, and other credentials—are created by groups of industry players for everyone's benefit. These types of certifications are usually called *vendor neutral* to indicate that they stress general knowledge as opposed to detailed knowledge of some particular vendor's proprietary products or technologies.

Given that certification is good for vendors and employers alike, you might ask, "What's in it for me?" Answering this question requires separating hype from reality. Many vendors will tell you that their certifications are the keys to career success, if not liberty and the pursuit of happiness. Employers like certification credentials because they define measurable steps up job ladders and because certifications make it easy for them to separate motivated, trained employees or job applicants from others.

However, the marketplace decides what a certification is really worth. If you don't see the initials for some certification program anywhere in the classifieds or if you've never even heard of a program, that might mean that it's not a very valuable credential. On the other hand, some of these seemingly innocuous strings of letters can be a ticket to a distinct improvement in your financial circumstances. However, certification is neither cheap, easy, nor free. This book should help you understand the details of the specific programs I cover, examine and evaluate other certification programs, and decide which ones are worthwhile—and which ones to ignore.

Interesting Certification Stats

Today, technical training and certification is an industry niche of its own. Like other such niches, it has its share of focused publications, including magazines such as *Certification, Professional Certification, Inside Technology Training, Microsoft Certified Professional Magazine, The NetWare Connection*, and numerous others. Industry analysts—such as the Gartner Group, IDC, and the Meta Group, among others—employ analysts to track this market niche, just as they track other such niches to look for trends, seek out revenue opportunities, and advise companies whether they should jump onto the training and certification bandwagon.

Based on reporting from these various sources, the answer to the question "Is training and certification a worthwhile business activity?" appears to be a resounding "Yes!" Without trying to edit or analyze some of the reporting I uncovered when researching this topic, here are some keen statistics about certification programs that you might find surprising:

➤ The total population of individuals in the United States today with computer certifications numbers about 4.5 million. By the year 2002, that number is expected to double. By the year 2010, that number is expected to jump to over 20 million. These are the kinds of numbers that not only attract interest but also spur serious investment.

➤ Many large companies—such as Microsoft, Novell, Oracle, Cisco, and others—make serious money from their training and certification programs. For larger companies, I'm talking hundreds of millions of dollars a year; for smaller companies, tens of millions of dollars annually—not enough to dominate the bottom line, but more than enough to constitute a worthwhile investment.

➤ Reports about the value of certification—especially those from vendors (and if you poke around the vendor Web sites I mention in this book, you can find plenty of these for yourself)—stress ROI (return on investment) for certified employees. In English, this means that they're more productive, fix problems faster, and don't need to wait on hold as often for technical support because they can fix problems for themselves.

➤ For individuals, certification can mean increases in pay or better jobs elsewhere. Vendor Web sites for certification programs invariably include profiles of certification overachievers, called "Success Stories." While it's wise to take some of these claims (and dollar figures) with a grain of salt, there's no denying that certification can boost your bottom line, too. Most salary surveys show that certified technical staff earn at least 15 to 20 percent more than their uncertified counterparts. The only caveat I'd add to this observation is that certification may get you in the door, but it's what you know that keeps you on the job. Be sure to learn how to use what you know, or you won't be able to stay on the job very long—this means that you must obtain hands-on experience, which takes extra time and effort.

I could go on with amazing and wonderful statistics for quite some time, but hopefully you get the idea: Certification is a growing market and creates plenty of opportunities for both certifiers and certificants. The devil is in the details, though, and that's what this book is supposed to help you with. So please, read on!

About This Book

This book consists of 13 chapters, followed by an appendix on job prospecting and capped with a glossary. Chapter 1 covers certification programs in a bit more detail and gives an overview of the numerous specific organizations I cover in Chapters 2 through 11. Starting with Microsoft's various and sundry certifications, the order of coverage proceeds to explore Novell's programs; followed by Oracle's, then Cisco's, then CompTIA's, and then Sun's Java certification programs; the Chauncey Group's certifications; ProsoftTraining.com's programs; Linux certifications; and a grab bag of various certification programs that you might find interesting but that aren't covered in detail elsewhere in this book. This takes you up through Chapter 11.

Chapter 12 provides a skills and experience assessment that you can use to figure out where you belong in the certification game, and Chapter 13 covers resources and techniques that have proven helpful for individuals preparing for one or more IT certifications. The glossary contains definitions of the terms you'll find throughout this book. There's also a companion Web site at **www.examcram.com/studyresource/** where you can create your own personal study page, take practice exams using an extensive database of test questions and analyses, sign up for daily questions and answers, read exam alerts, or send your questions to a team of Exam Cram Mentors. Spend some time exploring this resource. I think you will find it to be extremely valuable.

Each chapter in this book follows a regular structure and offers graphical cues about especially important or useful material. In fact, it's modeled on Certification Insider Press's popular *Exam Cram* series, which helps individuals prepare for most, if not all, of the certification exams mentioned in this book. Here's the structure—which I follow religiously—of a typical chapter:

➤ *Opening hot lists*—Each chapter begins with lists of the terms, tools, and techniques that you must learn and understand before you can be fully conversant with the chapter's subject matter. I follow the hot lists with one or two introductory paragraphs to set the stage for the rest of the chapter. Here, you'll find a brief description of the certification program you're about to dive into to help you get oriented.

➤ *Topical coverage*—After the opening hot lists, each chapter covers the various certification programs and exams for that chapter's focus. This includes an overview of the programs, including the number of tests, their costs, how much time you're allotted to take them, and so on. Then it covers each program individually. This includes overviews of the topics that are likely to appear in the qualifying exams and comments on the format and contents of these exams.

➤ *Visual elements*—Within each chapter, I use visuals to highlight particularly important or useful information about certification programs and exams. For example, the Exam Alert icon flags items of information that are particularly germane to the test-taking experience:

 This is what an Exam Alert looks like. In a regular *Exam Cram*, an Exam Alert stresses concepts, terms, software, or activities that are likely to appear in one or more certification test questions. In this book, however, they flag items that are particularly important to note or act on that relate to one or more certification tests.

➤ On the other hand, the Tip icon helps flag useful or helpful information that may or may not be test related but that certainly is worth noting because it can save you time, money, or effort:

 This is what a Tip looks like. In a regular *Exam Cram*, a Tip points out a shortcut, a time-saving technique, or some other fact that will save you time or effort. In this book, the Tip flags information that might help make your certification experience cheaper, faster, or easier.

➤ Even if material isn't flagged as an Exam Alert or a Tip, all the contents of this book are associated, at least tangentially, to something certification related. This book is lean to focus only on the essential elements of these certification programs; you'll find that what appears in the meat of each chapter is critical knowledge.

➤ *Details and resources*—Every chapter ends with a section titled "Need to Know More?" This section provides direct pointers to each vendor's or organization's certification program data, and also to third-party resources that offer further details on the certification program or programs covered in a chapter. Also, this section tries to rate the quality and thoroughness of a topic's coverage by each resource. If you find a resource you like in this collection, use it, but don't feel compelled to use them all. On the other hand, I recommend only resources I use regularly, so none of my recommendations should waste your time or money.

How to Use This Book

If you're interested in certification in general but don't have a specific area of technical expertise or experience, you might want to read this book from cover to cover. Some of the material that I present, to do proper justice to the certification programs I cover, gets pretty technical.

If you find yourself mystified by the terminology or concepts that I use to describe a certification program, chances are that you'll find the technical material necessary to obtain that certification downright opaque. For that reason, feel free to skip any material that doesn't make sense. However, if you really want to get to the bottom of anything, you can always visit the vendor's or organization's Web site to look for basic tutorials or to find information about introductory classes for a particular technology, product, or subject area. If you really want to learn any of this stuff, you can do it!

Given all the book's elements and its specialized focus, I've tried to create a tool to help you review the various certification programs I cover and to perform meaningful comparisons between these programs (that's one reason why I've tried to make each chapter as consistent with the others as possible). I hope that you can use it to help satisfy your curiosity about these programs and to guide your progress into one or more of these certification areas.

Still, I know that I can't please everyone, nor can I represent all this information completely or perfectly in a single work. Therefore, please share your feedback on the book with me, especially if you have ideas about how I can improve it for future readers. I'll consider everything you say carefully, and I'll respond to all suggestions. You can reach me via email at **ed.tittel@examcram.com**. Remember to include the title of this book in your message; otherwise, I'll be forced to guess which book you're making a suggestion about. It's also a good idea to list a page number that relates to your questions or comments. I don't like to guess—I want to *know* what you're thinking!

You should also visit Certification Insider's Web site at **www.examcram.com/ insider/**.

Thanks, and enjoy the book!

Certification Programs

Terms you'll need to understand:

✓ Microsoft Certifications (MCP, MCP+I, MCP+SB, MCDBA, MCSE+I, MCSD, MCT, MOUS)

✓ Novell Certifications (CNA, CNE, MCNE, CNI, CDE)

✓ Oracle Certifications (OCP)

✓ Cisco Career Certifications (CCNA, CCNP, CCIE, CCDA, CCDP)

✓ CompTIA Certifications (A+, Network+, i-Net+)

✓ Sun Java Certifications

✓ Chauncey Group Certifications (ATS, CTT)

✓ Prosofttraining.com Certifications (CIW)

✓ Red Hat Certifications (RHCE, RHCX)

✓ LPI Certifications (LPIC)

✓ Sair Linux and GNU Certifications (LCP, LCA, LCE, MLCE)

Techniques you'll need to master:

✓ Identifying certification programs

✓ Locating certification training information online and offline

✓ Deciding which certification programs meet your needs and those of your organization (or customer base)

Once you begin to pay attention to training and certification programs, you'll probably be amazed by the number of offerings available. You may even be a bit overwhelmed by the variety of programs to choose from, not to mention the many flavors of certification available. The key to success lies in selecting a certification credential that meets your career needs and matches your interests and abilities while also meeting the needs of current or prospective employers. In this chapter, you'll learn about the general characteristics of certification programs and about some of the players, both large and small, who are involved in this game.

General Program Characteristics

Although the details for each individual certification program differ, all of them incorporate numerous common elements. In fact, these programs usually include most, if not all, of the following characteristics:

➤ Identifies individuals who have demonstrated their knowledge and understanding of a particular technology or product.

➤ Defines a particular course of study, which may include supplementary materials. Such study materials can include classroom training, self-study materials, courseware, computer-based study materials, Web-based training, and privately published or trade books. Eventually, such a course of study leads to a series of one or more tests aimed at examining an individual's knowledge of the subject matter. Most such tests are computer based and are widely available through nationwide (and global) testing centers.

➤ Certifies those who pass a prescribed test or series of tests for as long as the certification period lasts. When new products or technologies replace old ones, currently certified individuals must often recertify to keep their certifications current. Otherwise, such certifications lapse and become worthless.

➤ Offers tests in a monitored environment, for a fee, to would-be certificants. Each time an individual takes a certification test (whether he or she passes or fails), the test-taker must pay that fee. Some programs also limit the number of tries at a test within a given time period, but all such programs permit individuals to retake tests as many times as necessary to pass.

➤ Each vendor or organization maintains the individual's certification status so it can be verified by current or potential employers.

Note: Some certifications are offered from software companies such as Novell and Microsoft, whereas others are offered from industry organizations such as the Computing Technology Industry Association (CompTIA). Therefore, I've differentiated between the two by using the word "vendor" when discussing certification programs offered from companies and "organization" when discussing those offerings from vendor-neutral organizations.

Certified experts are available to help install, service, support, and maintain whatever technologies or products fall within the scope of their certifications. This is important not only for vendors and industry organizations because of the impact it has on their customers, but also for those individuals who become certified. Access to a pool of certified experts adds to the credibility and usability of the products or technologies that these vendors and organizations support and also adds to the technical competence of those who obtain certification. It's a win-win game and a calculated way to maintain customer loyalty in all kinds of interesting ways, as you'll discover later in this chapter.

In addition to the common characteristics, there is another set of characteristics common to many certification programs:

➤ Certified individuals are granted the right to represent themselves as a "Certified _____," complete with camera-ready logo art for business cards, ad copy, and so on. As a result, such individuals can leverage the strength of their certification as a type of brand name.

➤ Certified individuals often are given special access to the vendor's or organization's technical support team. This includes discounts and information not made available to the general public.

➤ Certified individuals often qualify to receive evaluation copies of software products, participate in beta or early software release programs, and obtain access to password-protected Web sites, special mailing lists, and other sources of valuable "inside information."

 These perks add not just cachet to a certification, but also access to restricted or sensitive information, which can be of great value to individuals and the companies that employ them.

➤ Certified individuals who act as consultants may receive customer referrals from a certifying vendor or organization. In most cases, mailing lists and Web sites for certified individuals create well-informed groups of specialists.

➤ Certified individuals are often polled and surveyed to learn more about what they perceive and want, be it from products and services or from the certification programs themselves. This provides vendors with valuable information about their services and products from an educated user community. Also, certified individuals are often asked to participate in designing new elements for the certified curriculum and to contribute questions to certification tests, which ultimately introduce new elements into a certification program.

The net result of certification programs is to create individuals who not only identify with the technologies or products around which their certification is based, but who also wear their credentials with a certain amount of pride. In most certification programs, there's a considerable sense of community and of special status. After all, considerable time, expense, and effort are usually involved in obtaining a certification, and such certifications often increase the marketable value of those who obtain them.

In fact, certification is generally regarded as a valuable program for vendors and organizations, as an important credential for individuals to add to their resumes, and as an important checkbox for employers to add to their list of requirements for current and prospective employees. In the sections that follow, you'll learn more about what's at stake—and of value—for each of these separate constituencies and why certification is an area where so many interests can converge so successfully.

Why Vendors Like Certification Programs

Although what you're about to read applies to organizations nearly as much as it does to vendors, certification programs can be particularly appealing to vendors beyond the value that access to a pool of certified experts can provide. In fact, a survey conducted by IDC (International Data Corporation) indicated that nine of the top 10 software vendors offer some type of certification program. Many of these vendors certify instructors to teach their curricula and also offer some type of sales certification program whereby resellers, distributors, and other elements of the sales channel can also demonstrate their knowledge and understanding of products, sales programs, and so on.

Certification can be a powerful weapon in any vendor's arsenal. Here's why:

➤ Vendors make money at all stages of a certification program: Many maintain their own training operations and charge authorized training centers to use their materials. They also offer official approval for third-party training materials, study guides, and so on and charge for the seal that usually accompanies their blessing. They receive revenue from the testing centers that administer the tests. For large companies, such as Novell and Microsoft, training and certification is a business that generates hundreds of millions of dollars annually.

➤ Vendors maintain databases of all of their certified professionals and, therefore, automatically gain access to detailed demographic and employment information about the cream of the technical-professional crop. The value of these databases as sales and analysis tools is impossible to estimate.

➤ Those individuals who have shouldered the cost and effort involved in becoming certified are far more likely to want to maintain their certifications. This creates a captive audience of core business for future training and certification programs. Likewise, companies that fund employee certifications not only seek to maintain current certifications for those employees, but also often go to extraordinary lengths to retain them.

For vendors, certification adds up nicely: In addition to the money it generates, certification databases provide detailed information about key customers and guarantee the presence of "product champions" within those companies that employ certified professionals. I've observed three primary classes of vendors for whom certification is particularly useful or effective:

➤ Those who lead the market and wish to remain in that position

➤ Those who seek to capture a market and establish market dominance

➤ Those who seek to compete with market leaders on equal terms and are willing to bear the costs

Most vendors of any size in the high-tech marketplace fall into one of these categories, so the prevalence of certification programs should come as no surprise.

Why Individuals Like Certification Programs

In any profession, especially in high-tech organizations, good employees always seek to establish a professional advantage to elevate their status among their colleagues and peers. For technical employees, certifications have proven to be an effective tool in this effort. Certified employees tend to make more than their uncertified colleagues in similar job categories by anywhere from 10 to 25 percent.

However, there's more to certification than just money. In a marketplace full of mergers and acquisitions, restructurings and layoffs can produce sudden employment shifts that require a special edge to merit consideration in both new and current positions. Many high-tech types have jumped on the certification bandwagon as a way to help them maintain ongoing employment, despite the constant change of employment in any one organization. They definitely feel that certification makes it easier to find another job, no matter what circumstances may propel them into a job search.

Finally, for motivated high-tech workers, there's a sense that obtaining a professional certification involves overcoming a challenge or obtaining a badge of accomplishment. Certainly, there are plenty of individuals who are certified across many programs, and some overachievers no sooner finish one such program than they begin another.

Why Employers Like Certification Programs

Employers face the need for an increasingly diverse and complex array of skills in their employees, particularly in the areas of information technology (IT). Anything that can simplify their search for the right type of expertise—or that can help them bring existing employees up to the right level—is welcome.

That's why many companies require employees in key positions—such as network or system administrators, PC technicians, or database administrators—to obtain and maintain certifications from the vendors and industry groups in which the organizations make an investment. For some companies, the availability of training (if not certification) is a necessary precondition for purchasing a product or technology. "No certification, no sale" epitomizes the attitude in some boardrooms, in fact.

The Certification Programs

Now that you've explored the common ingredients for most certification programs and the benefits for all parties involved, it's time to introduce some key players in the game. In the sections that follow, you'll have a chance to read about some of the most profitable, best-run, and most highly regarded certification programs in the IT business.

Please note that not all technical professional certifications are covered in this book. For information about additional technical certifications, go to your favorite Internet search engine and search for keywords such as "certification," "training," and "exam." In addition, the best source of information on any certification is generally its sponsoring vendor or organization, so always check there first. Finally, I provide brief descriptions and pointers to additional certifications in Chapter 11.

Microsoft Certification Programs

Today, Microsoft's certification programs encompass the largest number of certificants and an extremely broad range of offerings. Also, as the "800-pound gorilla" of the software marketplace, Microsoft's programs generate the greatest interest and activity. As you'd expect from a company like Microsoft, it offers a dizzying array of certifications whose requirements range from completing a single test to passing as many as nine tests.

Today, Microsoft claims over 880,000 certified professionals across its many designations, a population that is unsurpassed by any other vendor's claims. You'll learn more about the details of Microsoft's certification programs in Chapter 2, but here's an overview of the nine different flavors of certification programs that are in store for you from the Microsoft camp:

➤ *Microsoft Office User Specialist (MOUS)*—This program is at the bottom of the hierarchy. It certifies individuals who are proficient with Word, Excel, PowerPoint, and Access, usually for workers in an office environment. It is possible to certify as proficient or an expert in any one of these applications, and an additional "master exam" on integrating multiple Office applications is also available.

➤ *Microsoft Certified Professional (MCP)*—Passing almost any of the over 60 exams available in this program (except Networking Essentials, exam 70-058, or any Office-related exam) qualifies an individual as an MCP. MCP status is a stepping-stone to the much-vaunted Microsoft Certified Systems Engineer (MCSE) credential, which requires passing six or seven tests.

➤ *MCP + Site Building (MCP+SB)*—This program aims to certify individuals who can design, build, and maintain corporate Web sites. It requires that an individual first become an MCP, then pass any two from a pool of three tests on FrontPage; Site Server 3.0, Commerce Edition; or Visual InterDev.

➤ *MCP + Internet (MCP+I)*—This program aims to certify individuals who can build and maintain an Internet presence using Microsoft Windows NT and related products. It requires passing tests on TCP/IP, Windows NT Server 4.0, and Internet Information Server.

➤ *Microsoft Certified Database Administrator (MCDBA)*—This program aims to certify those responsible for logical and physical design, implementation, maintenance, and administration of SQL Server databases. To obtain this certification, you must pass four or five required exams, depending on whether you certify in the Windows 2000 or Windows NT 4 track, respectively, plus one elective exam. The elective is from a range of four possible protocol, database, or implementation topics.

➤ *Microsoft Certified Systems Engineer (MCSE)*—This program aims to certify systems engineers who can support networks built around Microsoft products, most notably Windows NT and Windows 2000. This program requires individuals to pass six or seven tests. Of the four required exams for the Windows NT MCSE, one covers a desktop operating system, two are on Windows NT Server 4, and the last is on Networking Essentials. The remaining exams draw from a large pool of electives. The exams for a Windows 2000 MCSE are similar but include an extra exam on Directory Services.

➤ *MCSE + Internet (MCSE+I)*—This program aims to certify systems engineers who specialize in supporting networked environments that include an

Internet presence of some type. To obtain the MCSE+I, candidates must pass nine tests. Seven of these tests are required exams, including the core four required for the Windows NT 4 MCSE plus three additional Internet-focused required exams. Two electives, which may be drawn from a fairly limited pool, are also necessary.

➤ *Microsoft Certified Solution Developer (MCSD)*—This program aims to certify individuals who can develop custom applications for use on Microsoft networks. It requires passing four exams, including a basic Microsoft architecture exam, plus exams on desktop and distributed applications for the same programming language and a single elective drawn from a large pool of exams.

➤ *Microsoft Certified Trainer (MCT)*—MCTs are certified instructors who are authorized to deliver Microsoft Official Curriculum (MOC) elements (courses) at Microsoft-authorized training outlets of many kinds. Obtaining this certification means that instructors must meet specific instructional requirements and that they must pass the certification exams related to the courses they wish to teach. Meeting the instructional requirements means taking a Microsoft-authorized "train-the-trainer class" that includes an evaluation of a candidate's teaching skills or that the individual obtain a Certified Technical Trainer certification from the Chauncey Group (covered in Chapter 8).

Microsoft's exams are richly supported, both with official tools (built by or approved by Microsoft)—which include classroom training, self-study kits, computer-based training, online classes, and books—and through a broad range of unofficial tools that cover the same kinds of materials. Current industry trends indicate that Microsoft certifications are among the most sought after of all IT certifications; given the company's ubiquitous IT presence and its marketing muscle, this shouldn't surprise anyone.

Novell Certification Programs

Although Microsoft may be the "800-pound gorilla" of the certification market, Novell has been at this game longer than just about anybody else and boasts a large population of certified professionals (500,000 plus). Novell also boasts the largest installed base of any network operating system vendor.

Following the release of a new version of its flagship product, NetWare 5 (version 5.1 is now available), Novell's certified population must recertify soon (some exams expire as soon as August 31, 2000) to maintain current certification. This suggests an active and vigorous training and testing marketplace, and indeed most Novell-certified professionals appear to be vigorously pursuing recertification at the same time that a new generation of professionals is beginning its pursuit of certification around NetWare 5.1.

Novell currently recognizes five levels of professional certification, with various areas of specialization, plus a separate Internet certification:

➤ *Certified Novell Administrator (CNA)*—This credential is Novell's entry-level certification. Obtaining a CNA requires passing any one of five tests that cover basic administration for three versions of NetWare (5, 4/intraNetWare, or 3) or two versions of GroupWise (5 or 4).

➤ *Certified Novell Engineer (CNE)*—The most sought-after Novell certification is the CNE. CNEs specialize in a particular version of NetWare or GroupWise and must pass a battery of six or seven tests (depending on which certification the individual is seeking) to qualify, including five or six required courses and one elective course. The individual must take the Networking Technologies and Service and Support tests. The remaining required exams for the NetWare CNE certification are as follows:

➤ *NetWare X Administration*—A basic administration exam aimed at the version of NetWare for which the individual seeks certification.

➤ *NetWare X Advanced Administration*—An advanced administration exam aimed at the version of NetWare for which the individual seeks certification.

➤ *NDS Administration*—An exam on NetWare Directory Services (NDS) aimed at the version of NetWare for which the individual seeks certification.

➤ *NetWare X Installation Design and Configuration (for NetWare 3 and 4 certification only)*—An installation and configuration exam aimed at the version of NetWare (3 or 4) for which the individual seeks certification.

In addition to the Networking Technologies and Service and Support tests, additional exams are required for the GroupWise certification, which are selected from the following:

➤ *intraNetWare: NetWare 4.11 Administration*—An administration exam aimed at NetWare 4.11/intraNetWare.

➤ *GroupWise X Administration*—An administration exam aimed at the version of GroupWise for which the individual seeks certification.

➤ *GroupWise X Advanced Administration*—An advanced administration exam aimed at the version of GroupWise for which the individual seeks certification.

➤ *GroupWise Net Access and Connectivity (for GroupWise 5 certification)*—An exam on GroupWise gateways and agents; user access methods, protocols, and services; Internet access and gateways; installation; configuration; and management.

> ➤ *GroupWise 4 Async Gateway and GroupWise Remote (for GroupWise 4 certification)*—A test on principles of the GroupWise 4 dial-up gateway and use of GroupWise 4 remote access capabilities, including planning, design, installation, configuration, and management.

The electives cover topics that range from GroupWise administration to securing intranets using Novell's BorderManager product. Passing any one of these, in addition to the required exams, is what it takes to become a CNE.

➤ *Master CNE (MCNE)*—This is Novell's most elite certification. It designates recipients as specialists in one of seven areas of expertise. Requirements vary from specialty to specialty, but involve anywhere from four to six tests beyond CNE requirements.

➤ *CDE (Certified Directory Engineer)*—This high-level Novell credential seeks to supply the IT industry with directory-qualified networking experts. Obtaining a CDE requires that an applicant already attain some senior-level certification such as CNE, MCSE, ASE, CCNP, or CCIE, plus two core exams and a problem-solving, live laboratory exam. To keep their credentials, CDEs must recertify annually by retaking the laboratory exam.

➤ *CNI (Certified Novell Instructor)*—To obtain certification as a Novell instructor, candidates must meet an instructional requirement, which may be satisfied by taking a Novell "train-the-trainer" course or by obtaining certification as a CTT from the Chauncey Group (the CTT is covered in Chapter 8). In addition, would-be CNIs must pass a more difficult version of any Novell certification exam, aimed specifically at instructors, to be allowed to teach the related course within Novell's authorized education channels.

Even though Microsoft has passed Novell in terms of its certification programs' population and popularity, it's important to note that Novell pioneered this marketplace and that its education and certification programs have served as a model for many other vendors, including Microsoft. Even today, Novell's program is highly regarded and widely emulated. The Novell certification program is covered in detail in Chapter 3.

Oracle Certification Programs

Although Oracle might have to stretch to match Microsoft across all markets, no one can dispute its leadership in the database arena. In keeping with its stature, Oracle offers the Oracle Certified Professional program to certify professionals in one of several tracks:

➤ *Oracle8 Certified Database Operator (DBO)*—This is the entry-level Oracle certification designed for individuals who must manage or operate database applications built around the Oracle8 database environment. You must pass only a single test, the Oracle8 Database Operator exam, to obtain this credential.

➤ *Database Administrator (DBA)*—This is designed for individuals who must create and maintain Oracle databases. Obtaining this credential requires passing four or five tests. Oracle offers a variety of training vehicles to help individuals prepare for these tests, ranging from instructor-led training to a variety of online tutorials. The tests cover the following topics:

> ➤ *Introduction to Oracle: SQL and PL/SQL*—Covers basic database concepts and structures, plus basic programming in SQL.

> ➤ *Oracle7.3/8i: Oracle Database Administration*—Covers database architectures, creation, and maintenance; aimed at a particular version of Oracle (either 7.3, 8, or 8i, as is the case with the following two exams).

> ➤ *Oracle7.3/8i: Performance Tuning*—Covers techniques for monitoring, tuning, and optimizing Oracle database and server performance; aimed at a particular version of Oracle.

> ➤ *Oracle7.3/8i: Backup and Recovery*—Covers backup and recovery tools as well as strategies for Oracle databases; also aimed at a particular version of Oracle.

> ➤ *Oracle8/8i Network Administration*—Covers administration of Oracle8/8i servers as well as connection management.

Note: If you have compelling reasons to certify in the Oracle7.3 DBA track, do it quick! Oracle has announced that the Oracle7.3 DBA track exams will expire by August 31, 2000. After that, individuals desiring a DBA certification can pursue Oracle8 or Oracle8i only.

➤ *Oracle Certified Application Developer*—This is for developers who wish to establish their proficiency at developing Oracle-based applications using Oracle's Developer/2000 Release 1 or Release 2 development environment. Here again, Oracle offers a variety of training vehicles to help individuals prepare for the five tests required for this certification. The five tests cover the following topics:

> ➤ *Introduction to Oracle: SQL and PL/SQL*—Covers basic database concepts and structures, plus basic SQL programming.

> ➤ *Develop PL/SQL Program Units*—Covers developing and managing stored procedures, functions, packages, and database triggers.

➤ *Developer/2000 Forms I*—Covers using Developer/2000 tools and environment, plus basic forms development, including forms editors, modules, blocks, events, and more.

➤ *Developer/2000 Forms II*—Covers advanced forms development, including menu modules, function keys, managing windows and canvases, manipulating forms at runtime, and more.

➤ *Developer/2000 Reports*—Covers programming for Oracle's report generator, including designing, using, and maintaining reports, plus managing data models, layouts, parameters, triggers, and more.

➤ *Oracle Certified Java Developer*—Certification as an Oracle Java developer recognizes those Web developers who master using Oracle8i to create e-commerce, information delivery, and other Internet-related applications. Three levels of certification occur under this umbrella. They require up to five exams, including performance-based and essay exams, depending on which level you decide to pursue.

➤ *Oracle Certified Financial Applications Consultant*—Here, you'll find two certification levels aimed at those who work with Oracle's Procurement R11 or the Order Fulfillment R11 subsystems. Three exams are required, including two core exams plus an elective on either Procurement or Fulfillment.

Given that most Oracle installations cost upwards of half a million dollars, training and certification are quite customary in this environment (and often, training and consulting services are negotiated as part of an overall purchase agreement). As a result, certification is a key ingredient for hiring new database professionals and for ensuring that current employees maintain their skills. You'll learn more about Oracle Certified Professional exams, training, and resources in Chapter 4.

Cisco Certification Programs

Although less than 25,000 individuals currently hold some type of Cisco certification, these programs currently enjoy terrific cachet. This is primarily because Cisco Career Certifications are scarce, and certified individuals are in high demand, so that elite Cisco Career Certification candidates can expect to earn six-figure incomes immediately on obtaining their credentials. With a potential payday of this magnitude, Cisco certification remains a hot ticket.

The buzz aside, there are plenty of good reasons why Cisco certified professionals are in high demand. As the leading purveyor of routing, switching, and connectivity equipment, Cisco dominates the markets for Internet and intranet gear. Because its equipment and software are both sophisticated and powerful, certification is viewed as essential for those individuals entrusted to work on such mission-critical systems and software.

Cisco offers multiple certifications, each of which may be obtained across multiple disciplines. Each of these disciplines requires a strong general background in networking technologies and concepts, but each represents a specialized area of focus (please note that the last three specializations in the following list currently apply only to Cisco's elite CCIE certification):

➤ *Routing and Switching*—This discipline covers the use of routers and switches in enterprise-level internetworks and includes coverage of wide area network (WAN) technologies only insofar as they tie into organizational networks.

➤ *WAN Switching*—This discipline covers long-haul aspects of WAN links and includes coverage of routers and switches, a wide variety of WAN technologies, voice/data/video integration, plus Internet security issues.

➤ *ISP Dial*—This focuses on the kinds of internetworking issues more typical at an Internet Service Provider (ISP)—namely, some coverage of routers and switches, but also of telephony, modems and other remote communications devices, Web and Internet security issues, and communications servers.

➤ *CCIE SNA/IP Integration*—This covers Cisco Mainframe Channel Connectivity (CMCC) and System Network Architecture (SNA), IP and IP routing, and bridge- and switching-related technologies. Visit the Web page at **www.cisco.com/warp/public/625/ccie/certifications/sna_ip.html** for more details about this exam.

➤ *CCIE Design*—This covers design principles related to the Access, Distribution, and Core layers of large internetworks. It also requires that candidates have a thorough understanding of campus design, multiservice, SNA-IP, and network management–related design issues. Visit the Web page at **www.cisco.com/warp/public/625/ccie/certifications/design.html** for more information about this exam.

Across these disciplines, Cisco offers various certifications. Of the five in the following list, the first three represent a certification ladder for individuals who take an operating role in building and maintaining internetworks that incorporate Cisco components. The final two represent a certification ladder for those who seek to design and deploy such internetworks (likewise, the newly minted CCIE Design specialty defines a top-level track for network designers).

Typically, individuals would climb the first ladder at an organization that uses or operates such a network. Individuals would climb the second ladder at a consulting company or other organization that specializes in building and deploying networks for third parties.

Together, these five certifications include the following:

➤ *Cisco Certified Network Associate (CCNA)*—This is the entry-level operational certification and is aimed at individuals who must manage simple routed local area networks (LANs) or WANs, small ISPs, or smaller switched LAN or LANE environments. Passing a single multiple-choice exam is required to obtain this certification.

➤ *Cisco Certified Network Professional (CCNP)*—This is the middle-tier operational certification aimed at individuals who must install, configure, operate, and troubleshoot complex routed LANs, routed WANs, switched LAN networks, or Dial Access Services. Applicants must first obtain a CCNA and then take either two or four additional exams, depending on which test options they choose.

➤ *Cisco Certified Internetwork Expert (CCIE)*—This is the top-tier operational certification aimed at individuals with advanced technical skills and knowledge, who know how to configure networks for optimum performance, and who understand how to maintain complex, far-flung, multivendor networks. Applicants must pass only two exams for this certification: a written exam through normal channels and a laboratory evaluation at a Cisco certification lab.

Cisco's lab exams have the reputation of being the most challenging and difficult certification tests in the networking industry, bar none. In addition to their difficulty, the Cisco required lab exams are also the most expensive certification exams around. They are offered only at a small number of locations and usually involve travel expenses beyond the cost of the exam itself ($1,000).

➤ *Cisco Certified Design Associate (CCDA)*—This is the entry-level design credential. It requires individuals to be able to design and deploy simple routed and switched networks as well as configure, operate, and maintain them. To obtain this certification, applicants must pass a single exam (640-4419). (This certification is not an option for those seeking the WAN Switching specialization.)

➤ *Cisco Certified Design Professional (CCDP)*—This is the top-tier design credential. It requires individuals to be able to design and deploy complex routed LANs and WANs, plus switched LANs and LANE environments. Likewise, individuals must be able to configure, operate, and maintain such networks and connections. For those seeking the Routing and Switching specialization, applications must first obtain CCNA and CCDA certification and then pass either two or four exams, depending on which exam track they elect. For those seeking the WAN Switching specialty, they must first obtain CCNA and CCNP certification and then take one additional test.

You'll learn more about the requirements and expertise required for all Cisco certifications in Chapter 5.

CompTIA's A+, Network+, and i-Net+ Certification Programs

CompTIA stands for the Computing Technology Industry Association. Its members include most major PC hardware and software manufacturers. This organization offers the A+ certification to provide vendor-neutral credentials for PC technicians who are able to handle a broad variety of hardware, operating systems, and related matters. The Network+ exam aims to provide similar, vendor-neutral credentials for network technicians who work in complex, multivendor networked environments. Finally, the i-Net+ exam provides a vendor-neutral credential for internetworking professionals who interact with the Internet, company intranets, or other TCP/IP-based networks and services.

Obtaining A+ certification requires passing two exams:

➤ *Core*—Focuses on basic principles of computer operation, configuration, installation, and maintenance. The purpose of this test is to examine a candidate's knowledge and understanding of computer systems, peripherals, and components.

➤ *DOS/Windows*—Focuses on installation, configuration, maintenance, and troubleshooting of DOS and Windows (through Windows 95) operating systems. The purpose of this test is to examine a candidate's knowledge and understanding of the basic desktop PC operating systems and services.

Unlike the certification programs previously mentioned, CompTIA requires that both tests be taken and passed within a 90-day period. Otherwise, candidates must retake both tests to obtain A+ certification. You'll learn more about the details and requirements for this widely held computer certification in Chapter 6.

Obtaining Network+ certification requires passing a single exam, divided into two parts. The first part of the exam covers basic networking technologies, plus network security and TCP/IP basics. The second part tests basic knowledge about maintaining and troubleshooting a typical network.

Obtaining i-Net+ certification also requires passing a single exam, which covers six separate topical areas. The topics covered include Internet basics, Internet clients, Web development tools and technologies, basic IP protocols and networking concepts, Internet security issues and solutions, and e-commerce concepts and technologies.

You'll learn more about the details and requirements for these increasingly popular vendor-neutral certifications in Chapter 6.

Sun's Java Certification Programs

Given the immense popularity of Java as a programming language, it should come as no surprise that Sun (the subsidiary of Sun Microsystems, Inc., that's responsible for developing and promoting this technology) has instituted a Java certification program.

Currently, about 30,000 individuals have obtained one level of Java certification or another, and a great many more are expected to complete certification by the end of 2000. As companies like IBM, Novell, Oracle, and Sun undertake new development work in Java and seek to convert existing code to Java, demand for qualified Java programmers is exploding. Certified Java professionals are not as pricey as Cisco professionals, but they certainly command a premium in today's marketplace.

Sun offers three levels of Java certification:

➤ *Sun Certified Programmer for the Java Platform*—Individuals who seek this certification must take a written test aimed at a specific Java Development Kit (JDK). The most current test covers Java 2; other tests on JDK 1.1 are still available. Individuals who take this test must be familiar with basic Java language constructs and concepts and intimately familiar with APIs and tools in the JDK.

➤ *Sun Certified Developer for the Java Platform*—Individuals who seek this certification submit an application form and pay a fee to receive a set of specifications for a full-blown Java application. They must write code to meet those specifications and submit it to Sun for evaluation. Following a critique and analysis of their work, applicants who pass must write an essay about the application they created. Individuals who take these tests must first pass the Certified Java Programmer test and be familiar enough with Java programming and development techniques to complete the assignment and essay exam. The work involved can take from two to five days, according to those who've acquired this certification.

➤ *Sun Certified Enterprise Architect for Java 2, Enterprise Edition Technology*— Individuals who seek this newest Sun Java certification—it applies only to Java 2—must understand multilayered Java applications and development tools. This high-level Java certification involves passing two exams and a programming assignment, which cover a wide range of topics from multitiered database applications, through various Web-based and distributed programming approaches, object-oriented design and implementation strategies, specification and implementation of client/server applications, to migrating applications to Internet-based platforms. Those who wish to become Certified Java Architects must not only understand technologies and programming, but also apply business reasoning to guide and design complex development efforts.

Sun offers classroom training and an online tutorial to help individuals prepare for this test. If you've spent any time in a bookstore with a decent selection of computer titles lately, you're probably aware that books on Java constitute a heavily populated niche in the computer section. There's no lack of information or documentation available to those who seek this certification. For more details about Sun's programs and offerings, consult Chapter 7.

Chauncey Certifications

A subsidiary of the Educational Testing Service (ETS), itself well known for its college and graduate-level entrance exams, the Chauncey Group offers assessment and testing services, plus training materials. Chauncey's interests cover various subjects, including technical training and an entry-level, basic IT certification. Chauncey also offers services and performs educational assessments on behalf of organizations like the American Nursing Association, among other groups.

Chauncey is best known for its instructor certification, known as the Certified Technical Trainer (CTT) credential. Even though most vendor certifications—including those from Adobe, AOL/Netscape, Lotus, Microsoft, and Novell, among others—offer their own in-house, train-the-trainer programs, all these organizations accept the CTT as an alternative to their homegrown trainer certifications.

A CTT is quite valuable for these reasons:

➤ The CTT costs no more than half as much as most other vendor-specific certifications; this makes the CTT a real bargain.

➤ Because the CTT meets instructional requirements for numerous vendor trainer certifications, obtaining a CTT enables individuals to train for multiple programs based on only a single exam and in-class video submission. This makes the CTT a multifaceted tool for those who want to teach in multiple training programs.

In Chapter 8, you'll also learn about another Chauncey certification, known as the Associate Technology Specialist (ATS). ATS originated at the NorthWest Center for Emerging Technologies (NWCET), under the direction of the National Science Foundation, as a vendor-neutral, entry-level IT certification.

The ATS program includes a Core Skills exam that covers IT technology basics, problem-solving skills, project management processes, basic writing skills, and applied basic math and statistics. Beyond the core, individuals can select from exams in one of eight IT specialties, called career clusters. These elements include Network Design and Administration, Enterprise Systems Analysis and Integration, Database Development and Administration, Digital Media, Programming/Software Engineering, Technical Writing, Technical Support, and Web Development and Administration.

Because the ATS promises to be a useful credential for aspiring IT professionals, I cover it and the CTT program in Chapter 8.

Prosofttraining.com's Certified Internet Webmaster Program

Chapter 9 covers a Web-focused certification program created by Prosoft-training.com, called the Certified Internet Webmaster (CIW) program.

Basically, the Prosoft program uses an entry-level curriculum and exam called the "CIW Foundations Track" to test all students' knowledge of Internet basics. Interestingly, you can take either the Prosoft Foundations exam to meet the program's entry-level requirements or substitute CompTIA's i-Net+ exam instead. From there a student can take and pass any one of the CIW series exams to qualify for the CIW Professional designation. Finally, students can branch into three different areas of Web activity—Web administrators, Web developers, and Web designers—each of which culminates in an advanced Master-level certification.

Here's how the various tracks work:

➤ Starting with Foundations, a candidate passes any one of the CIW series exams to achieve CIW Professional status (two tests in all).

➤ Administrators continue on from Foundations into a track that starts with a Server Administrator course/test combination, then to an Internetworking Professional combination, and then to a Security Professional combination that culminates in certification as a Master CIW Administrator (four tests in all).

➤ Programmers continue on from Foundations to language course/test combinations on either Perl or JavaScript. From there, they tackle course/test combinations on Java Programming, Object-Oriented Analysis, Database Specialist, and Enterprise Developer topics. Completion of the series culminates in certification as a Master CIS Enterprise Developer (eight tests in all).

➤ Web designers continue on from Foundations to a Site Designer course/test combination, then to an E-Commerce Designer combination. This culminates in certification as a Master CIW Designer (three tests in all).

For a more complete description of the CIW program, consult Chapter 9. You can also visit **www.ciwcertified.com/default.htm** for more CIW information. For a great description of CIW requirements, tracks, and exams, see also **www.ciwcertified.com/certifications/ciw_program.htm**.

This program has been endorsed by the Association of Internet Professionals (AIP) and the International Webmasters Association (IWA). Both of these are nonprofit organizations of like-minded professionals. The CIW has not, however, been endorsed by another crucial body: the World Wide Web Consortium (W3C), which basically owns all the specifications for Web-related technologies.

Linux Certifications

Linux certifications come in many shapes and sizes. More than just another Open Source implementation of the Unix operating system, Linux is well on its way to becoming a marketing phenomenon in its own right. Although its market share still remains relatively low compared to Windows, Linux has gained enough momentum to attract interest from organizations, individuals, and vendors over the past year. I cover key Linux certifications in Chapter 10.

Just as there are many different versions of Linux itself available, there are also a number of Linux certifications competing for recognition and acceptance. Unfortunately, there's still some confusion in the marketplace about which Linux certification matters most. Although there are probably more Linux certifications available than the ones I mention in this book, there are at least three players who've mounted Linux certification efforts at present, with varying degrees of success:

➤ Red Hat is the largest commercial vendor for Linux (with about 70 percent of that market) and is clearly a major player in the Linux certification game. Right now, Red Hat offers its own certification program, which creates Red Hat Certified Engineers (RHCEs). See Chapter 10 for more details.

➤ Prometric (a leading purveyor of certification tests of all kinds, as you may already know) and Software Architecture Realization and Implementation (a leading Unix and Linux training company) have teamed up to define and deliver a global, vendor-neutral form of Linux and GNU certification. (Their program has been endorsed by numerous Linux vendors, including Caldera, the number two commercial provider of Linux.)

This effort has produced a complex certification scheme, with three levels of Linux and GNU certification. These levels span the range from a Linux Certified Administrator credential to a Master Linux Engineer who has passed four tests. Tests are multiple choice and may be administered at any Prometric testing center. See Chapter 10 for more details.

➤ The Linux Professional Institute (LPI) is a nonprofit, vendor-neutral Linux certification organization run by Dan York, a well-known industry figure and Unix expert. This group is also building a multileveled, highly professional Linux certification program that's quite similar to the Sair Linux and GNU program covered in the preceding list element. See Chapter 10 for more details.

Although the degree of acceptance and popularity for each of these various Linux certifications remains somewhat uncertain, it's pretty clear that some kind of Linux certification (perhaps even more than one) is bound to attain market acceptance in the next year or two. That's why I cover all the main contenders for this prize in Chapter 10.

But Wait, There's More!

Chapters 2 through 10 are each devoted to a particular set of vendor certification programs or cover important certifications for specific topic areas. Even so, this barely scratches the surface of the total IT certification landscape. That's why Chapter 11 is a kind of grab bag that mentions numerous other certifications that you may find of interest without quite covering them at the same level of detail as the programs covered in Chapters 2 through 10. Nevertheless, you may find some tasty tidbits in here that may be worthy of further investigation. That's why I also provide pointers to online information about every program that appears in this chapter.

Chapters 12 and 13 cap off the book with more general certification information. Chapter 12 provides a brief, but pointed, self-assessment tool that you can use to help determine which certifications might apply to your interests and career goals. Chapter 13 reviews some important tips, tricks, and techniques to help you prepare to take—and pass—whatever certification exams you decide to take on.

Summary

This concludes our overview of the various vendor and organization certifications that you'll encounter in this book. The remainder of this book is devoted to more detailed descriptions and discussions of their programs, exams, and supporting materials. Enjoy!

Need to Know More?

 www.microsoft.com/trainingandservices/default.asp?PageID=mcp This is the "mother of all Web pages" for topics and information related to Microsoft certification. Be sure to investigate the pointers on the left-hand side of this page where you'll find exam preparation guides, practice tests, and other kinds of self-assessment tools.

 http://services.novell.com This is a good point of departure to investigate Novell's certification programs, exams, and training options, all of which may be located under the "Valuable Education" heading at the top right of the page.

 http://education.oracle.com/certification/ This is where to begin investigating Oracle's certification programs, exams, and training. Be prepared to read tons of PDF files as you sift through its thorough, but fragmented, Web pages and downloads.

 www.chauncey.com Follow pointers from the home page to learn more about the CTT and ATS programs.

 www.cisco.com/warp/public/10/wwtraining/certprog/ This page describes Cisco's certifications in general, with pointers to other pages with details on courses, examinations, requirements, and other useful stuff. Cisco's online information is the only instance where I found lists of recommended reading and online resources to help individuals prepare for tests, for which Cisco gets lots of kudos.

 www.comptia.org Follow pointers to the A+, Network+, or i-Net+ certifications to learn more about these tests and their background requirements.

 www.linuxcertification.org Home to the Prometric/SAIR Linux and GNU certification effort, this for-profit, vendor-neutral organization offers lots of information about its multilevel Linux certification programs and exams.

 www.lpi.org Home to the Linux Professional Institute, this nonprofit, vendor-neutral organization offers lots of information about their multilevel Linux certification programs and exams.

www.prosofttraining.com Choose the Certification link under the Products menu item to check out their voluminous documentation on the Certified Internet Webmaster (CIW) program.

Microsoft Certification Programs

Terms you'll need to understand:

✓ MCP, MCP+I, MCP+SB, MCDBA, MCSE, MCSE+I, MCSD, MCT, MOUS

✓ Windows product family: Windows 95, Windows 98, Windows NT, Windows 2000

✓ System or network administrator

✓ Software developer

✓ Microsoft exam IDs

Techniques you'll need to master:

✓ Locating training and certification information on the Microsoft Web site

✓ Obtaining descriptions and objectives for specific Microsoft exams

✓ Locating practice tests to help you prepare for specific Microsoft exams

Of all the vendor programs you'll encounter in this book, Microsoft's certification programs are arguably the most numerous and varied. Definitely, no other vendor whose programs are covered in this book offers as many different exams (not to mention related classroom training, courseware, self-study kits, Web-based training, and books) as Microsoft does. In this chapter, you'll have a chance to examine Microsoft's many different certification options and to understand how one certification can sometimes lead to another.

Alphabet Soup

To begin, let's review the many acronyms that relate to certification, Microsoft style. After that, you'll have a chance to investigate each certification in some detail. Then, you'll be presented with a roadmap that shows how all the pieces fit together and learn how to sign up for tests, track certification progress, and so on.

Here's the list of key acronyms related to Microsoft certifications, with brief explanations for each one:

➤ *Microsoft Certified Professional (MCP)*—Anyone who's passed any one exam—other than Networking Essentials (exam 70-058) or any of the Office-related exams—on a current Microsoft application or operating system.

➤ *MCP + Internet (MCP+I)*—MCP candidates who prove their Internet expertise and qualify to plan security, installation, and configuration of server products; implement server extensions; and manage server resources. Three core exams are required to pass.

➤ *MCP + Site Building (MCP+SB)*—MCP candidates who prove their expertise in managing sophisticated, interactive Web sites, including databases, multimedia, and searchable content. To qualify, candidates must pass two of three required exams.

➤ *Microsoft Certified Database Administrator (MCDBA)*—Professionals who work with Microsoft SQL Server version 7.0 or higher and who manage databases or develop database applications will find this certification of interest. To qualify, candidates must pass four or five required exams, including two SQL exams and one or two core exams, plus an elective exam.

➤ *Microsoft Certified Systems Engineer (MCSE)*—Candidates who prove their expertise with desktop and server operating systems, networking components, and Microsoft BackOffice products. To qualify, candidates must pass six or seven exams—four or five core exams and two electives.

➤ *MCSE + Internet (MCSE+I)*—MCSE candidates who prove their expertise using Microsoft products and technologies in Internet or intranet environments.

As with the basic MCSE, candidates must pass the same four core MCSE exams, plus three Internet core exams and two Internet-specific electives.

➤ *Microsoft Certified Solution Developer (MCSD)*—Candidates who prove their abilities to build Web-based, distributed, or e-commerce applications. This program is aimed at developers rather than system or network managers. Knowledge of solution architectures, application-development strategies and techniques, and development tools is required of all candidates, who must pass three core exams and one elective exam to qualify.

➤ *Microsoft Certified Trainer (MCT)*—Individuals who are authorized to teach elements of the Microsoft Official Curriculum (MOC), usually at official, Microsoft-sanctioned training centers or academic affiliates. Individuals obtain MCT credentials on a topic-by-topic basis by passing the related MCP exam and meeting Microsoft's instructional requirements to demonstrate classroom teaching skills. MCTs must also maintain current certification as an MCSE to qualify to teach Microsoft courses.

➤ *Microsoft Office User Specialist (MOUS)*—Office workers such as temps, administrators, and clerical staff who prove their abilities to handle the Microsoft Office productivity suite (which includes Word, Excel, Access, and PowerPoint) in the Office 95, 97, or 2000 versions (is included in the Office 2000 exams). This program recognizes three levels of certification: a Proficient Specialist (Office 95 or 97) or Core Specialist (Office 2000) for Word and Excel, Expert Specialist for each of the Office components, and Microsoft Office Master for those who are experts in all Office components.

All the information in the preceding list, plus some additional details about the exams, is summed up in Table 2.1. Please note that information about the number of questions, the cost, and the time period is for each exam, not for all exams.

In the sections that follow, you'll examine each of these certifications in some detail and learn a little more about the exams that you must pass to qualify for each one. If you visit the URLs mentioned for each credential, in most cases you'll be able to jump straight to the details related to the required exams (and electives, where applicable).

Microsoft is now administering some MCP exams in an adaptive test format. Table 2.1 includes information about fixed-length, adaptive, and short-form exams. The number of questions and time allowed varies on adaptive exams but is never less than 15, as indicated in the table. See the section titled "Microsoft Testing" later in this chapter for more information.

Table 2.1 Microsoft certifications.					
Certification	Required Exams	Elective Exams	Questions	Cost	Time
MCP	1	0	15–72	$100	30–90 min.
MCP+I	3	0	15–72	$100	30–90 min.
MCP+SB	2	0	15–72	$100	30–90 min.
MCDBA†	3	1	15–72	$100	30–90 min.
MCDBA*	4	1	15–72	$100	30–90 min.
MCSE*	4	2	15–72	$100	30–90 min.
MCSE†	5‡	2	15–72	$100	30–90 min.
MCSE+I*	7	2	15–72	$100	30–90 min.
MCSD	3	1	15–72	$100	30–90 min.
MCT	2	0	15–72	Varies	Varies
MOUS	1–5	0	45–60	$60	30–60 min.

*Applies only to Windows NT 4.0.

†Marks a newer certification version specific to Windows 2000.

‡The number of exams for the Windows 2000 MCSE varies according to whether you are upgrading from a prior certification or have taken the three Windows NT 4.0 exams (70-067, 70-068, and 70-073) that qualify you for an accelerated Windows 2000 exam (70-240). See the section titled "MCSE" later in this chapter for details.

MCP

Anyone who passes any Microsoft certification exam—other than exam 70-058, Networking Essentials, or any of the Office-related exams—can become certified as an MCP. Because you'll learn about the range of exams that this broad category includes in the following sections, I won't list them here.

For a more detailed description of the requirements to become an MCP, visit Microsoft's MCP page at **www.microsoft.com/trainingandservices/default. asp?PageID=mcp.**

MCP+I

MCPs who want to specialize in Internet tools and technologies must pass three exams to demonstrate their technical proficiency and expertise. Microsoft designs these exams on the basis of input from industry professionals, and they are intended to reflect how Microsoft products are used in a business or organizational setting.

Individuals who obtain MCP+I certification are assumed to be qualified to plan Internet and network security, to install and configure Windows NT Server products, and to manage related resources. They should also be able to extend NT-based Web servers to run Common Gateway Interface (CGI) or Internet Server

Table 2.2 The MCP+I exams.	
Exam ID and Title	70-059 Internetworking with Microsoft TCP/IP on Microsoft Windows NT 4.0
Description	Covers NT 4 TCP/IP protocols, addressing, subnets, DNS, and WINS, plus services and utilities.
Exam ID and Title	70-067 Implementing and Supporting Microsoft Windows NT Server 4.0
Description	Covers basic Windows NT Server 4 planning, installation, configuration, and management.
Exam ID and Title	70-087 Implementing and Supporting Microsoft IIS 4.0
Description	Covers installation, configuration, and maintenance of IIS 4.0 and Index Server. Also covers security, content management, Web site design, and related IP services

API (ISAPI) scripts, monitor and analyze server performance, or troubleshoot problems. Table 2.2 summarizes the requirements for obtaining MCP+I certification.

For more information about this certification, visit Microsoft's Web page at **www.microsoft.com/trainingandservices/default.asp?PageID=mcp** and choose the MCP+I link.

 The MCP+I is specific to Windows NT 4.0. Like other Windows NT 4.0–related Microsoft certifications, the exams for this certification will retire on December 31, 2000, and this certification itself becomes obsolete on December 31, 2001 (one year after the exams retire).

MCP+SB

The MCP+SB credential is aimed primarily at Web site developers who seek to demonstrate their knowledge of related Microsoft tools and technologies. Individuals who hold the MCP+SB certification are judged to be qualified to build, maintain, and manage Web sites using Microsoft products and technologies. This credential will be of greatest value to those who manage complex, interactive Web sites that integrate a variety of content types (such as multimedia and database access) and that include searchable content. Requirements for obtaining an MCP+SB are covered in Table 2.3; to qualify, you need only pass any two of the three exams that are listed.

For more information about obtaining an MCP+SB, visit **www.microsoft.com/ trainingandservices/default.asp?PageID=mcp** and choose the MCP+SB link.

Table 2.3 The MCP+SB exams.		
Choose any two of the following three exams.		
Exam ID and Title	70-055	Designing and Implementing Web Sites with Microsoft FrontPage 98
Description		Covers FrontPage tools and utilities; Web site design, deployment, and maintenance; and extending Web site functionality and interactivity using FrontPage 98.
Exam ID and Title	70-057	Designing and Implementing Commerce Solutions with Microsoft Site Server 3.0, Commerce Edition
Description		Covers designing, implementing, managing, and securing an e-commerce presence on the Web and using Site Server 3 and its various commerce tools and extensions.
Exam ID and Title	70-152	Designing and Implementing Web Solutions with Microsoft Visual InterDev 6.0
Description		Covers working with Microsoft's Visual Development toolset for building Web extensions, including CGI programs, ISAPI programs, ActiveX controls, Active Server Pages, and so on.

MCDBA

The MCDBA credential is aimed primarily at database administrators and developers who work with Microsoft SQL Server and related products and technologies. Individuals who hold the MCDBA certification are judged to be qualified to design, build, maintain, and manage databases and related applications using Microsoft SQL Server. This credential will be of greatest value to those who develop database designs, construct logical data models, create physical databases, create services with Microsoft's Transact-SQL, manage and maintain databases, configure and manage database security, monitor and optimize databases, and install and configure Microsoft SQL Server.

Requirements for obtaining an MCDBA are covered in Table 2.4; to qualify, you must pass all of the required exams (four for the Windows NT 4.0 track, three for the Windows 2000 track), plus any one of the elective exams that are listed.

For more information about obtaining an MCDBA, visit **www.microsoft.com/trainingandservices/default.asp?PageID=mcp** and choose the MCDBA link.

 The Windows NT 4.0 exams for MCDBA will retire on December 31, 2000, and the NT 4.0 MCDBA certification will itself become obsolete on December 31, 2001.

Table 2.4   The MCDBA exams.

Required Exams (take both of these)

Exam ID and Title	70-028 Administering Microsoft SQL Server 7.0
Description	Managing, tuning, and maintaining SQL Server 7.0–based databases and applications.
Exam ID and Title	70-029 Designing and Implementing Databases With Microsoft SQL Server 7.0
Description	Designing, building, and troubleshooting SQL databases, plus SQL-based database applications.

Additional Windows 2000 Core Exams (take one)

Exam ID and Title	70-215 Installing, Configuring, and Administering Microsoft Windows 2000 Server
Description	Tests knowledge of basic Windows 2000 Server features, functions, and uses.
OR	
Exam ID and Title	70-240 Microsoft Windows 2000 Accelerated Exam for MCPs Certified on Microsoft Windows NT 4.0
Description	Covers the entire core exam content for the Windows 2000 MCSE (equivalent to 70-210, 70-215, 70-216, and 70-217).

Additional Windows NT 4.0 Core Exams (take both)

Exam ID and Title	70-067 Implementing and Supporting Microsoft Windows NT Server 4.0 (exam)
Description	Covers basic Windows NT Server 4.0 planning, installation, configuration, and management.
Exam ID and Title	70-068 Implementing and Supporting Microsoft Windows NT Server 4.0 in the Enterprise
Description	Covers advanced configuration and management topics aimed at large-scale enterprise-level networks and installations.

Elective Exams (take only one of these)

Only one elective exam is required; however, that exam must be valid for the category to which the candidate's MCDBA belongs (Windows 2000 or NT 4.0).

Windows 2000–only Electives (take one, if applicable)

Exam ID and Title	70-216 Implementing and Administering a Microsoft Windows 2000 Network Infrastructure
Description	Covers networking concepts, hardware, software, services, and protocols for Windows 2000–based networks. (Please note: 70-240 is also an acceptable Windows 2000 elective, but only if 70-215 is used as a Core element.)

Windows NT 4.0–only Electives (take one, if applicable)

Exam ID and Title	70-059 Internetworking with Microsoft TCP/IP on Microsoft Windows NT Server 4.0
Description	Basic principles and practices of using TCP/IP protocols and services with Windows NT 4.0.

(continued)

Table 2.4	The MCDBA exams *(continued)*.	
Exam ID and Title	70-087	Implementing and Supporting Microsoft Internet Information Server 4.0
Description		Covers installation, configuration, and maintenance of IIS 4.0 and Index Server and security, content management, Web site design, and related IP services.
Electives valid for either version of Windows		
Exam ID and Title	70-015	Designing and Implementing Distributed Applications with Microsoft Visual C++ 6.0
Description		Covers building, testing, and deploying client/server applications based on Visual C++ 6.0.
Exam ID and Title	70-019	Designing and Implementing Data Warehouses with Microsoft SQL Server 7.0
Description		Using SQL Server to build and manage large data repositories and related applications.
Exam ID and Title	70-155	Designing and Implementing Distributed Applications with Microsoft Visual FoxPro 6.0
Description		Covers building, testing, and deploying client/server applications based on Visual FoxPro 6.0.
Exam ID and Title	70-175	Designing and Implementing Distributed Applications with Microsoft Visual Basic 6.0
Description		Building networked client/server applications with Visual Basic 6.0.

MCSE

The MCSE credential is the most widely sought after of all the Microsoft certifications. Individuals who attain a Windows NT 4 MCSE must pass four core exams and two electives. Of the four core exams, two cover NT Server 4, one covers a desktop operating system (you have three choices, as shown in Table 2.5), and the last is the Networking Essentials exam. The two electives for a Windows NT 4 MCSE may be drawn from a broad range of choices, as shown in Table 2.6.

Table 2.5	Microsoft Windows NT 4 MCSE core exams.	
Exam ID and Title	70-067	Implementing and Supporting Microsoft Windows NT Server 4.0
Description		Covers basic Windows NT 4 Server planning, installation, configuration, and management.
Exam ID and Title	70-068	Implementing and Supporting Microsoft Windows NT Server 4.0 in the Enterprise
Description		Covers advanced configuration and management topics aimed at large-scale enterprise-level networks and installations.
Exam ID and Title	70-058	Networking Essentials
Description		Covers networking concepts, standards, terminology, and technology, with a special emphasis on Windows networking, local area networks, wide area networks, and wireless networking.

(continued)

Table 2.5	Microsoft Windows NT 4 MCSE core exams *(continued)*.	
Exam ID and Title	70-064	Implementing and Supporting Windows 95
OR		
Exam ID and Title	70-073	Implementing and Supporting Microsoft Windows NT Workstation 4.0
OR		
Exam ID and Title	70-098	Implementing and Supporting Microsoft Windows 98
Description		These tests cover each desktop operating system's features and functions as well as how to install, configure, and administer them on a network, both locally and remotely.

No Windows NT 4.0 core exams can be counted toward a Windows 2000 MCSE, except in qualifying for the 70-240 Accelerated Windows 2000 exam (where all three NT 4.0–related exams count).

If you have a strong networking background, we recommend that you take the exams in this order: Networking Essentials, Windows NT 4.0 Workstation, Windows NT 4.0 Server, and Windows NT 4.0 Server in the Enterprise. If you do not have a strong networking background, take the NT 4.0 exams in the specified order, and take Networking Essentials last.

Table 2.6	The Windows NT 4 MCSE elective exams.	
Choose any two items in this list, except for entries separated by the keyword **OR**, which indicates that only one of the items in that category may be counted as an MCSE elective.		
Exam ID and Title	70-013	Implementing and Supporting Microsoft SNA Server 3.0
OR		
Exam ID and Title	70-085	Implementing and Supporting Microsoft SNA Server 4.0
Description		Both tests cover Microsoft's IBM mainframe connectivity servers. Topics include terminal emulation, host sessions, LAN-to-host data transfer, and so on.
Exam ID and Title	70-018	Implementing and Supporting Microsoft Systems Management Server 1.2
OR		
Exam ID and Title	70-086	Implementing and Supporting Microsoft Systems Management Server 2.0
Description		Both tests cover Microsoft's BackOffice network management tool set and deal with topics including remote management, software distribution, network monitoring and management, and so on.
Exam ID and Title	70-019	Designing and Implementing Data Warehouses with Microsoft SQL Server 7.0
Description		Covers how to build and manage large-scale database applications using SQL Server 7.0.
Exam ID and Title	70-026	System Administration for Microsoft SQL Server 6.5
OR		
Exam ID and Title	70-028	Administering Microsoft SQL Server 7.0
Description		Covers database maintenance, programming, migration, and troubleshooting using Microsoft's SQL Server.

(continued)

Table 2.6	The Windows NT 4 MCSE elective exams *(continued)*.	
Exam ID and Title	70-027	Implementing a Database Design on Microsoft SQL Server 6.5
OR		
Exam ID and Title	70-029	Implementing a Database Design on Microsoft SQL Server 7.0
Description	Both tests cover Microsoft's BackOffice database engine and deal with topics including database design, testing, and deployment.	
Exam ID and Title	70-056	Implementing and Supporting Web Sites Using Microsoft Site Server 3.0
Description	Covers Microsoft's BackOffice intranet information-delivery environment. Topics include how to publish information, search for information, and deliver information to users via email, channels, or Web pages.	
Exam ID and Title	70-059*	Internetworking with Microsoft TCP/IP on Microsoft Windows NT 4.0
Description	Covers NT 4 TCP/IP protocols, addressing, subnets, DNS, and WINS, plus services and utilities.	
Exam ID and Title	70-076	Implementing and Supporting Microsoft Exchange Server 5
OR		
Exam ID and Title	70-081	Implementing and Supporting Microsoft Exchange Server 5.5
Description	Both exams cover Microsoft BackOffice's messaging engine and deal with topics that include design and deployment of email systems, Internet links, messaging-based applications, and so on. These are regarded as among the hardest of the exams.	
Exam ID and Title	70-078	Implementing and Supporting Microsoft Proxy Server 1.0
OR		
Exam ID and Title	70-088	Implementing and Supporting Microsoft Proxy Server 2.0
Description	Version difference aside, both exams cover maintaining Internet security, address translation, packet and address filtering, protocol and address filtering, plus proper use of related tools and utilities.	
Exam ID and Title	70-079	Implementing and Supporting Microsoft Internet Explorer 4.0 by Using the Internet Explorer Administration Kit
OR		
Exam ID and Title	70-080	Implementing and Supporting Microsoft Internet Explorer 5.0 by Using the Internet Explorer Administration Kit
Description	Both exams cover planning, installation (manual and auto-mated), configuration, and deployment of Internet Explorer on Windows and other desktops using the Internet Explorer Administration Kit (IEAK).	

(continued)

Table 2.6 The Windows NT 4 MCSE elective exams *(continued)*.	
Exam ID and Title	70-087* Implementing and Supporting Microsoft IIS 4.0
Description	Covers installation, configuration, and maintenance of IIS 4.0 and Index Server and security, content management, Web site design, and related IP services.

Items marked with an asterisk are not valid electives if you are upgrading from the Windows NT 4.0 MCSE to the Windows 2000 MCSE.

For the Windows 2000 MCSE certification, applicants are required to pass five core and two elective exams, or they can qualify to take the 70-240 Accelerated Windows 2000 exam (by passing all three Windows NT 4.0–related MCSE core exams). Table 2.7 summarizes Windows 2000 MCSE core exam requirements, and Table 2.8 lists valid electives for Windows 2000 MCSEs.

I don't cover Windows NT 3.51 certification exams because Microsoft retired these exams on June 30, 2000, following the introduction of the first wave of Windows 2000 exams.

Note that the Windows NT 4.0 MCSE certification, along with a number of related exams, are scheduled for retirement on December 31, 2000. After that date, Microsoft will offer only Windows 2000–related exams and exams not yet scheduled for retirement. If you want to certify sooner rather than later, I recommend completing the Windows NT 4.0 certification quickly. If you take the three Windows NT 4.0 exams (70-067, 70-068, and 70-073), you qualify for 70-240 Accelerated Windows 2000 when you upgrade your MCSE credential. You must upgrade your Windows 4.0 MCSE by December 31, 2001, which is the date when the Windows NT 4.0 MCSE expires and becomes invalid.

Table 2.7 Windows 2000 MCSE core exams.	
You can take the 70-240 Accelerated Windows 2000 exam only if you've already taken the three Windows NT 4.0 exams: 70-067, 70-068, and 70-073 (see Table 2.5). If you can't take 70-240, you MUST take all four Core Platform Windows 2000 exams: 70-210, 70-215, 70-216, and 70-217.	
Core Platform Windows 2000 Exams	
Take all four of these exams or take 70-240 Accelerated Windows 2000.	
Exam ID and Title	70-210 Installing, Configuring, and Administering Microsoft Windows 2000 Professional
Description	Covers Windows 2000 Professional, Microsoft's premier desktop platform, in depth.
Exam ID and Title	70-215 Installing, Configuring, and Administering Microsoft Windows 2000 Server
Description	Covers Windows 2000 Server, Microsoft's primary server platform, in depth.

(continued)

Table 2.7 Windows 2000 MCSE core exams *(continued)*.		
Exam ID and Title	70-216	Implementing and Administering a Microsoft Windows 2000 Network Infrastructure
Description		Covers network implementation, management, services, and troubleshooting for Windows 2000.
Exam ID and Title	70-217	Implementing and Administering a Microsoft Windows 2000 Directory Services Infrastructure
Description		Covers directory services implementation, management, services, and troubleshooting for Windows 2000.
Accelerated Windows 2000 Exam		
Take this exam only once (at no cost) if you've already taken 70-067, 70-068, and 70-073.		
Exam ID and Title	70-240	Microsoft Windows 2000 Accelerated Exam for MCPs Certified on Microsoft Windows NT 4.0
Description		A condensed and intensive combination of coverage from all four of the Core Platform Windows 2000 exams: 70-210, 70-215, 70-216, and 70-217.
Windows 2000 Additional Core Exams (take only one)		
Exam ID and Title	70-219	Designing a Microsoft Windows 2000 Directory Services Infrastructure
Description		Covers planning, designing, and deploying a Windows 2000 Active Directory environment.
Exam ID and Title	70-220	Designing Security for a Microsoft Windows 2000 Network
Description		Covers planning, designing, and deploying security schemes for Windows 2000 and hybrid Windows networks.
Exam ID and Title	70-221	Designing a Microsoft Windows 2000 Network Infrastructure
Description		Covers planning, designing, and deploying networking technologies, protocols, and services for Windows 2000 and hybrid Windows networks.

If you meet the prerequisites for the 70-240 Accelerated Windows 2000 exam, you get to take it for free—but only once! Passing this exam can save you $400, so study HARD!

Table 2.8 Windows 2000 MCSE elective exams.		
You must take two electives to meet requirements for a Windows 2000 MCSE. Because all valid Windows NT 4.0 MCSE electives that have not been announced for retirement also count for the Windows 2000 MCSE, refer to Table 2.6 to determine the list of such eligible electives.		
Any of the following that are core exams may be used as an elective, but can be counted only once (thus, if you take a second core exam, it counts as an elective).		
Exam ID and Title	70-219	Designing a Microsoft Windows 2000 Directory Services Infrastructure
Description		Covers planning, designing, and deploying a Windows 2000 Active Directory environment.
Exam ID and Title	70-220	Designing Security for a Microsoft Windows 2000 Network
Description		Covers planning, designing, and deploying security schemes for Windows 2000 and hybrid Windows networks.
Exam ID and Title	70-221	Designing a Microsoft Windows 2000 Network Infrastructure
Description		Covers planning, designing, and deploying networking technologies, protocols, and services for Windows 2000 and hybrid Windows networks.
Exam ID and Title	70-222	Migrating from Microsoft Windows NT 4.0 to Microsoft Windows 2000
Description		Covers issues involved in planning, automating, installing, and deploying upgrades from a Windows NT 4.0–based network to a Windows 2000–based network.

The MCSE+I exams retire on December 31, 2000, and the cerification becomes obsolete on December 31, 2001. Before you take any elective that you want to count toward a Windows 2000 credential, be sure to double-check the Microsoft Web page that lists retired MCP exams, along with all those scheduled for retirement, at **www.microsoft.com/trainingandservices/default.asp?PageID=mcp** (choose the Exams To Be Retired link on the left-hand side of the page). DO NOT take any exams that appear on this page—they won't count!

The goal of MCSE certification is to produce a class of professionals who are thoroughly confident working with Microsoft desktop and server operating systems as well as being knowledgeable about modern network design, implementation, and maintenance. Those with MCSE certification are deemed able to plan, design, and implement network-based business information systems and to handle related technologies and products, in particular Microsoft's BackOffice suite.

For complete details about MCSE certification, visit the Microsoft site at **www.microsoft.com/trainingandservices/default.asp?PageID=mcp** and choose the MCSE link.

MCSE+I

Although the plain-vanilla MCSE might be the most sought-after Microsoft certification, MCSE+I is certainly the most demanding. It requires passing nine exams: the core four required for the regular MCSE, three additional core exams (most of which are valid electives for a plain Windows NT 4.0 MCSE), and two Internet-specific electives. The MCSE+I credential adds to the ordinary MCSE's understanding of internal systems and networks—a thorough knowledge and appreciation of the tools, products, and problems that one is likely to encounter when working with the Internet.

Rather than repeating all the information from the MCSE section, Table 2.9 lists only the additional core requirements for MCSE+I. Likewise, the electives for MCSE+I are listed in Table 2.10. Please note that only the Windows NT 4 track applies to MCSE+I; that certification does not accept the 3.51 Windows NT track for its four core requirements. Microsoft has also announced that this certification will become obsolete on December 31, 2001, when all Windows NT 4.0–related Microsoft credentials will expire.

Table 2.9 Additional MCSE+I required core exams.		
You must take three of the four exams listed here to meet additional MCSE+I core requirements, as well as all core exams required for the Windows NT 4.0 MCSE. Exams 70-059 TCP/IP and 70-087 IIS are valid MCSE electives and are by far the most popular choices for MCSEs simply because they eliminate two-thirds of the additional required MCSE+I core exams.		
Exam ID and Title	70-059*	Internetworking with Microsoft TCP/IP on Microsoft Windows NT 4.0
Description	Covers NT 4 TCP/IP protocols, addressing, subnets, DNS, and WINS, plus services and utilities.	
Exam ID and Title	70-079	Implementing and Supporting Microsoft Internet Explorer 4.0 by Using the Internet Explorer Administration Kit
OR		
Exam ID and Title	70-080	Implementing and Supporting Microsoft Internet Explorer 5.0 by Using the Internet Explorer Administration Kit
Description	These exams cover planning, installation (manual and automated), configuration, and deployment of Internet Explorer on Windows and other desktops using the Internet Explorer Administration Kit (IEAK).	
Exam ID and Title	70-087*	Implementing and Supporting Microsoft IIS 4.0
Description	Covers installation, configuration, and maintenance of IIS 4.0 and Index Server and security, content management, Web site design, and related IP services.	

Exams marked with an asterisk do not count toward the Windows 2000 MCSE.

For more information about the MCSE+I credentials and requirements, visit **www.microsoft.com/trainingandservices/default.asp?PageID=mcp** and choose the MCSE+I link.

The MCSE+I retires on December 31, 2000, and becomes obsolete on December 31, 2001. That's probably why it's not as popular as it used to be!

Table 2.10 MCSE+I elective exams.		
Choose any two items in this list, except for entries separated by the keyword **OR**, which indicates that only one of the items in that category may be counted as an MCSE+I elective.		
Exam ID and Title	70-026	Administering Microsoft SQL Server 6.5
OR		
Exam ID and Title	70-028	Administering Microsoft SQL Server 7.0
Description		Both tests cover Microsoft's BackOffice database engine and deal with what happens when design and deployment leave off—namely, database maintenance, programming, migration, and troubleshooting.
Exam ID and Title	70-027	Implementing a Database Design on Microsoft SQL Server 6.5
OR		
Exam ID and Title	70-029	Implementing a Database Design on Microsoft SQL Server 7.0
Description		Both tests cover Microsoft's BackOffice database engine and deal with topics including database design, testing, and deployment.
Exam ID and Title	70-056	Implementing and Supporting Web Sites Using Microsoft Site Server 3.0
Description		Covers Microsoft's BackOffice intranet information-delivery environment. Topics include how to publish information, search for information, and deliver information to users via email, channels, or Web pages.
Exam ID and Title	70-076	Implementing and Supporting Microsoft Exchange Server 5
OR		
Exam ID and Title	70-081	Implementing and Supporting Microsoft Exchange Server 5.5
Description		Both exams cover Microsoft BackOffice's messaging engine and deal with topics that include design and deployment of email systems, Internet links, messaging-based applications, and so on. Regarded as among the hardest of all Microsoft exams.

(continued)

Table 2.10 MCSE+I elective exams *(continued)*.		
Exam ID and Title	70-078	Implementing and Supporting Microsoft Proxy Server 1.0
OR		
Exam ID and Title	70-088	Implementing and Supporting Microsoft Proxy Server 2.0
Description		70-078 covers Proxy Server 1; 70-088 covers the current version. For both exams, topics include maintaining intranet security using Proxy Server, packet and address filtering and exceptions, managing protocols, and working with related tools and utilities.
Exam ID and Title	70-085	Implementing and Supporting Microsoft SNA Server 4.0
Description		Covers Microsoft's IBM mainframe connectivity servers. Topics include terminal emulation, host sessions, LAN-to-host data transfer, IP connectivity, and so on.

MCSD

The MCSD credential is aimed at software developers who seek to construct business solutions using Microsoft development tools, technologies, and platforms. As a result, this particular program has very little overlap with those you've examined so far in this chapter. MCPs and MCSEs may design and build systems around specific Microsoft components and products, but if they develop content, its software component is more incidental or supplementary rather than central. However, for MCSDs, building or customizing software solutions is assumed to be their primary activity.

MCSDs are required to pass three core exams and one elective exam. The core technology exams require candidates to demonstrate their competence with Microsoft's solution architecture and with developing desktop and distributed applications. The elective exams allow individuals to use their knowledge of programming languages or development environments. Table 2.11 lists the core requirements for the MCSD; Table 2.12 lists the electives.

Table 2.11 MCSD required core exams.		
Take one desktop application exam, one distributed application exam, and the solutions architecture exam for a total of three MCSD core exams.		
Desktop Applications Requirement (choose any one of the following)		
Exam ID and Title	70-016	Designing and Implementing Desktop Applications with Microsoft Visual C++ 6.0
Exam ID and Title	70-156	Designing and Implementing Desktop Applications with Microsoft Visual FoxPro
Exam ID and Title	70-176	Designing and Implementing Desktop Applications with Microsoft Visual Basic 6.0

(continued)

Table 2.11 MCSD required core exams *(continued)*.		
Distributed Applications Exams (take one)		
Exam ID and Title	70-015	Designing and Implementing Distributed Applications with Microsoft Visual C++ 6.0
Exam ID and Title	70-155	Designing and Implementing Distributed Applications with Microsoft Visual FoxPro 6.0
Exam ID and Title	70-175	Designing and Implementing Distributed Applications with Microsoft Visual Basic 6.0
Solutions Architecture Requirement		
Exam ID and Title	70-100	Analyzing Requirements and Defining Solution Architectures
Description		Covers application planning, analysis, and design; includes implementation tools, environments, and strategies; also covers all important Microsoft Application Programming Interfaces (APIs).

Table 2.12 MCSD elective exams.		
Choose any item in this list, except for entries separated by the keyword **OR**, which indicates that only one of the items in that category may be counted as an MCSD elective. Note that an exam used to fulfill a core requirement cannot be used to also fulfill an elective requirement.		
Exam ID and Title	70-015	Designing and Implementing Distributed Applications with Microsoft Visual C++ 6.0
Exam ID and Title	70-016	Designing and Implementing Desktop Applications with Microsoft Visual C++ 6.0
Exam ID and Title	70-019	Designing and Implementing Data Warehouses with Microsoft SQL Server 7.0
Exam ID and Title	70-024	Developing Applications with C++ Using the Microsoft Foundation Class Library
Exam ID and Title	70-025	Implementing OLE in Microsoft Foundation Class Applications
Exam ID and Title	70-027	Implementing a Database Design on Microsoft SQL Server 6.5
Exam ID and Title	70-029	Designing and Implementing Databases with Microsoft SQL Server 7.0
Exam ID and Title	70-055	Designing and Implementing Web Sites with Microsoft FrontPage 98
Exam ID and Title	70-057	Designing and Implementing Commerce Solutions with Microsoft Site Server 3.0, Commerce Edition
Exam ID and Title	70-069	Application Development with Microsoft Access for Windows 95 and the Microsoft Access Developer's Toolkit

(continued)

Table 2.12 MCSD elective exams *(continued)*.		
Exam ID and Title	70-091	Designing and Implementing Solutions with Microsoft Office 2000 and Microsoft Visual Basic for Applications
Exam ID and Title	70-097	Designing and Implementing Database Applications with Microsoft Access 2000
Exam ID and Title	70-105	Designing and Implementing Collaborative Solutions with Microsoft Outlook 2000 and Microsoft Exchange Server 5.5
Exam ID and Title	70-152	Designing and Implementing Web Solutions with Microsoft Visual InterDev 6.0
Exam ID and Title	70-155	Designing and Implementing Distributed Applications with Microsoft Visual FoxPro 6.0
Exam ID and Title	70-156	Designing and Implementing Desktop Applications with Microsoft Visual FoxPro 6.0
Exam ID and Title	70-165	Developing Applications with Microsoft Visual Basic 5.0
Exam ID and Title	70-175	Designing and Implementing Distributed Applications with Microsoft Visual Basic 6.0
Exam ID and Title	70-176	Designing and Implementing Desktop Applications with Microsoft Visual Basic 6.0

Because there are so many electives for the MCSD, and nearly all of them have been covered elsewhere in this chapter, I will forgo the brief description that has accompanied exam listings up to this point. For more information about this older program and the tests mentioned in Table 2.12, visit **www.microsoft.com/ trainingandservices/default.asp?PageID=mcp** and choose the MCSD link.

MCT

The Microsoft Certified Trainer (MCT) credential is designed to identify those individuals who are qualified to teach elements of the Microsoft Official Curriculum (MOC) within the Microsoft training channel. Training outlets within this channel may be identified as Certified Technical Education Centers (CTECs) or as Authorized Academic Training Partners (AATPs). Basically, instructors who wish to teach MOC elements at either kind of outlet must be certified as MCTs.

Unlike other elements of the Microsoft curriculum, obtaining an MCT is a bit more convoluted and subject to a greater number of potential alternatives. That's why I present these requirements in the form of a bulleted list rather than in table form, as with most other elements in this book. The MCT certification requirements are as follows:

➤ Prospective candidates must submit a completed MCT application form (download this form from **www.microsoft.com/trainingandservices/downloads/mct00app.doc**).

➤ Prospective candidates must meet Microsoft's instruction requirement to verify that they possess the necessary classroom training skills. You can meet this requirement in one of three ways:

➤ Complete a Microsoft preapproved training workshop (download the list of such workshops from the bottom of the Web page named in the preceding list element).

➤ Produce trainer credentials from Novell, Lotus, SCO, Banyan Vines, Cisco Systems, or Sun Microsystems.

➤ Produce credentials for the Chauncey Certified Technical Training (CTT) certification.

➤ Prospective candidates must produce a copy of their MCP transcript (available through the MCP Web page at **www.microsoft.com/trainingandservices/default.asp?PageID=mcp**) to demonstrate completion of the exams related to the courses they wish to teach and to document their current MCP status.

In addition, candidates must also complete a Microsoft course preparation checklist for each MOC element they wish to teach. Completion of this checklist means that they must meet the following requirements:

➤ *Pass any prerequisite MCP exams to measure current technical knowledge.* For many MOC elements, this means that candidates must have completed a current MCSE (for Windows 2000 elements, this will ultimately mean completing a Windows 2000 MCSE, but because those exams are still being rolled out, you must check individual courses on a case-by-case basis). If there is no MCP exam associated with a specific course, you may have to pass a Microsoft trainer exam for that course instead. This requires ordering the Trainer Kit for the course and examining its contents to determine the exact requirements.

➤ *Prepare to teach the MOC course.* Instructors must familiarize themselves with the contents of the Trainer Kit for that course and ready themselves to present it in the classroom either through self-study or by attending the course at a CTEC or an AATP. You can attend either a trainer preparation (T-prep) course at a Microsoft CTEC or any offering of the same course to the public (be sure to bring your own Trainer Kit with you as you attend).

➤ *Complete additional exam requirements.* Once you are prepared to teach the course, you may have to take an additional MCP or trainer exam to meet that course's specific completion requirements. Check the Trainer Kit for the details.

➤ *Submit a course preparation checklist to Microsoft to obtain accreditation to teach the course.* Even after meeting the previously mentioned requirements, you must submit a completed course preparation checklist to Microsoft, and your MCP transcript updated to reflect accreditation to teach the class, before you become authorized to teach the MOC element at a CTEC or an AATP. Brand-new MCTs must also attend at least one public MOC course at a CTEC so that they can become familiar with required course flow and timing elements and observe interaction between MCTs and their students. The course you attend must be taught by an accredited MCT with two or more years of classroom experience.

Accredited MCTs have access to a private MCT Web site where they can order Trainer Kits, obtain access to beta and instructor-only information, and so on. The MCT is rightly regarded as one of Microsoft's premier credentials.

MOUS

The MOUS program is designed to provide a cadre of certified individuals who can function in today's workplace. Because the skills that a MOUS can document are in such high demand, Microsoft has announced that it seeks to certify over one million individuals for some level of MOUS certification by the end of 2001.

The MOUS program recognizes three levels of proficiency, as follows:

➤ *Microsoft Office Proficient Specialist (Office Core)*—This level indicates that users can handle a wide range of everyday tasks and requires working knowledge of both Microsoft Word and Microsoft Excel (Office 97 or 2000 versions). This certification is known as the Core Certification for Office 2000 software.

➤ *Microsoft Office Expert Specialist (Office Expert)*—This level indicates that users can handle complex assignments that involve advanced formatting and functionality. This certification applies to any of the four primary components of Office 97 (Word, Excel, PowerPoint, and Access) or the Word and Excel components of Office 2000. Thus, an individual could claim to be a Microsoft Expert Specialist in Excel and Word, for instance. For Office 2000, this certification is called Office Expert Certification.

➤ *Microsoft Office Master*—This level indicates that users have attained Master Specialist status in all four of the Office 97 or five of the Office 2000 components for which testing is currently available: Word, Excel, PowerPoint, and Access (and Outlook for the Office 2000 certification only). This is the highest-level MOUS certification available. The name of this certification is the same for both Office 97 and Office 2000.

Unlike other Microsoft tests mentioned so far in this chapter, MOUS tests rely almost entirely on simulation techniques and task-oriented assignments to assess the test taker's skills. That is, most of the questions involve manipulating a mock-up of one or more Office applications' interfaces and require individuals to complete a battery of assignments within a period of time.

At present, a battery of Microsoft tests for the various MOUS certifications is available for Office 97 (visit **www.mous.net** for more information). Of the six exams for Office 97 components currently available, two are at the "Proficient" level for Microsoft Word 97 and Microsoft Excel 97, and four are at the "Expert" level for all four major office components: Word 97, Excel 97, PowerPoint 97, and Access 97.

Although there are a number of Microsoft tests for many Office 97 applications, Office 2000 supports the greatest number of individual exams. For more information, go to **www.mous.net/include/levels_2000_include.htm** (Office 2000 Exam listing) or **www.mous.net/include/levels_97_include.htm** (Office 97 Exam listing).

Microsoft has made a lot of noise about how important and strategic MOUS certification can be, but you should be prepared to do some digging to find your way into this program.

Microsoft Testing

By now, you've certainly read about a sizable number of Microsoft tests. You're probably wondering what's involved in signing up for or taking such tests. Nothing could be easier than to explain how this process works.

For all the MCP, MCSE, and MCSD tests, you may sign up with one of two testing companies that handle testing for Microsoft certification:

➤ *Prometric*—You can sign up for a test through the company's Web site (current exams only, no beta exams through the Web) at **www.2test.com**, or you can register by phone at 1-800-755-EXAM (in the United States or Canada).

➤ *Virtual University Enterprises*—You can sign up for a test or get the phone numbers for local testing centers through the Web page at **www.vue.com/ms/**.

To sign up for a test, you must possess a valid credit card or contact either company for mailing instructions to send them a check (in the United States). You can register for a test only when payment is verified or a check has cleared.

To schedule an exam, call or visit either of the Web pages that appear in the preceding list at least one day in advance. To cancel or reschedule an exam, you must call at least 12 hours before the scheduled test time or before close of business the preceding working day (or you may be charged, even if you don't show up to take the test). When you want to schedule a test, have the following information ready:

➤ Your name, organization, and mailing address.

➤ Your Microsoft Test ID. (In the United States, this means your social security number; citizens of other nations should call ahead to find out what type of identification number is required to register for a test.)

➤ The name and number of the exam you wish to take.

➤ A method of payment.

Once you sign up for a test, you'll be informed as to when and where the test is scheduled. Try to arrive at least 15 minutes early. You must supply two forms of identification, one of which must be a photo ID.

All Microsoft exams are closed book. In fact, you won't be allowed to take anything with you into the testing area; you'll be furnished with a blank sheet of paper and a pen. I suggest that you immediately write down whatever you've memorized for the test before you actually begin to take the test. You'll have some time to compose yourself and to record this information.

Microsoft is increasingly using adaptive and short-form rather than fixed-length exams. Adaptive exams are set up to determine a test taker's testing level by adjusting the level of difficulty, depending on whether your answer to a question is correct (next question is more difficult) or incorrect (next question is easier). Short-form exams determine the exam questions that most fully test a candidate's knowledge of the subject on the basis of the results of statistical analyses of other tests. For more information, visit the Microsoft site at **www.microsoft.com/ trainingandservices/default.asp?PageID=mcp** and choose the Testing Innovations link on the left-hand side of the page.

The test subject matter in both adaptive and fixed-length exams is the same, but each offers different numbers of questions and different time limits. In an adaptive test, the number of questions you need to answer depends on the number of questions you get right or wrong. An incorrect answer on such tests results in the next question being different from the one that comes up after a correct answer. Essentially, this means that you can't return later to a question, as you can in the short-form or fixed-length tests.

Two other kinds of Microsoft tests are relatively new in the testing scene. The select-and-place test calls on candidates to synthesize information across a number of subjects and to use their results in answering exam questions. The other kind of exam is based on case studies (scenarios) and relies heavily on descriptions of different situations in posing test questions. For this kind of exam, candidates have to put their knowledge to work in the situation that an exam question postulates. Both kinds of exams are designed to do away with rote memorization as a test factor as well as to force candidates to use what they know in solving theoretical problems.

To sign up for a MOUS test, you must identify a local MOUS testing center and call it directly to schedule the test you want to take. To do this, you can call one of these two numbers to identify which testing center you should call:

➤ 1-800-933-4493 in North America

➤ #0800 389 7793 or #0345 002 000 in the United Kingdom

Elsewhere, call Microsoft's main number at 1-425-882-8080 and ask to be connected to a Microsoft Office User Specialist program coordinator. Or, if you prefer, you can use the online test center locator available through the Locate button on the home page at **www.mous.net**. Expect most of the financial terms and restrictions to be like those I've described for the other Microsoft tests earlier in this section.

Tracking MCP Status

As soon as you pass any Microsoft operating system exam, you'll attain MCP status. Microsoft also generates transcripts that indicate the exams you've passed and your corresponding test scores. You can order a transcript by sending an email to **mcp@msprograms.com**. You can also obtain a copy of your transcript by calling the Microsoft Certified Professional program's customer service number at 1-800-636-7544 in North America. Outside North America, contact the Microsoft location nearest you for more information.

Becoming an MCSE

Once you pass the necessary set of six or seven exams, you'll be certified as an MCSE. Official notification normally takes anywhere from four to six weeks, so don't expect to get your credentials overnight. When the package arrives, it will include a Welcome Kit that contains a number of elements, including the following:

➤ An MCSE certificate, suitable for framing, along with an MCSE Professional Program membership card and lapel pin.

➤ A license to use the MCP logo, which allows you to use the logo in documents, advertisements, promotions, letterhead, business cards, and so on. An MCP logo sheet, which includes camera-ready artwork, comes with the license. (Note that before using any of the artwork, individuals must sign and return a licensing agreement that indicates that they'll abide by its terms and conditions.)

➤ A half-price subscription to TechNet—a collection of CDs that includes software, documentation, service packs, databases, and more technical information than you can digest in a month. In my mind, discount access to TechNet is the best and most tangible benefit of attaining MCSE status.

➤ A subscription to *Microsoft Certified Professional* magazine, which provides ongoing data about testing and certification activities, requirements, and changes to the program.

Many people believe that the benefits of MCSE certification go well beyond the perks that Microsoft provides to newly anointed members of this elite group. It's not at all uncommon to see job listings that request or require applicants to have an MCSE, and many individuals who complete the program can qualify for increases in pay and/or responsibility. As an official recognition of hard work and broad knowledge, MCSE certification is a badge of honor in many IT organizations. Likewise, the same is true of MCSE+I and MCSD certifications.

Tracking MOUS Status

At present, Microsoft hasn't automated access to MOUS status and test results as it has for its other certifications (I expect that to change before the end of 2001, however, given Microsoft's ambitious recruitment objectives). Right now, you must call one of the following phone numbers to obtain MOUS status information:

➤ 1-800-933-4493 in North America

➤ #0800 389 7793 or #0345 002 000 in the United Kingdom

Elsewhere, call Microsoft's main number at 1-425-882-8080 and ask to speak with a Microsoft Office User Specialist program coordinator.

How to Prepare for a Microsoft Exam

At a minimum, you should use the following to prepare for a Microsoft exam:

➤ For most exams, Microsoft offers self-study kits or computer trade books. Microsoft Press publishes both types of materials. You can search for such information using the search facilities at your favorite online bookstore or at the Microsoft Press site at **mspress.microsoft.com**.

➤ Exam preparation materials, practice tests, and self-assessment exams are available for most, if not all, tests on the Microsoft Training and Services—Certification page at **http://www.microsoft.com/trainingandservices/default.asp?PageID=mcp** (choose the appropriate pointer under Exams on the left-hand side of the page). Find these materials, download them, and use them!

➤ Check the Certification Insider Press *Exam Cram* and *Exam Prep* books. The *Exam Cram*s are the first and last things you should read before taking an exam. They are complete with practice questions, study tips, additional resources, and a sample test. *Exam Prep*s are detailed study guides to help those not already familiar with a test's subject to learn that subject matter and prepare to take that test. Each chapter breaks down a subject area and concludes with hands-on projects and review questions. A CD-ROM that contains two sample tests is also included.

In addition, you'll probably find any or all of the following materials useful in your quest for Microsoft expertise:

➤ *Study guides*—Numerous publishers offer so-called MCSE study guides of one kind or another.

➤ *Microsoft Resource Kits*—Although not every Microsoft test is the subject of one of these publications (nor of their supplements, three of which are available for Windows NT Server at this writing), all of them include valuable information about Microsoft terminology, products, and technologies. Resource Kits are available from Microsoft Press and are usually must-have resources, not just for test preparation but also for living with these products once you've passed the tests.

➤ *Classroom training*—CTECs, academic institutions, and unlicensed third-party training companies (such as Wave Technologies, American Research Group, Learning Tree, and Data-Tech) offer classroom training on Microsoft exam topics. These companies aim to help prepare network administrators to understand Microsoft's requirements and pass the tests. Although such training runs upwards of $350 per day in class, most individuals who are lucky enough to partake (including your humble author, who's even taught such courses) find them to be quite worthwhile.

➤ *Other publications*—You'll find plenty of other publications and resources if you take the time to look around on the Web or in your local bookstore; there's no shortage of materials available about Microsoft exams.

➤ *TechNet*—TechNet is a monthly CD subscription available from Microsoft. TechNet includes all the Windows NT BackOffice Resource Kits and their product documentation. In addition, TechNet provides the contents of the Microsoft Knowledge Base and many kinds of software, white papers, training materials, as well as other good stuff. TechNet also contains all service packs, interim release patches, and supplemental driver software released since the last major version for most Microsoft programs and all Microsoft operating systems. A one-year subscription costs $299—worth every penny, if only for the download time it saves. For an additional $150, you can sign up for TechNet Plus and get beta versions of all Microsoft products as part of your monthly CD delivery as well.

The previous set of required and recommended materials represents a nonpareil collection of sources and resources for Microsoft exam topics and software.

Need to Know More?

For convenience, I include all the URLs mentioned so far in this chapter, along with pointers to a few other resources worth investigating for information about Microsoft certification, exams, training, and more:

 www.microsoft.com/trainingandservices/default.asp?PageID=mcp This is the ultimate resource for information related to all Microsoft certification. To learn about the requirements for each certification, click on the appropriate link on the left-hand side of this page. Be sure to check out the Exams section for exam preparation guides, practice tests, and other kinds of self-assessment tools.

 www.microsoft.com/train_cert/mct/ This is the home page for the MCT program, where you can download the application form, course preparation checklist, program details, and more.

 www.mous.net This is the home page for the MOUS program. It includes information on upcoming tests and events, an electronic newsletter open to all subscribers, and general program information.

 www.officecert.com This is a third-party MOUS site operated by QuickStart Technologies, Inc. It features exam information, online study groups, access to domain experts, and more. It's worth spending time on if you're chasing any MOUS credentials.

 www.prometric.com This is the home page for Prometric's testing centers and can provide information about this company's locations, charges, and policies.

 www.2test.com This is the home page for Prometric testing centers and has information about company locations, costs, and policies.

 www.vue.com/ms/ This is the home page for Virtual University Enterprises' Microsoft testing area and can provide information about this company's locations, charges, and policies for such tests.

 www.mcpmag.com This URL points to the home page for *Microsoft Certified Professional Magazine*, a third-party publication that covers news, products, training materials, study guides, and other information related to Microsoft certification.

www.microsoft.com/technet/ This URL points to the online version of Microsoft's fabulous TechNet CD library.

 www.sunbelt-software.com/index.htm This URL points to Sunbelt Software's online resources for MCSE preparation, which includes an informative and active mailing list focused on MCSE issues, plus pointers to all kinds of study and preparation materials.

Novell Certification
Programs

Terms you'll need to understand:

✓ CNA

✓ CNE

✓ MCNE

✓ CNI

✓ CDE

✓ NetWare product family: NetWare 3,
  NetWare 4/intraNetWare, NetWare 5

✓ System administrator

✓ Network administrator

Techniques you'll need to master:

✓ Locating training and certification information on the
  Novell Web site

✓ Obtaining descriptions and objectives for specific
  Novell exams

✓ Locating practice tests to help you prepare for specific
  Novell exams

Novell has been in the training and certification game long enough to be considered a pioneer, although it may not have the most complex or voluminous set of offerings of all the vendors you'll encounter in this book. Novell's certification program pre-dates Microsoft's by at least three years, and the number of certified professionals—currently estimated at over 660,000 and growing—is the second largest of any certification program. In this chapter, you'll examine Novell's various certification options.

Alphabet Soup

To begin, let's review the numerous acronyms that relate to Novell's certification credentials. After that, you'll have a chance to investigate each certification in some detail, including the elements that lead to each one. Along the way, you'll be presented with a series of tables that show how the pieces fit together. Then, you'll learn how to sign up for tests, track certification progress, and prepare for each test.

Here are the acronyms related to Novell certifications, with brief explanations:

➤ *Certified Novell Administrator (CNA)*—Candidates who demonstrate their skills in any of a number of areas of expertise. This certification requires passing one test in any of five tracks (three are specific to NetWare versions, and two are specific to GroupWise versions). This is Novell's entry-level certification.

➤ *Certified Novell Engineer (CNE)*—Candidates who demonstrate their skills in installing and managing NetWare networks. This certification is obtained by passing six or seven exams, including five or six (depending on which track you are pursuing) required core exams and a single elective. This is Novell's most sought-after certification.

➤ *Master CNE (MCNE)*—Candidates must first prove their basic expertise by obtaining CNE certification. To obtain an MCNE certification, they must then pass four to six tests in any of seven specialized areas. This is Novell's most elite certification.

➤ *Certified Novell Instructor (CNI)*—Candidates must meet both an instructional requirement and training and examination requirements for whatever courses they may wish to teach. Basic requirements are simple, but per-course requirements must also be weighed whenever you consider what courses you might want to teach.

➤ *Certified Directory Engineer (CDE)*—Achieving a senior-level certification such as CNE, MCSE, ASE, CCNP, or CCIE is a prerequisite to this credential. The CDE requires completion of two core exams in addition to a hands-on live lab exam (similar to the CCIE lab exam). CDEs must recertify annually by retaking the live lab exam (and other exams as announced).

	Required	Elective			
Certification	**Exams**	**Exams**	**Questions**	**Cost**	**Time**
CNA	1	0	15–90	$95	30–90 min.
CNE	5–6	1	15–90	$95	30–90 min.
MCNE	4–6	0–1	15–90	$95	30–90 min.
CNI	CNE/MCNE + 1	0	Varies	Varies	Varies
CDE	3	0	Varies	$95 and TBD	30–90 min./ 2 hours

Table 3.1   Novell certifications, exams, and more.

All the information in the preceding list, plus some additional details about the exams, is summed up in Table 3.1.

 The number of questions, the cost, and the time period are for each exam, not for all exams.

Novell uses two different types of tests in its certification exams: program tests and adaptive tests. *Program tests* use traditional, multiple-choice questions, graphical exhibits, and simulations. They follow a regular, predictable sequence of questions, drawn at random, by category, from a database of potential questions. Each test taker sees the same number of questions and gets an equal amount of time to finish.

Adaptive tests recognize when test takers answer a question incorrectly and react by asking a simpler question on the same topic, asking gradually more difficult questions on that topic until a test taker's expertise in the category is established. For this reason, adaptive tests can end in as little as 30 minutes or can take longer than an hour to complete.

Because the length of an adaptive test is related to the test taker's familiarity with the subject matter, it's more important to prepare thoroughly for an adaptive test than for a program test. Adaptive behavior also makes it impossible to predict exactly how many questions you'll see on any particular adaptive test or how long a test will take. That's why Table 3.1 shows broad variation in the number of questions and time required for the various exams it lists. For details on the type and number of questions for any Novell test, visit **http://education.novell.com/ testinfo/testdata.htm**.

Live lab exams involve certificants interacting with a simulated networking environment and making requisite design and implementation changes and troubleshooting setup problems. These exams are designed to test knowledge and skills associated with operating actual networks. The CDE is the only Novell credential that currently requires a live lab exam.

In the sections that follow, you'll examine each of Novell's certifications in more detail, and learn a little more about the related exams that you must pass. If you visit the URLs mentioned for each credential, in most cases you'll be able to jump straight to the details related to the required exams (and electives, where applicable).

 Although Web locations change over time, they're worth chasing down because Novell's Web site is the final authority on certification information and requirements.

CNA

When it comes to options, CNAs have an awful lot to choose from. However, because CNAs provide onsite network and systems administration in a variety of working conditions, this variety makes sense. In general, CNAs are usually responsible for everyday administration and oversight of some installed Novell networking product, be it NetWare 5, intraNetWare or NetWare 4, NetWare 3, GroupWise 5, or GroupWise 4. These specific product responsibilities also match the tracks that prospective CNAs must follow to attain this particular certification.

 You may notice throughout this chapter that I use NetWare 4 to refer to the intraNetWare track. This is because Novell uses both names for the same product—namely, intraNetWare and NetWare 4.11 or 4.2—but the network operating system software is more often called NetWare 4 or 4.x to cover all versions.

Table 3.2 covers the requirements for each CNA category. However, note that Novell recommends that prospective CNAs meet certain knowledge prerequisites: NetWare CNAs of all stripes should know basic PC and networking concepts and terminology and be familiar with DOS and Windows; GroupWise CNAs of all stripes should know basic NetWare administration and NetWare Directory Services (NDS).

For a more detailed description of these requirements, visit the CNA home page at **http://education.novell.com/cna/**. For a detailed roadmap of courses, tests, and certifications into which the various CNA tracks feed (and Novell is very good about pointing out how these various tracks can lead to more advanced Novell certifications), download the CNA Progress Chart from the CNA home page.

Table 3.2	CNA tracks and associated exams.	
Exam ID and Title	50-639	NetWare 5 Administration
OR		
Exam ID and Title	50-645	NetWare 5 Administration 1.01
Track	NetWare 5	
Description	Both exams cover basic NetWare 5 planning, installation, configuration, and administration.	
OR		
Exam ID and Title	50-638	NetWare 4.11 to NetWare 5 Update*
Track	NetWare 5	
Description	Prepares NetWare Administrators certified in 4.11 to upgrade to 5 and to integrate across versions.	
Exam ID and Title	50-613	intraNetWare: NetWare 4.11 Administration
Track	NetWare 4	
Description	Covers basic NetWare 4.11/intraNetWare planning, installation, configuration, and administration.	
OR		
Exam ID and Title	50-615	intraNetWare: NetWare 3.1x to NetWare 4.11 Update
Track	NetWare 4	
Description	Prepares NetWare Administrators certified in 3.1x to upgrade to 4.11 and to integrate NetWare across versions.	
Exam ID and Title	50-130	NetWare 3.1x Administration
Track	NetWare 3	
Description	Covers basic NetWare 3.x (current version is 3.12) planning, installation, configuration, and administration.	
Exam ID and Title	50-618	GroupWise 5 Administration
OR		
Exam ID and Title	50-633	GroupWise 5.5 System Administration
Track	GroupWise 5	
Description	Both exams cover GroupWise 5x features, functions, and architecture; planning; installation; administration; user management; libraries; documents; and more.	
Exam ID and Title	50-154	GroupWise 4 Administration
Track	GroupWise 4	
Description	Covers GroupWise 4 features, functions, and architecture; planning; installation; administration; user management; libraries; documents; and more.	

Applies only to individuals already certified as a CNE.

CNE

Individuals who obtain a CNE are assumed to be qualified to plan, install, configure, and manage the systems and services that fall within the track they are pursuing. Except for a single exam, the CNE remains very much a NetWare- or GroupWise-focused certification (only the version of NetWare or GroupWise that a CNE specializes in may vary; otherwise, the testing regimen is the same).

Table 3.3 lists the exams for those seeking certification in NetWare (version 3, 4, or 5) and in GroupWise (version 4 or 5).

Note: The same tracks apply to the CNE that apply to the CNA.

Table 3.3 Exams required for NetWare CNE certifications.
Applicants must take and pass five or six required exams (five for NetWare 5, six for all other tracks) and one elective to obtain a CNE. The first two exams listed below are mandatory for all tracks. Read each entry for track information to determine exact track requirements. When following a higher-numbered version of software (such as NetWare 5), Novell recommends taking the highest numbered exam in a category in which there are multiple options.

Core Requirements

Exam ID and Title	50-632	Networking Technologies
Track	All	
Description	Covers networking concepts and terminology, plus networking installation, operations, and troubleshooting for current networking technologies, topologies, and media. The CompTIA Network+ or MCSE certification is acceptable in lieu of Novell's Networking Technologies exam (visit **http://education.novell. com/waiver/waiverform.pdf** to download a waiver form).	

Exam ID and Title	50-635	Service and Support
Track	All	
Description	Measures skills necessary to support network installation, configuration, troubleshooting, and maintenance issues. Many experts regard this as among the most difficult of all Novell exams.	

NetWare-Specific Exams

Exam ID and Title OR	50-639	NetWare 5 Administration
Exam ID and Title OR	50-645	NetWare 5 Administration 1.01
Exam ID and Title	50-653	NetWare 5.1 Administration
Track	NetWare 5	
Description	These exams cover basic NetWare 5 and 5.1 planning, installation, configuration, and administration.	

Exam ID and Title OR	50-640	NetWare 5 Advanced Administration
Exam ID and Title	50-654	NetWare 5.1 Advanced Administration
Track	NetWare 5	
Description	These exams cover advanced NetWare topics, including automated installation, complex configurations, enterprise design and deployment issues, remote administration, and heterogeneous networking situations.	

(continued)

Table 3.3   Exams required for NetWare CNE certifications (continued).

Exam ID and Title	50-634 NDS Design and Implementation
Track	NetWare 5
Description	Covers NDS directory planning, design, deployment, and management, as well as use of complex directory trees and directory-enabled applications.
Exam ID and Title	50-613 intraNetWare: NetWare 4.11 Administration
Track	intraNetWare/NetWare 4
Description	Covers installing, configuring, and managing NetWare 4.11.
Exam ID and Title	50-614 intraNetWare: NetWare 4.11 Advanced Administration
Track	NetWare 4
Description	Covers advanced NetWare 4.11 topics, including automated installation, complex configurations, enterprise design and deployment issues, remote administration, and heterogeneous networking situations.
Exam ID and Title	50-634 NDS Design and Implementation
Track	NetWare 4
Description	Covers NDS directory planning, design, deployment, and management, plus use of complex directory trees and directory-enabled applications.
Exam ID and Title	50-617 intraNetWare: NetWare 4.11 Installation and Configuration
Track	NetWare 4
Description	Covers planning and performing upgrades and migrations from NetWare 3.12, and new installations of NetWare 4.11 systems and servers.
Exam ID and Title	50-130 NetWare 3.1x Administration
Track	NetWare 3
Description	Covers installing, configuring, and managing NetWare 3.1x networks.
Exam ID and Title	50-131 NetWare 3.1x Advanced Administration
Track	NetWare 3
Description	Covers advanced NetWare 3.1x topics, including automated installation, complex configurations, enterprise design and deployment issues, remote administration, and heterogeneous networking situations.
Exam ID and Title	50-615 intraNetWare: NetWare 3.1x to NetWare 4.11 Update
Track	NetWare 3
Description	Prepares NetWare Administrators certified in 3.1x to upgrade to 4.11 and to integrate NetWare across versions.
Exam ID and Title	50-132 NetWare 3.1x Installation and Configuration
Track	NetWare 3
Description	Covers planning and performing upgrades, migrations, and new installations of NetWare 4.11 systems and servers.

(continued)

Table 3.3   Exams required for NetWare CNE certifications *(continued)*.

Exam ID and Title	50-613 intraNetWare: NetWare 4.11 Administration
Track	GroupWise 5
Description	Covers installing, configuring, and managing NetWare 4.11.
OR	
Exam ID and Title	50-639 NetWare 5 Administration
OR	
Exam ID and Title	50-645 NetWare 5 Administration 1.01
OR	
Exam ID and Title	50-653 NetWare 5.1 Administration
Track	GroupWise 5
Description	These exams cover basic NetWare 5 and 5.1 planning, installation, configuration, and administration.
Exam ID and Title	50-633 GroupWise 5.5 System Administration
Track	GroupWise 5
Description	Covers planning, installing, administering, and troubleshooting GroupWise 5.5, plus using features and functions of GroupWise, such as documents, libraries, and email-enabled applications.
Exam ID and Title	50-643 GroupWise 5.5 Advanced Administration
Track	GroupWise 5
Description	Covers planning, configuring, and installing GroupWise applications, workflow, and document management for local and enterprise-wide uses.
Exam ID and Title	50-620 GroupWise Net Access and Connectivity
Track	GroupWise 5
Description	Covers installation, configuration, and management of agents and gateways, along with Internet and local access methods, services, and protocols.
Exam ID and Title	50-613 intraNetWare: NetWare 4.11 Administration
Track	GroupWise 4
Description	Covers NetWare 4.11 installation, configuration, and management.
Exam ID and Title	50-154 GroupWise 4 Administration
Track	GroupWise 4
Description	Covers GroupWise 4 planning, installation, and management; using features and functions; and managing users, documents, libraries, and email-enabled applications.
Exam ID and Title	50-612 GroupWise 4 Async Gateway and GroupWise Remote
Track	GroupWise 4
Description	Covers installing and configuring Async Gateway in GroupWise, managing remote clients, and troubleshooting.
Exam ID and Title	50-604 GroupWise 4 Advanced Administration
Track	GroupWise 4
Description	Covers planning, configuring, and installing GroupWise applications, workflow, and document management for local and enterprise-wide uses.

(continued)

Table 3.3	Exams required for NetWare CNE certifications *(continued)*.		
CNE Electives				
For brevity's sake, I provide no exam descriptions here. Visit the Novell Web site at **http://education.novell.com/testinfo/objectives/crsindex.htm** for more detailed information. Except where noted, these electives apply to all CNE tracks.				
Exam ID and Title	50-656	Desktop Management with ZENworks
Exam ID and Title	50-642	Securing Intranets with BorderManager
Exam ID and Title	50-650	Internet Security Management with BorderManager: Enterprise Edition 3.5
Exam ID and Title	50-641	Network Management Using ManageWise 2.6
Exam ID and Title	50-649	TCP/IP for Networking Professionals
Exam ID and Title	50-644	Integrating NetWare and Windows NT
Exam ID and Title	50-633	GroupWise 5.5 System Administration (not applicable for GroupWise 5 track)
Exam ID and Title	50-436	Oracle Database Operator for NetWare

Note that the requirements for the NetWare 4 and 5 tracks overlap considerably but that the NetWare 3 track includes several of its own special elements. Unless you work in an environment that is tied to NetWare 3 for a special reason, you should seek certification on a more recent version of NetWare, preferably NetWare 5.

For more information about the CNE certification, visit Novell's CNE home page at **http://education.novell.com/cne/**. Pay special attention to the CNE Progress Chart.

MCNE

Novell calls the individuals who attain this credential "the industry's leading integration specialists." Given that passing six exams and obtaining a CNE are merely prerequisites to entering the MCNE program and that four to six additional exams are necessary to make the grade, it may have a point. Suffice it to say that only those with a real appetite for test taking tend to attain this exalted status.

MCNE exams are broken into three categories, as follows:

➤ *Core*—All MCNEs must take two core exams on internetworking and NDS design and implementation. This is to ensure that all candidates have a solid background in complex, heterogeneous network environments. Some MCNE specialties involve one additional core exam.

➤ *Target*—Each area of specialization involves one or two target tests to ensure specialists' expertise in their chosen areas.

➤ *Elective*—Most specializations involve one or two elective tests to ensure that specialists are well rounded in important Novell or networking technologies.

All relevant tests for the MCNE appear in Table 3.4, broken down by the areas of specialization. Target exams vary by specialty. The table also includes the number of electives required by specialty, where applicable.

Table 3.4   Exams required for Master CNE certifications.

These exams are separated by the categories Core, Target, and Elective. Where tracks apply to an exam, the track is named by its abbreviations as it appears in the preceding list. Where an exam applies to all tracks, its category is listed as All. Where any one of several exams may be taken, such exams will be grouped and separated by the keyword **OR** in a single table entry.

Core Exams

Exam ID and Title	50-611 Fundamentals of Internetworking
Track	All
Description	Comprehensive internetworking exam on the OSI reference model, networking equipment and practices, routing, gateways, network addressing schemes, security models, and more.
Exam ID and Title	50-634 NDS Design and Implementation
Track	All
Description	Covers NDS directory planning, design, deployment, and management, plus use of complex directory trees and directory-enabled applications.
Exam ID and Title	50-145 NetWare TCP/IP Transport
Track	Int,Unix, WinNT
OR	
Exam ID and Title	50-649 TCP/IP for Networking Professionals
Track	Int, Unix, WinNT
Description	These exams cover IP protocols, practices, and principles, plus related services; IP addressing issues; and integration with older NetWare networks where IP is not a native protocol (it is native for NetWare 5 and higher).
OR	
Exam ID and Title	90-054 SCO OpenServer Release 5 Network Administration
OR	
Exam ID and Title	90-554 SCO OpenServer Release 5 Network Administration
Track	Unix
Description	Covers installing, configuring, and maintaining SCO's UnixWare or OpenServer operating systems and administering a network using SCO's OpenServer platform.

(continued)

Table 3.4	Exams required for Master CNE certifications *(continued)*.
Exam ID and Title	50-637 NetWare for SAA
Track	AS/400
Description	Basic principles of IBM's Systems Applications Architecture and SNA-related networking protocols, practices, and principles.
Target Exams	
The only track that requires two target exams rather than one for an MCNE is the Internet/Intranet Solutions track, abbreviated below as "Int."	
Exam ID and Title	50-641 Network Management Using ManageWise 2.6
Track	Mgmt
Description	Basic principles of network monitoring and management, including remote and local management, and integrating ManageWise with other third-party management environments.
Exam ID and Title	50-642 Securing Intranets with BorderManager
OR	
Exam ID and Title	50-650 Internet Security Management with BorderManager
Track	Conn
Description	Basic principles and practices for managing intranet or Internet security, including planning, installation, and management of BorderManager, used as a firewall, gateway, and proxy server.
Exam ID and Title	50-643 GroupWise 5.5 Advanced Administration
OR	
Exam ID and Title	50-623 GroupWise 4.1 to 5 Differences
Track	Msg
Description	Advanced deployment, configuration, and applications based on GroupWise 5.5, covering the differences involved in installing, configuring, managing, and troubleshooting GroupWise 5 compared to GroupWise 4, respectively. The second exam is recommended only for those who already know GroupWise 4 (or who are cross-certifying for MCNE status in both GroupWise versions).
Exam ID and Title	50-710 Web Server Management
Track	Int
Description	Design, installation, configuration, management, and trouble shooting of NetWare-based Web sites, including document issues, programming concerns, and day-to-day operations and maintenance tasks.
Exam ID and Title	50-712 Managing Netscape Enterprise Server for NetWare
Track	Int
Description	Installation, configuration, maintenance, and management of the Netscape Enterprise Server for NetWare, including site hosting and multihosting, content management, programming issues, and more.

(continued)

Table 3.4 Exams required for Master CNE certifications *(continued)*.

Exam ID and Title **Track** **Description**	00-051 IBM 1100 intraNetWare and AS/400 Integration AS/400 Installation, configuration, management, and troubleshooting of hybrid AS/400-NetWare installations, including attachment types, protocol conversions, downstream logical and physical units, and more. This is an IBM exam, not a Novell exam, and is no longer available. Only individuals who have already taken this exam can complete this track.
Exam ID and Title **OR** **Exam ID and Title** **Track** **Description**	90-161 SCO OpenServer Release 5 ACE for Master CNE 90-078 SCO UnixWare 7 ACE for Master CNE Unix Exams testing administrative skills and NetWare integration skills on SCO Unix releases, including installation, configuration, maintenance, resource sharing, and troubleshooting topics. Consult the Novell Master CNE Progress Chart for information about other alternative Unix exams.
Exam ID and Title **Track** **Description**	50-644 Integrating NetWare and Windows NT WinNT Covers issues involved in using NetWare and Windows NT 4.0 in hybrid networks, including resource sharing, client software, NetWare tools and utilities, Windows NT tools and utilities, and more.

Master CNE Elective Track Requirements

The short table section that follows indicates the number of elective exams for each Master CNE track. The table section that follows it provides a list of possible elective exams.

Number Required	Track(s)
0	AS/400, Unix
1	Int, WinNT
2	Mgmt, Conn, Msg

Master CNE Elective Exams

For brevity's sake, we provide only exam IDs and titles here. Visit the Novell Web site at **http://education.novell.com/testinfo/objectives/crsindex.htm** for more detailed information. Except where noted or where an exam is used for a core or target requirement, these electives apply to all MCNE tracks.

Exam ID and Title	50-606	Fundamentals of Network Management
Exam ID and Title	50-622	Printing in an Integrated NetWare Environment
Exam ID and Title	50-145	NetWare TCP/IP Transport
Exam ID and Title	50-649	TCP/IP for Networking Professionals
Exam ID and Title	50-160	NetWare NFS Services: Management, Printing and File Sharing—NetWare 4 Edition

(continued)

Table 3.4 Exams required for Master CNE certifications *(continued)*.		
Exam ID and Title	50-637	NetWare for SAA
Exam ID and Title	50-641	Network Management Using ManageWise 2.6
Exam ID and Title	50-642	Securing Intranets with BorderManager
Exam ID and Title	50-650	Internet Security Management with BorderManager: Enterprise Edition 3.5
Exam ID and Title	50-656	Desktop Management with ZENworks

Seven areas of specialization apply to the MCNE:

➤ *Management*—For MCNEs who wish to specialize in network management, operations, and troubleshooting. In addition to the two core exams, this specialty requires one target test and two electives, for a total of five exams. (Abbreviated as Mgmt in Table 3.4.)

➤ *Connectivity*—For MCNEs who wish to specialize in managing communications and access on complex intranets, usually with WAN as well as LAN connections. In addition to the two core exams, this specialty requires one target exam and two electives, for a total of five exams. (Abbreviated as Conn in Table 3.4.)

➤ *Messaging*—For MCNEs who wish to specialize in email systems or messaging-based applications, usually involving multiple email systems (and gateways) that include GroupWise in their number. In addition to the two core exams, this specialty requires one target exam and two electives, for a total of five exams. (Abbreviated as Msg in Table 3.4.)

➤ *Internet/Intranet Solutions*—For MCNEs who wish to specialize in IP-based networks and services, whether for internal (intranet) use or involving Internet access. In addition to the three core exams, this specialty requires two target exams and one elective, for a total of six exams. (Abbreviated as Int in Table 3.4.)

➤ *Client/Network Solutions: intraNetWare and AS/400 Integration*—For MCNEs who wish to specialize in networks that involve both NetWare and AS/400 systems. In addition to the three core exams, this specialty requires one target exam, for a total of four exams. (Abbreviated as AS/400 in Table 3.4.)

This track is being discontinued as of October 1, 2000. That's because the target exam is no longer available. Only those who've already taken the target exam can qualify for this track.

➤ *Client/Network Solutions: intraNetWare and Unix Integration*—For MCNEs who wish to specialize in networks that involve both NetWare and SCO Unix systems. In addition to the three core exams, this specialty requires one target exam, for a total of four exams. (Abbreviated as Unix in Table 3.4.)

➤ *Client/Network Solutions: intraNetWare and Windows NT Integration*—For MCNEs who wish to specialize in networks that involve both NetWare and Windows NT systems. In addition to the three core exams, this specialty requires one target exam and one elective, for a total of five exams. (Abbreviated as WinNT in Table 3.4.)

Note that if an elective is required as a core or a target exam for a specialty, it may not also be counted for elective credit. For further details on the requirements, visit the MCNE home page at **http://education.novell.com/mcne/**. Here again, the Master CNE Progress Chart will help to spell out all the requirements and other details.

CNI

Novell's instructor certification is widely regarded as a premier certification in the IT industry. Novell instructors must first obtain a NetWare 4 or NetWare 5 CNE (NetWare 5 is recommended for maximum certification longevity) before they can enter the CNI program. Then, they must meet stringent instructional and subject matter requirements to qualify to teach specific Novell courses (and to prepare students for the exams that go with these courses).

Instructional requirements for the CNI may be satisfied only by meeting the following requirements:

➤ CNIs must be employed at a Novell Authorized Education Center (NAEC) or at a Novell Authorized Education Partner (NAEP) or declare themselves to be freelance instructors by designating their employment status as "contract instructor." Any CNI must belong to one and only one of these employment categories.

➤ CNIs must submit a complete CNI Application and a signed CNI Certification Agreement.

➤ CNIs must attend the base-level certification course for NetWare 4 (course 520, exam 50-613) or NetWare 5 (course 560, exam 50-639, 50-645, or 60-653).

➤ CNIs must also pass the related NetWare exams at the instructor level (exam 50-813, 50-839, or 50-853).

➤ Instructors must either attend a Novell Instructor Performance Evaluation (IPE) class or must submit evidence of current Certified Technical Trainer (CTT) credentials to meet in-class presentation and training skills requirements.

Once they obtain certification, CNIs are not limited to the types of courses they can instruct. Because the ability to teach any given Novell course depends on passing the instructor-level exam for that course—designed to be more demanding and detail oriented than the normal certification exams for the same courses— passing the instructor exam, along with CNI or MCNI credentials, suffices to obtain authorization from Novell to teach any of its official course materials.

Novell even offers a Master CNI (MCNI) credential. It requires two years of documented classroom experience as a CNI, plus completion of all requirements for Novell's Master CNE (MCNE) certification. The MCNI is one of the most elite IT certifications available in today's marketplace. Visit Novell's CNI Web pages at **http://education.novell.com/cni/** for more information about the CNI and MCNI programs.

CDE

Novell's newest certification program, CDE, is meant to supply the IT industry with a group of elite, directory-knowledgeable networking professionals. People who obtain this certification can use NDS and related directory technologies in managing applications, operating systems, and enterprise-level installations. CDEs can apply directory solutions to meet real-world business needs.

Applicants pursuing the CDE have to first complete a premier IT certification, such as CNE, MCSE, CCNP, CCIE, or Compaq ASE. In addition, they must complete two core exams and take a live, hands-on laboratory exam stressing real-world design, implementation, and problem-solving skills. Novell has not yet announced how much time it will take to complete the laboratory exam— known as the Novell Practicum—or how much this exam will cost. Be prepared for changes and refinements as the CDE program builds momentum. Consult the CDE home page at **http://education.novell.com/cde/** for updates on this program. Table 3.5 summarizes the CDE certification core exams.

Table 3.5 CDE core exams.	
Exam ID and Title **Description**	50-648 Advanced NDS Tools and Diagnostics Using NDS Health Check, server logging, troubleshooting tools, replicas, directory tree management, and NDS 8 migrations and upgrades.
Exam ID and Title **Description**	50-655 Directory Server Technologies Using NDS to design, create, install, configure, and troubleshoot directory-based and directory-enabled applications and working with advanced directory services, tools, and technologies.

Novell Testing

By now, you've certainly read about a sizable number of Novell tests. You're probably wondering what's involved in signing up for or taking such tests. Nothing could be easier than to explain how this process works!

You may sign up with one of two testing companies that handle testing for Novell certification:

➤ *Prometric Testing Centers*—Sign up through the company's Web site at **www.2test.com** or register by phone at 1-612-820-5706 or 1-800-RED-EXAM.

➤ *Virtual University Enterprises (VUE)*—Sign up at **www.vue.com/novell/** or register by phone at 1-952-995-8970 or 1-800-TEST-CNE.

To sign up for a test, you must have a valid credit card or contact either company for mailing instructions to send the company a check or money order. You can register for a test only when payment is verified or your check has cleared.

To schedule an exam, call or visit the Web page at least one day in advance. To cancel or reschedule an exam, you must call at least 12 hours before the scheduled test time or before the close of business on the preceding working day (otherwise you may be charged, even if you don't show up for the test).

To schedule a test, have the following information:

➤ Your name, organization, and mailing address.

➤ Your Novell Education Testing ID and PIN. Inside the United States, the ID is your social security number; citizens of other nations should call ahead to find out what type of identification is needed. The PIN is a number you select when you first sign up to take a Novell certification exam with either Prometric or VUE. Be sure to write this down somewhere and have it ready when you sign up.

➤ The name and number of the exam you wish to take.

➤ A method of payment.

Once you sign up for a test, you'll be told when and where the test is scheduled. Try to arrive at least 15 minutes early. You must supply two forms of identification, one of which must be a photo ID.

All Novell exams are closed book. In fact, you can't take anything with you into the testing area. You'll be given a blank sheet of paper and a pen. I suggest that you immediately write down whatever you've memorized for the test before you begin. You'll have some time to compose yourself, to record this information, and even to take a sample orientation test before you begin the real thing. I suggest that you take the orientation exam before taking your first real Novell exam. They're all more or less the same in terms of layout, behavior, and controls, so you won't need to do this more than once or twice before it's quite familiar.

As soon as you complete a Novell exam, the software tells you whether you've passed or failed. Even if you fail, I suggest you ask for—and keep—the detailed score report that the test administrator can print for you. This will tell you which areas you need to work on. If you happen to fail, you'll have to contact Prometric or VUE to schedule another test.

Tracking Novell Certification Status

As soon as you pass any of the CNA exams, you'll attain Certified Novell Administrator status. Novell also maintains a Personal Certification Requirements History (PCRH), which indicates the exams you've taken and those you've passed. You can check your PCRH through the secured Novell Power PIN login page at **http://certification.novell.com/pinlogin.htm**. It takes Novell up to seven business days after an exam to update your PCRH.

In addition to providing access to certification information and test records, Novell operates secured Web sites for CNA, CNE, and CDE candidates. These sites provide access to all types of information aimed at certified users. This information includes special news, software utilities, operating system updates and tools, and opportunities to sign up for beta tests and beta software. You'll find much more than simply access to your certification progress reports. You'll be furnished with details on how to access these sites—which require your Testing ID and PIN to gain access—when you complete any Novell certification exam that qualifies you for potential certification (thus, aspiring CNEs who finish a test can get access to the site, as can already certified CNEs).

You can also contact Novell's education operation at 1-800-233-EDUC (outside the United States or Canada, call 1-801-429-7000 and ask for Novell education) or send email to **edcustomer@novell.com**.

How to Prepare for Novell Exams

At a minimum, you should use the following materials to prepare for a Novell exam:

➤ For most exams, Novell offers one or more instructor-led training classes. Novell recommends that you attend such training at a NAEC or a NEAP. However, other study options are available, including self-study kits, computer-based training, Web-based training, and computer trade books. Novell recommends that you discuss these options with a nearby training center professional.

➤ Because Novell publishes both course and test objectives, you should also become familiar with these items before taking any test. Course objectives are available through Novell's education product listings, which you can access through the Course Catalog button at **http://education.novell.com/certinfo/**; test objectives are available at **http://education.novell.com/testinfo/objectives/crsindex.htm**.

➤ Novell publishes The Guide CD, which you can get from any local testing center at no charge. It contains practice exams with questions much like those that appear on the actual exams. In fact, it's produced by the same people who write those exams. These are worth taking, if only to get the feel for the real thing. For more information, visit The Guide CD Web page at **http://education.novell.com/theguide/**.

In addition, you'll probably find any or all of the following materials useful in your search for Novell expertise:

➤ *Study guides*—Numerous publishers offer CNE or CNA study guides of some type. A search at your favorite online bookstore will help in locating these.

➤ *Other publications*—You'll find plenty of other publications and resources if you take the time to look around on the Web or in your local bookstore; there's no shortage of materials available about Novell.

➤ *The Network Support Encyclopedia, Professional Edition (NSEPro)*—The NSEPro is a monthly CD subscription that includes all types of technical documentation and training materials about Novell products and technologies, plus summaries of technical support issues and software patches and fixes. A single-user NSEPro license is $495 per year, and site licenses cost $995 per year. However, CNEs can purchase a single-user subscription directly from Novell for $295 per year. To subscribe to the NSEPro, contact an authorized Novell reseller—call 1-800-828-3362 for a reseller in your area or 1-800-377-4136 or 1-303-297-2725 to order from Novell directly or to receive your CNE discount.

This set of materials represents a stellar collection of sources and resources for Novell exam topics and software.

Need to Know More?

For convenience, I include the most important URLs mentioned so far in this chapter, along with pointers to a few other resources worth investigating:

 http://education.novell.com/certinfo/index.htm Start here to get to the home pages for the CNA, CNE, MCNE, CNI or CDE certifications. There, you'll find requirements, progress charts, and more.

 www.netboss.com This is the home page for Novell's Certified Internet Professional programs. It lists the requirements for and steps necessary to attain all of the CIP-related certifications.

 http://education.novell.com/testinfo/ This is the home page for all Novell certification testing information (except for CIP-only tests). Use this to find objectives, analyze test types, obtain question counts, and more.

 http://certification.novell.com/pinlogin.htm This is the Power PIN login page. Once you obtain a Novell Education Testing ID and PIN, visit this page to check your certification status, obtain news about new certification tests and objectives, sign up for beta tests, and so on.

 http://support.novell.com This is the home page for Novell Technical Support. It is also an excellent source of technical data, including a meaty and worthwhile set of NetWare 5 white papers.

 comp.os.netware.connectivity This is the key technical Usenet newsgroup on Novell technologies and NetWare topics. Other members of this hierarchy are **comp.os.netware.security** (covers NetWare security topics), **comp.os.netware.announce** (covers Novell and third-party NetWare-related announcements), and **comp.os.netware.misc** (covers other NetWare topics that don't fit under the other NetWare newsgroups).

Oracle Certification Programs

Terms you'll need to understand:

✓ Oracle Certification Professional (OCP)

✓ Database Operator (DBO) track

✓ Database Administrator (DBA) track

✓ Application Developer track

✓ Financial Applications Consultant track

✓ Oracle product family: Oracle7, Oracle8/8i

✓ Java Developer track

✓ Instructor-Led Training (ILT)

✓ Media-Based Training (MBT)

✓ Oracle Learning Architecture (OLA)

Techniques you'll need to master:

✓ Locating training and certification information on the Oracle Web site

✓ Obtaining descriptions and objectives for specific Oracle exams

✓ Identifying training and self-study options related to specific Oracle exams

Alphabet Soup

To begin, let's review the numerous acronyms that relate to Oracle's certification credentials. After that, you'll have a chance to investigate each certification in some detail, including the elements that lead to each one. Along the way, you'll be presented with a series of tables that show how the pieces fit together and learn how to sign up for tests, track certification progress, and so on.

Here are the acronyms related to Oracle certifications, with brief explanations:

➤ *Oracle Certified Professional (OCP)*—This is a catchall term that identifies anyone who obtains an Oracle certification, either as a DBA (database administrator) or as an Oracle software developer. DBA candidates must demonstrate their abilities to install, configure, manage, and maintain Oracle databases; software developer candidates must demonstrate their knowledge of Oracle design and development principles, plus important Application Program Interfaces (APIs), report generators, forms-based development tools, and so on.

➤ *Database Operator (DBO)*—Someone who handles routine day-to-day database maintenance, backups, and restores and who also provides traffic, activity, and database reports.

➤ *Database Administrator (DBA)*—Someone who handles the design, implementation, maintenance, upgrades, and updates of corporate databases.

➤ *Instructor-Led Training (ILT)*—This refers to Oracle Education's comprehensive set of classroom courses for exam preparation and general training. Ultimately, the Oracle exams are derived from classroom experience with students, and Oracle indicates that each ILT class covers all the material necessary to take and pass the related test.

➤ *Media-Based Training (MBT)*—This is Oracle's term for self-paced, computer-based training materials. There's a substantial overlap between MBTs available from Oracle and the various certification exams, but sometimes it's necessary to complete two MBTs to adequately prepare for an exam.

➤ *Oracle Learning Architecture (OLA)*—This is Oracle's term for its Web-based training materials. Although these are largely self-paced and entirely computer-based, OLA training also includes the opportunity to interact with an instructor via email or online chat. Thus, OLA strikes a balance between the ILT and MBT approaches.

Table 4.1 breaks down the five tracks in terms of number of exams, time, and cost.

Oracle's tests are based on multiple-choice questions, most of which relate to usage- or data-based scenarios. Thus, answering questions involves applying your

Table 4.1 Oracle certifications, exams, and more.				
Certification	Exams	Questions	Cost	Time
OCP, Database Operator track	1	70	$125	90 min.
OCP, Database Administrator track	4–5	60–65	$125	60–90 min.
OCP, Application Developer track	5	50–60	$125	60–90 min.
OCP, Java Developer	5	60–70	$125/$175*	60–120 min.
OCP, Oracle Financials	3	61–77	$125	60–90 min.

*The Java Developer certification includes third-party tests from Sun (among others) that cost $175 (and take up to 120 minutes). The number of questions, the cost, and the time period are for each exam, not for all exams.

knowledge of Oracle concepts, terminology, tools, and techniques to select among a range of possibilities the best alternative, or requires analyzing different implementation or design approaches to determine which is most effective.

Each test is between 50 and 77 questions. Although the tests are designed to be finished in approximately 60 minutes, test takers are allowed 90 minutes (up to 120 minutes for the Java Developer exam). It is important to read each question carefully and thoroughly and to try to anticipate what constitutes "best practices" or "optimal results" when determining how to answer.

In the sections that follow, you'll examine the various Oracle OCP certifications in more detail and learn a little more about the exams required to qualify for each. If you visit the URLs mentioned for each credential, in most cases you'll be able to jump straight to the details related to the required exams.

Although Web locations change over time, they're worth chasing down because Oracle's Web site is the most up-to-date source for certification information and requirements.

Oracle normally requires OCPs to recertify within six months of a new database version's release. However, even though Oracle8 has been available since late 1998, the company is permitting both certifications to run in parallel until August 31, 2000, when the Oracle7 DBA track is retired. Individuals are encouraged to upgrade their Oracle7 certification. For more information, download the Oracle7.3 to Oracle8 Candidate Guide at **http://education.oracle.com/certification/pdf/ cg738.pdf**.

OCP-DBO Track

This track applies only to Oracle8 and aims to identify those individuals who can perform simple, operational tasks on an Oracle database, with basic understanding of Oracle database software and related graphical management utilities. The certification covers the kinds of skills that an individual who assists an Oracle DBA needs, including the following:

➤ Installing Oracle database software

➤ Creating and configuring Oracle databases

➤ Loading and managing data for Oracle databases

➤ Setting up and managing user access and accounts

➤ Managing routine activities, such as backups and performance checks

To obtain OCP-DBO certification, individuals must pass only a single test: 1Z0-401, the Oracle8 Database Operator exam. For more information, download the DBO Candidate Guide from **http://education.oracle.com/certification/dbo_track.html**.

OCP-DBA Track

This track, formally called the OCP Certified Database Administrator track, aims to identify those individuals who understand how to maintain an Oracle database in an enterprise business-computing environment. The certification covers a broad range of skills that include the following:

➤ Writing routine Oracle queries, analyses, and reports

➤ Handling everyday requirements for Oracle database administration

➤ Understanding basic Oracle database architectures

➤ Planning, creating, maintaining, and migrating Oracle databases

➤ Monitoring, tuning, and optimizing Oracle database server performance

➤ Handling Oracle database server backup and recovery, including backup and recovery strategies, tools, and techniques

Obtaining this certification requires passing four or five tests, which may pertain to Oracle7.3, Oracle8, or Oracle8i (individuals must follow one track; however, mixing tests across versions does not qualify them for certification). These tests are documented in Table 4.2.

For a more detailed description of these requirements, visit the Oracle Education home page at **http://education.oracle.com/certification/**. There you will find hyperlinks for the various Oracle tracks (7.3, 8 or 8i).

Table 4.2	OCP-DBA track required tests.
Common Core Exam: All Oracle Versions	
Exam ID and Title	1Z0-001 Introduction to Oracle: SQL and PL/SQL
Description	Covers basic SQL and PL/SQL concepts, terminology, and programming, plus writing queries and using Procedure Builder, Data Manipulation Language (DML), and Data Definition Language (DDL).
Required Oracle7.3-specific exams	
Exam ID and Title	1Z0-003* Oracle7.3 Database Administration
Description	Covers Oracle7.3 database architectures, plus design, creation, migration, and management of Oracle databases and related database schemas.
Exam ID and Title	1Z0-005* Oracle7.3 Backup and Recovery
Description	Covers backup and recovery for Oracle7.3 databases, including roll-back and roll-forward recovery techniques and applying recommended backup and recovery approaches and related Oracle tools.
Exam ID and Title	1Z0-004* Oracle7.3 Performance Tuning
Description	Covers performance measurement, evaluation, optimization, and tuning for Oracle7.3 databases, applications, and underlying systems and servers.
Required Oracle8-specific exams	
Exam ID and Title	1Z0-013 Oracle8 Database Administrator
Description	Covers Oracle8 database architectures, plus design, creation, migration, and management of Oracle databases and related database schemas.
Exam ID and Title	1Z0-015 Oracle8 Backup and Recovery
Description	Covers backup and recovery for Oracle8 databases, including roll-back and roll-forward recovery techniques and applying recommended backup and recovery approaches and related Oracle tools.
Exam ID and Title	1Z0-014 Oracle8 Performance Tuning
Description	Covers performance measurement, evaluation, optimization, and tuning for Oracle8 databases, applications, and underlying systems and servers.
Exam ID and Title	1Z0-016 Oracle8 Network Administration
Description	Covers planning, setup, and configuration of Oracle servers, plus client management, database names and agents, and managing connections and security matters.
Required Oracle8i-specific exams	
Exam ID and Title	1Z0-023 Oracle8i Architecture and Administration
Description	Covers Oracle8i database architectures, plus design, creation, migration, and management of Oracle8i databases and related database schemas.

(continued)

Table 4.2	OCP-DBA track required tests *(continued)*.	
Exam ID and Title	1Z0-025	Oracle8i Backup and Recovery
Description	Covers backup and recovery for Oracle8i databases, including roll-back and roll-forward recovery techniques and applying recommended backup and recovery approaches and related Oracle8i tools.	
Exam ID and Title	1Z0-024	Oracle8i Performance Tuning
Description	Covers performance measurement, evaluation, optimization, and tuning for Oracle8i databases, applications, and underlying systems and servers.	
Exam ID and Title	1Z0-026	Oracle8i Network Administration
Description	Covers planning, setup, and configuration of Oracle8i servers, plus client management, database names and agents, and managing connections and security matters.	

This exam is scheduled to retire on August 31, 2000.

 Individuals who are already certified as Oracle7.3 DBAs may recertify for Oracle8 by passing Exam 1Z0-010 Oracle8: New Features for Administrators. Individuals already certified as Oracle8 DBAs may recertify for Oracle8i by passing Exam 1Z0-020: New Featurs for Administrators. When the time comes to recertify, this information may come in handy. Also, individuals who obtain Chauncey DBA Certification for Oracle7 need only complete exams 1Z0-004 and 1Z0-005 to obtain OCP DBA credentials, but you must take and pass them by August 31, 2000.

OCP-Application Developer Track

The formal name for this Oracle certification is the Oracle Certified Application Developer Track for Developer/2000, which is now available in two flavors: Release 1 (works with Oracle7.3) and Release 2 (works with Oracle8). Developer/ 2000 is the name of Oracle's Y2K-ready development environment. This certification focuses on preparing database professionals to use Oracle's Developer/2000 tools and technologies to build state-of-the-art, database-driven applications. This process requires knowledge of Oracle's reporting and user interface design tools, including forms, and understanding of business transactions, SQL, and PL/SQL.

The Oracle Certified Application Developer credential therefore requires mastering a broad range of skills, including the following:

➤ A thorough understanding of Oracle's query language and procedure-building tools, especially SQL and PL/SQL.

➤ Ability to develop, manage, and use stored procedures and functions, packages, and database triggers.

➤ Total familiarity with Oracle's forms-based design and editing tool for creation of editors, windows, canvases, views, triggers, and input validation, plus event- and error-handling techniques.

➤ A thorough knowledge and appreciation of the capabilities of Oracle's Developer/2000 reporting tool, including designing, building, and running reports in a variety of simple and complex formats and layouts.

Obtaining this certification requires passing five tests, which vary depending on whether a candidate is seeking certification for Developer/2000 Release 1 or Release 2 (as before, individuals cannot mix exams across the two sets but must go entirely one way or the other). These tests are outlined in Table 4.3.

For more details about these requirements, visit the Oracle Education home page at **http://education.oracle.com/certification/** and click on the Application Developer Track hyperlink for Release 1 or 2. From there, you can download files that discuss this track in detail.

Individuals who have already completed the OCP Certified Application Developer credential for Release 1 of Developer/2000 can recertify for Release 2 simply by passing Exam 1Z0-120: Developer/2000 Release 2 New Features.

Table 4.3 OCP-Application Developer track required tests.	
Common Core Exams: All Versions of Developer/2000	
Exam ID and Title **Description**	1Z0-001 Introduction to Oracle: SQL and PL/SQL Covers basic SQL and PL/SQL concepts, terminology, and programming, plus writing queries and using Procedure Builder, Data Manipulation Language (DML), and Data Definition Language (DDL).
Exam ID and Title **Description**	1Z0-101 Develop PL/SQL Program Units Covers PL/SQL development topics, including stored procedures, developing and calling packages, and developing specific trigger functions. Also covers managing procedures, functions, and dependencies.
Required Exams: Developer/2000 Release 1	
Exam ID and Title **Description**	1Z0-111 Developer/2000 Forms 4.5 I Covers simple forms applications, including form tool navigation, managing form layouts, and building form applications. Also covers client/server PL/SQL, forms modules, processing user inputs, triggers, and events.

(continued)

Table 4.3 OCP-Application Developer track required tests *(continued)*.	
Exam ID and Title	1Z0-112 Developer/2000 Forms 4.5 II
Description	Covers complex forms applications, dynamic form layouts, and multitiered form applications. Also covers advanced processing of user inputs, triggers, and events.
Exam ID and Title	1Z0-113 Developer/2000 Reports 2.5
Description	Covers report generation issues, including designing, implementing, and creating reports. Also covers data models, report layouts and properties, triggers, and cross-platform properties.
Required Exams: Developer/2000 Release 2	
Exam ID and Title	1Z0-121 Developer/2000 Build Forms I
Description	Covers simple forms applications, including form tool navigation, managing form layouts, and building form applications. Also covers client/server PL/SQL, forms modules, processing user inputs, triggers, and events.
Exam ID and Title	1Z0-122 Developer/2000 Build Forms II
Description	Covers complex forms applications, dynamic form layouts, and multitiered form applications. Also covers advanced processing of user inputs, triggers, and events.
Exam ID and Title	1Z0-123 Developer/2000 Build Reports
Description	Covers report generation issues, including designing, implementing, and creating reports. Also covers data models, report layouts, and properties, triggers, and cross-platform properties.

OCP-Java Developer Track

This track's formal name is OCP Java Technology Certification Track, a separate developer track that Oracle has developed because the company is increasingly emphasizing the use of Oracle8i as a development platform for Web-enabled information delivery, e-commerce, and other Internet-oriented applications. The OCP-Java Developer track is part of a multivendor effort (involving Sun, IBM, Novell, and AOL/Netscape) to establish enterprise Java developer credentials called the Certification Initiative for Enterprise Development, which Oracle refers to as the jCert Initiative.

The OCP-Java Developer track includes three certification levels that require up to five exams each. If you want to follow the Certification Initiative for Enterprise Development, three of the exams relate to all initiative participants regardless of vendor affiliation; two others are Oracle specific. See Table 4.4 for more details.

For more detailed information about this track's requirements, go to the Oracle education home page at **http://education.oracle.com/certification/**. Click on the Oracle Java Developer hyperlink to download files covering all the details.

Table 4.4	Java Developer tracks and required exams.
Level 1: Sun Certified Programmer for the Java 2 Platform	
Exam ID and Title	1Z0-501 Java Programming
Description	Candidates demonstrate ability to create Java applications and applets and incorporate object-oriented principals.
Level 2: Oracle Certified Solution Developer	
Exam ID and Title	1Z0-502 Oracle JDeveloper: Develop Database Applications or 1Z0-512 with Java
Description	Candidates demonstrate ability to create visual, data-aware applets and applications; develop and deploy stored procedures and triggers; and work with JDBC and SQLJ protocols for database access (Oracle 8i only) using the Oracle JDeveloper 2.0 environment.
Exam ID and Title	1Z0-503 Object-Oriented Analysis and Design or 1Z0-513
Description	Requires candidates to interpret analysis and design materials related to object-oriented, real-world design problems (based on an IBM application development test). See **http://www-4.ibm.com/software/ad/certify/des089e.html** for more details.
Level 3: Oracle Certified Enterprise Developer-Oracle Internet Platform	
Exam ID and Title	1Z0-504 Enterprise Connectivity with J2EE
Description	Design, implementation, and use of Java distributed computing technologies, including JDBC, security measures, Java Remote Method Invocation (RMI), object serialization, CORBA inter-operability, Enterprise JavaBeans (EJB), and the Java Servlet API.
Exam ID and Title	1Z0-505 Enterprise Development on the Oracle Internet Platform
Description	This exam is still under development at this writing. Visit **http://education.oracle.com/certification/javatrack.html** for a quick status update.

If you'd like more information about the Certification Initiative for Enterprise Development, visit **www.jcert.org**.

OCP-Financial Applications Consultant Track

This certification's formal title is Oracle Certified Applications Consultant, Oracle Financials R11. The certification is based wholly on the Oracle database add-on package, which is designed to handle complex organizational or corporate accounting, financial reporting, and analysis functions. In most cases, only organizations that use Oracle for their line of business applications use this package, so this certification is somewhat rarer than other Oracle certifications.

To obtain this certification, you must pass three exams: two core exams and one elective exam on either Order Procurement or Fulfillment. Table 4.5 summarizes these exams.

For more details about the requirements for this track, go to the Oracle education home page at **http://education.oracle.com/certification/**. Click on the Oracle Financial Applications hyperlink to obtain access to download files that cover all the details.

Table 4.5 OCP-Financial Applications Consultant exams.	
Required Core Exams (take both)	
Exam ID and Title	1Z0-210 Oracle Financial Applications: Financial Management R11
Description	Oracle financial applications implementation and setup, integration of Oracle financial applications, and work with general ledgers and assets, charts of accounts, books, journal entries, and more.
Exam ID and Title	1Z0-220 Oracle Applications: Applied Technology R11
Description	Covers the development process for creating custom Oracle financial applications, including security issues, concurrency and reporting, profile option management, system resource audits, document sequencing, and more.
Elective Exams (take one)	
Exam ID and Title	1Z0-230 Oracle Financial Applications: Procurement R11
Description	Covers the procurement process, plus the development process for creating custom procurement applications, including multiorganization support, locations, organizations, and items; units of measure; item definitions; supplier information; purchase requisitions; and more.
Exam ID and Title	1Z0-240 Oracle Financial Applications: Order Fulfillment R11
Description	Covers the order fulfillment process, plus the development process for creating custom order fulfillment applications, including customer setup and management, processing orders, fulfilling and shipping orders, invoicing and closing orders, order entry, transactions, handling receipts and past due receivables, reconciling and closing receivables, and more.

Oracle Testing

By now, you've read about quite a number of Oracle tests. You probably want to know what's involved in signing up for or taking such tests. Nothing could be easier than to explain how this works!

For all these certification tests, you can sign up with the following testing center:

➤ *Prometric Testing Centers*—To register for an OCP exam, call Prometric at 1-800-891-EXAM or visit the Prometric Web site at **www.2test.com**. To locate a testing center near you, click the Find A Test Center link at the top of the Prometric page. You can also email **itech@prometric.com** outside North America to contact Prometric's headquarters directly.

To sign up for a test, you must have a valid credit card or contact Prometric for mailing instructions to send the company a check or money order. You can register for a test only after payment has been verified or a check has cleared.

To schedule an exam, call at least one day in advance. To cancel or reschedule an exam, you must call at least one day before the scheduled test time (or you may be charged, even if you don't show up for the test). Note that if you fail an OCP exam, you must wait 30 days before you can register to retake the test.

To schedule a test, have the following information:

➤ Your name, organization, and mailing address.

➤ A unique identifier that only you may use. (In the United States, this is your social security number. If you live outside the United States, call Prometric to ask what kind of identification you need to provide when you take an OCP exam.)

➤ The name and number of the exam you wish to take and the name of the track to which it belongs.

➤ A method of payment.

Once you sign up for a test, you'll be told when and where the test is scheduled. Try to arrive at least 15 minutes early. You must supply two forms of identification, one of which must be a photo ID.

All Oracle exams are closed book. In fact, you can't take anything with you into the testing area. You'll be furnished with a blank sheet of paper and a pen. I suggest that you immediately write down whatever you've memorized for the test before you begin the test. You'll have some time to compose yourself, to record this information, and even to take a sample orientation test before you begin the real thing. I suggest that you take the orientation exam before taking your first real Oracle exam; they're all more or less the same in terms of layout, behavior, and controls, so you won't need to do this more than once or twice before it's quite familiar.

As soon as you complete an Oracle exam, the software tells you whether you've passed or failed. It even provides detailed diagnostics information to indicate which areas you should study and which Oracle training materials provide this information. Even if you fail an Oracle exam, I suggest you ask for—and keep—the detailed test results that the test administrator can print for you. This tells you which areas you need to work on. If you happen to fail, you'll have to contact Prometric and schedule another test.

Tracking Oracle Certification Status

As soon as you pass the sequence of exams for either Oracle certification track, you'll attain OCP status. Prometric currently keeps track of this status information, so you'll need to contact Prometric by phone to request such information if you ever need it.

Note: It takes Prometric up to 10 business days after an exam to update your certification status.

Also, it takes about 30 days for Prometric to mail your OCP certificate once you pass all the necessary tests (be sure to keep this certificate in a safe place; replacements cost $10 each). You should also keep copies of your test results in case there's a question of whether you passed a certain test or tests. You can contact Prometric via email (**fulfillment@prometric.com**) with questions about your certificate.

How to Prepare for Oracle Exams

At a minimum, you should use the following materials to prepare for an Oracle certification exam:

➤ For most exams, Oracle offers corresponding ILT classes. The company recommends that you attend such training through an Oracle-authorized education outlet, which you can arrange through Oracle Education at 1-800-633-0575 (outside North America, call 1-650-506-7000 and ask for Oracle Education). For all OCP topics, however, MBTs and OLAs are also available; call Oracle Education for the details. Oracle also operates an OCP Help Desk, which you can use to register for future exams. Call it at 1-800-529-0165.

➤ Because Oracle publishes both course and test outlines, it also recommends that you familiarize yourself with these items prior to taking any test. Course objectives and test outlines appear in Oracle's program guides for both of its certification tracks. You can download them from **http://education. oracle.com/certification/index.html**.

➤ Oracle offers assessment tests for aspiring OCPs. If you visit the Download Assessment Test Web page at **http://education.oracle.com/cgi-bin/ certform.cgi** and fill out the form, you can download practice exams. Because these exams contain questions much like those that appear on the real tests, they are worth taking. At the Oracle site, you'll also find pointers to Self-Test Software (choose the Practice Tests link). This well-known provider of practice exams now offers Oracle practice tests as well. Visit the Web site at **www.stsware.com** and click on the Oracle button to investigate related practice test offerings.

In addition, you'll probably find any or all of the following materials useful in your search for Oracle expertise:

➤ *Study guides*—Numerous publishers offer Oracle DBA and Application Developer study guides of some type, including Certification Insider Press, which offers *Exam Cram* titles for many of the exams listed in this chapter. A search at your favorite online bookstore will help in locating these.

➤ *Other publications*—You'll find plenty of other publications and resources if you take the time to look around on the Web or in your local bookstore; there's no shortage of materials available about Oracle database technology.

The preceding set of materials represents a manageable collection of sources and resources for OCP exam topics and related information.

Need to Know More?

For convenience, I include the most important URLs mentioned so far in this chapter, along with pointers to a few other resources worth investigating for information about Oracle certification, exams, training, and more:

 http://education.oracle.com/certification/ This is the home page for OCP information and includes ready access to program guides for both OCP tracks, test-taking information, and self-assessment tests. This should be your first stop in any search for OCP information.

 Oracle also provides Candidate Guides for all OCP tracks. All of these documents are worth downloading and reading and provide some of the most detailed and cogent information about the exams, including course and exam outlines.

 Your favorite online bookstore A quick search using "Oracle" calls up a number of Oracle-specific books. These should offer some insight into the exam topics, questions, and the exam writers' mind-sets.

 listserv@kbs.net If you send a message that reads "SUBSCRIBE ORACLE-L YOUR NAME" to this address, it signs you up for one of the best all-around Oracle mailing lists.

 The following Usenet newsgroups cover Oracle's products and technologies:

> ➤ **comp.databases.oracle** Oracle SQL database products

> ➤ **comp.databases.oracle.marketplace** Oracle-related jobs and so on

> ➤ **comp.databases.oracle.server** Oracle database and server administration

> ➤ **comp.databases.oracle.tools** Oracle software tools and applications

> ➤ **comp.databases.oracle.misc** Miscellaneous Oracle information

Cisco Certification Programs

Terms you'll need to understand:

✓ Cisco Certified Network Associate (CCNA)

✓ Cisco Certified Network Professional (CCNP)

✓ Cisco Certified Internetwork Expert (CCIE)

✓ Cisco Certified Design Associate (CCDA)

✓ Cisco Certified Design Professional (CCDP)

✓ Certification ladder

✓ Laboratory evaluation

Techniques you'll need to master:

✓ Locating training and certification information on the Cisco Web site

✓ Understanding Cisco's individual certifications and its certification ladder

✓ Obtaining descriptions and objectives for specific Cisco exams

✓ Identifying training and self-study options related to specific Cisco exams

To maintain its position as the market leader in the routing, switching, and connectivity business, Cisco offers its Cisco Career Certification programs, chief among them the Cisco Certified Internetwork Expert (CCIE) credential. It also offers two additional levels of networking credentials and two design credentials, for a total of five separate certifications. All Cisco certifications require advanced skills in supporting a variety of networking topologies and technologies; as you climb their certification ladder, these requirements grow increasingly complex and demanding.

Alphabet Soup

To begin, let's review Cisco's certification programs. After that, you'll have a chance to investigate each of the tracks and each individual certification in some detail, including the elements that lead to each one. Along the way, you'll be presented with a table that shows how the pieces fit together and learn how to sign up for tests, track certification progress, and so on.

At present, there are five acronyms related to Cisco certification. They describe three certifications related to networks or internetworks and two certifications related to design:

➤ *Cisco Certified Network Associate (CCNA)*—This is the entry-level operational certification and is aimed at individuals who must manage simple routed LANs or WANs, small ISPs, or smaller switched LAN or LANE environments. Applicants must pass one exam (640-507 for CCNA 2.0 for the Routing and Switching track or 640-410 for the WAN Switching track) to obtain this certification.

➤ *Cisco Certified Network Professional (CCNP)*—This is the middle-tier operational certification, aimed at individuals who must install, configure, operate, and troubleshoot complex routed LANs, routed WANs, switched LAN networks, or Dial Access Services. Applicants must first obtain a CCNA and then take either two or four additional exams, depending on which test option they select.

➤ *Cisco Certified Internetwork Expert (CCIE)*—This is the top-tier operational certification aimed at individuals who have advanced technical skills and knowledge and who must know how to configure networks for optimum performance. They must also understand how to maintain complex, far-flung, multivendor networks. Applicants must pass only two tests for this certification: a written exam and a laboratory evaluation. No prior certification from Cisco is required to obtain a CCIE, but many individuals elect to obtain a

CCNA and/or a CCNP before attempting the CCIE. CCIE credentials are available for ISP Dial, WAN Switching, SNA/IP Integration, Routing and Switching, and Design areas.

➤ *Cisco Certified Design Associate (CCDA)*—This is the entry-level design credential; it requires individuals to be able to design and deploy simple routed and switched networks as well as configure, operate, and maintain such networks. To obtain this certification, applicants must pass one exam (640-441). This certification is available only for the Routing and Switching specialty.

➤ *Cisco Certified Design Professional (CCDP)*—This is the middle-tier design credential that requires individuals to be able to design and deploy complex routed LANs and WANs, plus switched LANs and LANE environments. Individuals must also be able to configure, operate, and maintain such networks and connections. To obtain this certification, applicants must typically obtain a CCNA for all tracks, a CCDA for the Routing and Switching track, and a CCNP for the WAN Switching track; and then pass one, two, or four more exams, depending on which exam option they elect (I will provide the exam numbers later in this chapter).

A CCNA can lead to either an entry-level design credential (CCDA) or a middle-tier network credential (CCNP) if the candidate takes a few additional tests. Likewise, both the CCNA and the CCDA lead to the CCDP. And, although the CCIE comes with no prerequisites elsewhere in Cisco's ladder, it is clearly the ultimate Cisco certification and is where many individuals who obtain other Cisco certifications aim their highest aspirations.

This combination of programs creates a "certification ladder," as shown in Figure 5.1.

All the exam-related information that applies to obtaining a Cisco certification, plus some additional details about the exams, is summed up in Table 5.1. Note that information about the cost and the time period is for each exam, not for all exams.

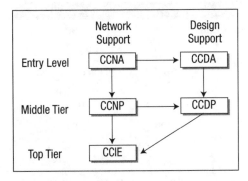

Figure 5.1 The Cisco certification ladder.

Details about specific test numbers for the CCNP, CCIE, and CCDP certifications are covered later in this chapter. The CCNP and CCDP certifications offer two options; to the left of the slash is the information about Test Option 1, and to the right is the information about Test Option 2. For the CCIE certification, the entries for cost and time reflect separate entries for the written test (these appear to the left of the slash) and for the laboratory evaluation (these appear to the right of the slash).

Cisco's Tracks and Specializations

Cisco organizes its entire certification program around two primary topical tracks: (1) Routing and Switching and (2) WAN Switching. These two tracks apply to all five of the Cisco certifications: CCNA, CCNP, CCIE, CCDA, and CCDP. As far as topical coverage goes, the Routing and Switching track aims to identify those individuals who understand how to manage a complex internetworked environment that incorporates high-end routers and switches. The WAN Switching specialty aims to identify those individuals who understand how to manage a complex internetworked environment that incorporates high-end routers and WAN links and who are focused on managing long-haul communications, leased lines, and telephony-related issues.

Other tracks are sometimes called "Specializations" (especially as they apply to the CCNP and CCDP certifications); for the CCIE, Cisco calls these topical areas "tracks" as well. These Specializations cover a number of topical areas that vary from one Cisco certification to the next. They include the following named areas (which I define briefly and associate with specific certifications):

➤ *Design (CCIE)*—Seeks to identify those individuals who understand how to design and manage large internetworks that incorporate campus design, multiservice, and SNA/IP.

➤ *ISP Dial (CCIE)*—Seeks to identify those individuals who understand how

Table 5.1	Cisco certifications, exams, and more.			
Certification	Prerequisites	Required Exams	Cost	Time*
CCNA	None	1	$100	90 min.
CCNP	CCNA	2/4	$100–$200	75–180 min.
CCIE	None	2	$200 $1,000	120 min. 2 days
CCDA	None	1	$100	120 min.
CCDP**	CCDA, CCNA	2/4	$100–$200	75–180 min.

*Exams are computer generated so the number of questions varies; therefore, the time allotted to take the exams changes frequently. These details can be verified prior to taking an exam by contacting Cisco at 1-800-829-6387.

**Note that this applies only for the Routing and Switching and Specializations tracks. For the WAN CCDP certification, you only need to have a CCNA, CCNP, and pass one exam.

to manage a typical internetworked Internet Service Provider (ISP) environment that incorporates routers and WAN links and is focused on managing
short-haul communications, modem banks, and related issues.

➤ *LAN ATM (CCNP)*—Seeks to identify those individuals who install, configure, and manage high-speed, ATM-based LANs and work with related
switches and management software.

➤ *Network Management (CCNP)*—Seeks to identify individuals who implement
and support network management solutions for multilayer (routing and LAN
switching) networks.

➤ *Security (CCNP)*—Seeks to identify individuals who must build and maintain
Cisco security solutions, including standalone firewall products and Cisco
IOS software features.

➤ *SNA/IP Integration (CCIE, CCNP, CCDP)*—Seeks to identify individuals who
must implement and support SNA/IP network management solutions for
multilayer (routing and LAN Switching) networks.

➤ *SNA/IP Network Management (CCNP)*—Seeks to identify individuals who
must install, configure, implement, and troubleshoot Cisco routers in SNA
environments.

➤ *Voice access (sometimes called "Voice over IP"; CCNP)*—Seeks to identify individuals who must implement and support data and voice integration solutions at the network-access level. Includes IP, ATM, and Frame Relay uplink
access products.

At present, the Specializations track applies only to the CCNP, CCIE, and CCDP
certifications (for specifics, each Specialization—called a "track" when applied to
CCIEs—is identified in the preceding bulleted list) but to neither the CCNA
nor the CCDA certification. The Routing and Switching track applies to all
Cisco certifications regardless of designation. The WAN Switching track applies
to all Cisco certifications, except for CCDA.

Individuals typically obtain certification in only one of these topical areas, no
matter which of the five certifications they pursue. In this chapter, you'll have a
chance to examine Cisco's various certification credentials and to understand what
each of the various Cisco certification specialties can prepare you to handle.

CCNA and CCDA

Both CCNA and CCDA certifications require that you pass only one test. CCDAs
can design simple routed LANs and WANs and switched networks. They can
also install, configure, and maintain such simple networks. As with the CCNA,
obtaining a CCDA requires passing only a single exam, as follows:

➤ *CCNA Exam 640-507*—Exam 640-507: Cisco Certified Network Associate 2.0 is the updated version of 640-407 in the Routing and Switching track. This exam covers the same ground, but addresses newer Cisco software and hardware. Test details are not yet forthcoming, but check Cisco's Exam List at **www.cisco.com/warp/public/10/wwtraining/certprog/testing/exam_ list.htm** for more information.

➤ *CCNA Exam 640-410*—Exam 640-410: Cisco Certified Network Associate 1.0 WAN Switching covers WAN basics, subnets and IP addressing, and WAN security, plus configuring and operating WAN routers, along with other topics. To view these CCNA exam objectives, visit **www.cisco.com/warp/public/ 10/wwtraining/certprog/wan/programs/ccna.html**.

➤ *CCDA Exam 640-441*—Exam 640-441: Designing Cisco Networks covers the same sort of material in the design area as the CCNA tackles in the network management area. That is, the CCDA test covers the same subject matter range and objectives as the CCNA test, but it focuses on designing and implementing the relevant technologies, tools, and hardware rather than on their operation.

Note: As of this writing, there is no CCDA certification for the WAN Switching track.

For a complete listing of all Cisco exams, plus related information, visit **www.cisco.com/warp/public/10/wwtraining/certprog/testing/exam_list.htm**.

CCNP

Although the subject matter for all the tracks varies, the exams across these tracks remain the same for the CCNP 2.0. For all specialty tracks, you have two or three exam sequence options. Note that the Foundation exam, explained in Step 2 of Test Option 1 for the Routing and Switching track, is actually the same as the three tests in Step 2 of Test Option 2; the Foundation exam has just been separated into its three counterparts in Test Option 2. At $300 for the required exams beyond the CCNA certification, Test Option 1 is a better deal than Test Option 2, at $400, for individuals pursuing the Routing and Switching track.

Test Option 1 for Routing and Switching

➤ *Step 1: CCNA 1.0 or 2.0 Certification*—The CCNA certification is a prerequisite for CCNP certification and must be completed for any test option.

➤ *Step 2: Foundation (FNDN) 2.0 Exam (640-509)*—This test covers fundamentals and operation of routers and switches and related Cisco products in excruciating detail. At this writing, the Foundation exam is in beta mode so some exam details, such as the length of time allotted to take the exam, are not yet available but the cost has been set at $200. Be sure to watch the Cisco Exam List and Outlines Web page at **www.cisco.com/warp/public/10/ wwtraining/certprog/testing/exam_list.htm** for future updates.

 The FNDN exam costs $200; however, the alternative is taking replacement exams to the tune of $300 (see Option 2). Exam 640-509 exists to save you money!

➤ *Step 3: Support (SUPRT) 2.0 Exam (640-506)*—This test covers the fundamentals and basic principles of network troubleshooting and of troubleshooting-related Cisco products. This exam can last as long as 75 minutes and costs $100. For more information about this test, consult the Exam List and Outlines page at Cisco's Web site at **www.cisco.com/warp/public/10/ wwtraining/certprog/testing/exam_list.htm**.

Test Option 2 for Routing and Switching

➤ *Step 1: CCNA 1.0 or 2.0 Certification*—The CCNA certification is a prerequisite for CCNP certification and must be completed for any test option.

➤ *Step 2:* Applicants must complete three tests, as follows:

➤ *Routing (RTING) 2.0 Exam (640-503)*—This exam covers all the details involved in installing and configuring Cisco routers across the entire product family. This exam can take as long as 75 minutes and costs $100.

➤ *Switching (SWTCH) 2.0 Exam (640-504)*—This exam covers installing, configuring, and troubleshooting Cisco's LAN switches. It can take as long as 180 minutes and costs $100.

➤ *Remote Access (RMTAC) 2.0 Exam (640-505)*—This exam covers remote access issues from installation and configuration, through operation and troubleshooting. This exam can take as long as 75 minutes and costs $100.

➤ *Step 3: Support (SUPRT) 2.0 Exam (640-506)*—This test covers the fundamentals and basic principles of network troubleshooting and of troubleshooting-related Cisco products. This exam can last as long as 75 minutes and costs $100. For more information about this test, consult the Exam List and Outlines page at Cisco's Web site at **www.cisco.com/warp/public/10/ wwtraining/certprog/testing/exam_list.htm**.

Specializations Track

If you want to follow the CCNP Specializations track, you need to obtain first a CCNA, then focus on one of these areas: Network Management, Voice Access, SNA/IP Network Management, SNA/IP Integration, or Security. Selecting Security means taking an extra exam, 640-442: Managing Cisco Network Security, in addition to the CCNP Switching and Routing requirements. Selecting Voice Access requires an extra exam, 640-447: Cisco Voiceover Frame Relay, in addition to the Switching and Routing requirements. There are two options for Network Management: one that calls for two additional exams (640-443: Managing Cisco Routed Internetworks and 640-444: Managing Cisco Switched Internetworks), the other calling for one combined extra exam (640-601: Network Management). For SNA/IP Network Management, one additional exam is required, 640-455: Managing SNA Networks. SNA/IP Integration requires two additional exams, 640-445: SNA Configuration for Multiprotocol Administrators and 640-456: SNA Foundation.

Consult **www.cisco.com/warp/public/10/wwtraining/certprog/special/ course.html** for updates on these specializations details.

Test Option for WAN Switching Track

➤ *Step 1: CCNA Certification*—The CCNA certification is a prerequisite for CCNP certification and must be completed for any test options.

➤ *Step 2:* Applicants must complete three tests, as follows:

  ➤ *Multiband Switch and Service Configuration (MSSC) Exam (640-419)*— This exam covers installation, setup, configuration, and troubleshooting of the Cisco multiband switch products, including IGX capabilities, traffic management, line and trunk management, and so on.

  ➤ *BPX Switch and Service Configuration (BSSC) Exam (640-425)*—This exam covers installation, setup, configuration, and troubleshooting of the Cisco BPX switch products, including IGX capabilities, traffic management, line and trunk management, plus voice and data configuration and troubleshooting.

  ➤ *MGX ATM Concentrator Configuration (MACC) Exam (640-411)*—This exam covers basic understanding of MGX features and functions, MGX installation, configuration, and setup, plus line and trunk management, inverse multiplexing, and more.

➤ *Step 3:* Applicants must complete one or the other of two tests, as follows:

  ➤ *Strata View Implementation and Operation (SVIO) Exam (640-451)*—This exam will retire on August 31, 2000. It will be replaced with Exam 640-459.

➤ *Cisco WAN Manager Installation and Operations (CWMIO) Exam (640–459)*—
This exam covers installation, configuration, management, and troubleshooting of the Cisco WAN Manager.

 To learn more about Cisco exam objectives, visit **www.cisco.com/ warp/public/10/wwtraining/certprog/testing/exam_list.htm**.

CCDP

The CCDP 2.0 represents a logical step up from the CCNA and CCDA in the Cisco certification ladder, moving over from the CCNA and up from the CCDA; perhaps that's why both of these credentials are normally prerequisites to obtaining CCDP certification. Note that the Foundation exam explained in Step 3 of Test Option 1 is actually the same as the three tests in Step 3 of Test Option 2; the Foundation exam has just been separated into its three counterparts in Test Option 2. At $300 for the required exams beyond the CCDA and CCNA certifications, Test Option 1 is a better deal than Test Option 2, at $400. You'll also note that the CCNP and CCDP certifications sometimes overlap in that both require the Foundation exam or its three separate counterparts (as with other elements of the Cisco certification program, this is not true for the WAN Switching track but does apply to the Routing and Switching track).

Test Option 1 for Routing and Switching

➤ *Step1: CCDA Certification*—The CCDA certification is another prerequisite for CCDP certification and must be completed for all test options.

➤ *Step 2: CCNA Certification*—The CCNA certification is a prerequisite for CCDP certification and must be completed for all test options.

➤ *Step 3: Foundation (FNDN) 2.0 Exam (640-509)*—This test covers fundamentals and operation of routers and switches and related Cisco products in excruciating detail. At this writing, the Foundation exam is in beta mode so some exam details, such as the length of time allotted to take the exam, are not yet available but the cost has been set at $200. Be sure to watch the Cisco Exam List and Outlines Web page at **www.cisco.com/warp/public/10/ wwtraining/certprog/testing/exam_list.htm** for future updates.

➤ *Step 4: Cisco Internetwork Design (CID) 3.0 Student Level Exam (640-025)*—The exam is based on the Cisco CID class, which covers internetwork troubleshooting in depth, including Cisco hardware, software diagnostics, and monitoring and measurement tools. It can last as long as 120 minutes and costs $100.

Test Option 2 for Routing and Switching Track

➤ *Step 1: CCDA Certification*—CCDA credentials are required for CCDP certification (except the WAN Switching track).

➤ *Step 2: CCNA Certification*—CCNA credentials are required for CCDP certification, and candidates must hold this certification for any CCDP test option.

➤ *Step 3:* Candidates must pass these three tests:

➤ *Routing (RTING) 2.0 Exam (640-503)*—This exam covers all the details involved in installing and configuring Cisco routers across the entire product family. This exam can take as long as 75 minutes and costs $100.

➤ *Switching (SWTCH) 2.0 Exam (640-504)*—This exam covers installing, configuring, and troubleshooting Cisco's LAN switches. It can take as long as 180 minutes and costs $100.

➤ *Remote Access (RMTAC) 2.0 Exam (640-505)*—This exam covers remote access issues from installation and configuration, through operation and troubleshooting. This exam can take as long as 75 minutes and costs $100.

➤ *Step 4: Cisco Internetwork Design 3.0 Student Level (CID) Exam (640-025)*— The Cisco CID class is the foundation of the CID exam and emphasizes software diagnostics, Cisco hardware, in-depth troubleshooting of internetworks, and measurement and monitoring tools. The exam can take up to 120 minutes to complete and costs $100.

Specializations Track: SNA/IP Integration

➤ *Step 1: CCNA Certification*—CCNA credentials are required for CCDP certification, and candidates must hold this certification for any CCDP test option.

➤ *Step 2: CCDA Certification*—CCDA credentials are required for CCDP certification (except the WAN Switching track).

➤ *Step 3: SNA to IP Migration (SNAMI) Exam (640-457)*—The SNAMI exam emphasizes designing, tuning, and managing an integrated SNA and IP network. The exam can take up to 90 minutes to complete and costs $100. If you would like more details, go to **www.cisco.com/warp/public/10/wwtraining/ certprog/special/course.html** and click on the Exam Information button at the bottom of the page.

Test Option for WAN Switching Track

➤ *Step 1: CCNA Certification*—The CCNA certification is a prerequisite for CCDP certification and must be completed for all test options.

➤ *Step 2: CCNP Certification*—The CCNP (WAN Switching) certification is a prerequisite for CCDP WAN Switching certification.

➤ *Step 3: Designing Switched WAN Voice Solutions (DSWVS) Exam (640-413)*— This test covers design, installation, and operation of voice applications on Cisco switches and related Cisco products, plus integration with data traffic, in some detail. This exam can last as long as 60 minutes and costs $100. For a complete list of objectives, consult **www.cisco.com/warp/public/10/ wwtraining/certprog/testing/pdf/dswvs.pdf**.

CCIE

Although Cisco requires that candidates pass only two tests to obtain a CCIE no matter what track is involved, they're both formidable. In the sections that follow, I'll discuss each of these important pieces to the CCIE puzzle.

The CCIE Qualification Exam

The written exam, called the CCIE Qualification Exam, is one of the longer exams offered by Prometric, which administers the written exam (see the section "Signing Up for the Written Exams" later in this chapter). However, only three other elements of the Cisco testing regimen exceed its length. No matter what track you might follow, the CCIE Qualification Exam is regarded as a challenging test of one's Cisco product knowledge as well as one's general knowledge of networking and communications.

The written exam consists of 120 multiple-choice questions or more, many of which are scenario based. The nature of a typical exam question makes it important to read it carefully and thoroughly and to try to anticipate what constitutes "best practices" or "optimal results" when selecting an answer. The exam is graded pass/fail, and candidates are informed of whether they passed at its conclusion. You must pass the CCIE Qualification Exam before you can sign up for the second exam.

The Laboratory Evaluation

None of the other vendor programs offers an exam anything like Cisco's second CCIE test: a two-day laboratory evaluation, offered at a limited number of testing labs worldwide, for $1,000. Here, would-be CCIEs are subjected to a variety of simulated situations that test their hands-on abilities and diagnostic skills. They must do the following:

➤ Implement a network or a communications environment from scratch

➤ Reconfigure existing environments

➤ Troubleshoot multiple environments that have been deliberately misconnected, misconfigured, or otherwise messed with

I'm told that each of this test's two days can sometimes be quite long and that the situations posed require extensive product knowledge, manual dexterity, and serious networking skills, along with an ability to think and act quickly and decisively.

In fact, Cisco's tests are so demanding that Cisco publishes the following list of prerequisites to prospective CCIE candidates, no matter what track they may seek to follow:

➤ A minimum of two years of internetwork administration, if not more

➤ Hands-on experience with internetwork installation and troubleshooting

➤ Strong knowledge of Cisco products, including related product and service documentation

➤ Extensive hands-on experience with Cisco products in a production environment

None of the other vendors is quite so forthcoming about informing prospective candidates that experience is not only advisable, but also necessary. But then, none of the other vendors has such demanding certification requirements, either.

Cisco Testing

By now, you've read about many different Cisco tests. You probably want to know what's involved in signing up for or taking such tests. Nothing could be easier than to explain how this works, as long as you remember that one process is required to sign up for the written tests and another to sign up for the CCIE laboratory evaluation.

Signing Up for the Written Exams

You can take the written exams only through Prometric. To register for a written Cisco certification exam, either visit Prometric's Web site at **www.2test.com** or call the company at 1-800-204-3926; outside North America, contact Prometric's headquarters directly by email at **itech@prometric.com**. You can also check the registration page of Cisco's Web site at **www.cisco.com/warp/public/10/ wwtraining/certprog/testing/register.htm** for a list of contact numbers for use outside North America.

To sign up for a test, you must possess a valid credit card or contact Prometric for mailing instructions to send the company a check or money order. You'll be able to register for a test only after payment is verified or your check has cleared.

To schedule an exam, call at least one day in advance. To cancel or reschedule an exam, you must call at least one day before the scheduled test time (or you may be charged, even if you don't show up to take the test).

When you want to schedule a test, have the following information ready:

➤ Your name, organization, and mailing address.

➤ A unique identifier that only you may use. (In the United States, this is your social security number. If you live outside the United States, call Prometric to ask what kind of identification you need to provide when you take a Cisco exam.)

➤ The name and number of the exam you wish to take.

➤ A method of payment.

Once you sign up for a test, you'll be informed as to when and where the test is scheduled. Try to arrive at least 15 minutes early. You must supply two forms of identification to be admitted into the testing room, one of which must be a photo ID.

All Cisco written exams are closed book. In fact, you can't take anything with you into the testing area; you'll be furnished with a blank sheet of paper and a pen. I suggest that you immediately write down whatever you've memorized for the test before you start the test. You'll have some time to compose yourself, to record this information, and even to take a sample orientation test before you begin the real thing. I suggest that you take the orientation exam; it'll help you get more comfortable when you take the real Cisco test.

As soon as you complete your exam, the software tells you whether you've passed or failed. It also provides a report about your performance on various areas. Even if you fail the exam, I suggest you ask for—and keep—the detailed test results that the test administrator can print for you. You can use these results to help you prepare to retake a test, if necessary. If you're pursuing CCIE certification, you'll also need to send Cisco the results to verify that you've passed the written exam so that you may sign up for the laboratory exam. Alas, if you do need to retake an exam, you'll have to schedule another test and pay the fee again.

Tracking certification progress for Cisco exams also involves following one of two paths: To check on any written exam, you can call Prometric to obtain a transcript of your test record (a fee of $10 will be charged for each such request). To check on your test record for the lab exam, you'll have to call the test center where you took that exam to obtain the results.

Signing Up for the CCIE Laboratory Evaluation

The laboratory evaluations must be scheduled through and taken at Cisco's facilities. To begin, full payment must be received at least 21 days before the laboratory evaluation date (28 days for purchase orders in Europe); otherwise, prospective candidates will be dropped. Typically, this means signing up at least two months in advance, if not sooner. Cancellations must be received at least 21 days prior to the test (28 days in Europe); otherwise, the payment is forfeited. Finally, if you fail a laboratory evaluation, you must wait at least 30 days before making another attempt.

To sign up for either the Routing and Switching or the WAN Switching CCIE laboratory evaluations, you must call one of the CCIE departments at Cisco at the testing center where you want to take the test. At corporate headquarters in San Jose, California, that number is 1-800-829-6387; you can also fax Cisco at 1-408-527-8588 or send an email to **ccie_usa@cisco.com**. For testing locations and contact information, consult the Web page at **www.cisco.com/warp/public/ 625/ccie/exam_preparation/lab.html#3**.

Before you can schedule any laboratory evaluation, the CCIE administrator at Cisco must receive proof that you've passed the CCIE Qualification Exam. The usual approach is to fax the printout of your exam results to the CCIE laboratory evaluation location of your choice or to 1-408-527-8588 for the ISP Dial test. Be sure to include your name, address, phone, and fax number so that your requests can be answered.

How to Prepare for Cisco Exams

At a minimum, you should use the following study materials to prepare for Cisco certification:

➤ For most exams, Cisco offers several corresponding classes. The company recommends that you attend such training through a Cisco Learning Partner. You can arrange to do so through your local Cisco account representative or through your nearest Cisco location. In North America, call 1-800-829-6387; outside North America, call 1-408-526-4000 and ask to speak to an education representative. You can also locate a Cisco Learning Partner near you by visiting Cisco's Training and Certifications Web page at **www.cisco.com/train- ing/** and then click on the Learning Locator button on the left-hand side.

➤ Because Cisco publishes both course and test outlines and objectives, it also recommends that you familiarize yourself thoroughly with these items prior to taking any test. Course objectives and test outlines are accessible through the various certification pages mentioned earlier in this chapter.

➤ Each of Cisco's certification pages includes pointers to practice tests. Because these exams contain questions much like the real exams, they're worth taking.

In addition, you'll probably find any or all of the following materials useful in your search for Cisco expertise:

➤ *Study guides*—Most large computer-book publishers offer Cisco certification-related titles.

➤ *Other publications*—You'll find plenty of other publications and resources if you take the time to look around on the Web or in your local bookstore, but there's no shortage of materials available about Cisco technologies and Cisco certification preparation. A quick visit to a major online bookstore turned up 57 titles using "Cisco" as a search term. Of course, Certification Insider Press now offers *Exam Cram*s for several Cisco exam topics as well.

This set of materials represents a formidable collection of sources and resources for Cisco exam topics and related information.

Need to Know More?

For convenience, I include the most important URLs mentioned so far in this chapter, along with pointers to a few other resources worth investigating for information about Cisco certification, exams, training, and more:

 www.cisco.com/warp/public/10/wwtraining/certprog/index.html This is the home page for all Cisco certification information and includes ready access to guides for all certification programs, certification tracks, test-taking information, and self-assessment tests. This should be your first stop in any search for Cisco certification information.

 www.cisco.com/warp/public/625/ccie/certifications/routing.html This site points to online details on Routing and Switching CCIE certification. It also includes pointers to sample questions for practice.

 www.cisco.com/warp/public/625/ccie/certifications/wan.html This site points to online details on the WAN Switching CCIE certification. It also includes pointers to sample questions for practice.

 www.ccprep.com The site's name says it all—it's entirely devoted to helping its users take and pass the CCIE exams. Although a fee is required to subscribe to this site, it's a great place to go looking for information outside the Cisco umbrella and includes great information about laboratory evaluation scenarios.

CompTIA Certifications

Terms you'll need to understand:

✓ A+

✓ Network+

✓ i-Net+

✓ Computing Technology Industry Association (CompTIA)

Techniques you'll need to master:

✓ Locating training and certification information on the CompTIA Web site

✓ Obtaining descriptions and objectives for CompTIA exams

✓ Identifying training and self-study options related to CompTIA exams

The story behind the A+, Network+, and i-Net+ exams differs from what you've read about so far. There's no single vendor standing behind these tests; rather, they result from the efforts of the Computing Technology Industry Association (CompTIA), an industry trade association that currently involves more than 10,000 members around the world.

As a result, a committee composed of numerous vendors and organizations defines the A+, Network+, and i-Net+ certifications, as opposed to one vendor deciding how best to position, support, and promote its products. Thus, the A+ exam is a test designed to certify that individuals are competent PC technicians and that their knowledge covers hardware and software products, principles, and technologies from many vendors. Likewise, the Network+ test is designed to certify that those who pass it are competent network technicians who have an understanding of networking hardware, devices, and TCP/IP, at a minimum. The i-Net+ exam is designed to identify applicants who are familiar with Internet and Web protocols, authoring, management, and services and who have the equivalent of at least 24 to 36 months of related experience. The official designation for these tests is, in fact, "vendor neutral."

CompTIA offers another certification—the Certified Document Imaging Architech (CDIA)—but that credential doesn't attract a sufficiently large audience to merit coverage in this book. (For more information, the home page for this certification is **www.comptia.org/certification/cdia/cdia.asp**.) I cover three CompTIA exams in this book: the A+ credential (which, for once, doesn't stand for anything) for PC technicians, the Network+ credential for network technicians, and the i-Net+ credential for intranet-, Internet-, or extranet-knowledgeable professionals.

A+ Details

To begin, let's review the A+ certification program. After that, you'll have a chance to review each of the two tests you must pass to obtain this credential, including an overview, objectives, and so on. Along the way, you'll be presented with a table that shows how the pieces fit together. You'll also learn how to sign up for the tests, track progress toward A+ certification, and keep tabs on late-breaking news from CompTIA.

The A+ certification is intended to identify individuals as qualified entry-level PC technicians. The official definition of A+ (taken from CompTIA's page at **www.comptia.org/certification/aplus/aplus.asp**) reads as follows: "Earning A+ certification means that the individual possesses the knowledge, skills, and customer relations skills necessary for a successful entry-level (six months' experience) computer service technician."

To be a bit more specific, obtaining an A+ certification requires passing two tests:

➤ A Core exam, which stresses basic PC hardware, networking interfaces and connections, and customer support skills

➤ A DOS/Windows exam, which stresses basic DOS and Windows architectures, installation, configuration, maintenance, and networking skills

Thus, someone who obtains an A+ certification is expected to have a broad and thorough understanding of basic PC hardware and software, including assembly or installation, setup and configuration, management, troubleshooting, and end-user support issues.

The A+ certification exam-related information is summarized in Table 6.1, which lists the number of questions, the cost, and the time period for each of the two current A+ exams.

The lower costs apply only to companies or individuals who belong to CompTIA. If you or your company are not CompTIA members, you must pay the higher price. Also note that you don't need to take both tests on the same day, only within 90 days of each other.

In the sections that follow, you'll examine A+ certification tests in more detail and learn more about what's on each of those exams. If you visit the URLs mentioned for each exam, you'll be able to jump straight to the nitty-gritty details about each one.

 Although Web locations change over time, they're worth chasing down because CompTIA's Web site is the most up-to-date source for A+ certification information and requirements. The home page for A+ information is **www.comptia.org/certification/aplus/aplus.asp**. From here, you can find all the details you might want. Note also that the banner advertisements that run on this site provide links to companies that offer A+ training, preparation materials, practice tests, and more.

Table 6.1 A+ exams.				
Certification	Questions	Cost (Members)	Cost (Nonmembers)	Time
Core	69	$78	$128	60 min.
DOS/Windows	70	$78	$128	75 min.

A+ Core Exam

This exam covers basic PC hardware knowledge and related skills. It aims to identify those individuals who understand how to assemble, configure, and maintain PCs, and who can also handle basic networking hardware and end-user support issues. This test was developed from an industry-wide task force of PC technicians. Over 5,000 already-certified A+ technicians were also surveyed on the questions to verify their accuracy. The topics covered in this 69-question exam may be broken down as follows:

➤ Thirty percent of the questions relate to installing, configuring, and upgrading PCs.

➤ Twenty percent of the questions relate to diagnosing problems and troubleshooting PCs.

➤ Ten percent of the questions relate to PC safety and preventive maintenance issues.

➤ Ten percent of the questions cover issues related to PC motherboards, CPUs, and memory installation, configuration, and upgrades.

➤ Ten percent of the questions cover issues related to PC-based printers, including cabling, drivers and installation, operation, maintenance, and troubleshooting.

➤ Five percent of the questions deal with portable PC systems, such as notebooks and laptop computers.

➤ Five percent of the questions deal with basic networking, primarily network interfaces, connectors, and cabling issues, in keeping with the hardware focus of this test.

➤ Ten percent of the questions cover customer satisfaction issues, and touch on basic end-user communications, support, and relationship skills.

For more information about test topics and sample questions from each category of questions, click on the Core button on the A+ Certification Objectives page. The exam code for the Core exam is 220-101.

DOS/Windows Exam

This exam covers PC operating system knowledge and deals with DOS versions 6 and 7, Windows 3.x, and Windows 95. It aims to identify those individuals who understand how to install, configure, maintain, and troubleshoot these operating systems and who can handle basic networking software and related configuration issues. This test was developed in the same way as the Core exam. Topics covered in this 70-question exam include the following:

➤ Thirty percent of the questions relate to the function, structure, and operation of DOS, Windows 3.x, and Windows 95, plus file system management.

➤ Ten percent of the questions relate to understanding DOS and Windows memory organization, managing memory conflicts, and optimizing memory usage on PCs.

➤ Thirty percent of the questions relate to installing, configuring, and upgrading operating system software on PCs and cover boot sequences for each operating system mentioned.

➤ Twenty percent of the questions cover issues related to diagnosing or troubleshooting DOS, Windows 3.x, and Windows 95, including recognizing error messages during the boot sequence, operating system startup, and so on, and identifying steps to correct such problems. Also covered in this segment are printing issues, viruses, startup and INI files, and more.

➤ Ten percent of the questions deal with DOS and Windows networking topics, including sharing files and printers, working with network interfaces and protocols, and basic Internet access and service issues.

For more information about test topics and sample questions from each category of questions, visit the DOS/Windows exam objectives by clicking on the DOS/Windows button on the A+ Certification Objectives page. The exam code for the DOS/Windows exam is 220-102.

At this time, new versions of both A+ exams are scheduled for release in December 2000 and will be updated to include coverage of more current versions of Windows (Windows 98, Windows NT 4.0, and Windows 2000) and Linux, among other updates.

Network+

The Network+ exam tests for the same kind of basic competency and knowledge for network technicians that A+ defines for PC technicians. The level of knowledge and expertise is greater because CompTIA states that its investigation attempts to identify individuals with at least 18 to 24 months of experience as network technicians (the A+ exam identifies individuals with only six months of experience or more).

Released in late March 1999, the Network+ exam involved many major players in the computer networking industry, including Banyan, Compaq Computers, *ComputerWorld* magazine, DataTrain, Fluke, the Information Technology Training Association (ITTA), Lotus, Microsoft, the Network Professional Association (NPA), Novell, Softbank, U.S. Robotics, US West, Vanstar, and Wave Technologies.

Beyond its vendor neutrality, the Network+ certificate recognizes its holders' knowledge and understanding of networking tools, technologies, hardware, and software. Given the population of participating vendors and organizations, this testing regimen covers these bases quite well.

Unlike A+ certification, obtaining Network+ certification requires passing only a single exam. This exam consists of 65 questions on a variety of networking topics and requires an 82 percent score (54 questions correct) to pass. Once you start, you'll have 90 minutes to complete this test, which costs $135 for CompTIA members and $185 for nonmembers.

According to the test objectives for this exam, it covers the following topics:

➤ The four lower layers of the OSI Reference Model: Physical, Data Link, Network, and Transport

➤ TCP/IP protocols, services, and addressing

➤ Remote connectivity

➤ Network security

➤ Installing a network

➤ Maintaining and supporting a network

➤ Troubleshooting a network

For more information, visit the Network+ home page at **www.comptia.org/certification/networkplus/networkplus.asp**, then click on the Objectives button. The exam code for the Network+ exam is NK-N10-001.

i-Net+

The i-Net+ exam's goal is to identify qualified, entry-level professionals who are "comfortable" with the Internet and related services, technologies, and protocols. CompTIA's official blurb describes the focus of the i-Net+ exam in this way: "The exam is designed to test Internet technical professionals who are hands-on specialists responsible for implementing and maintaining Internet, Intranet and Extranet infrastructure and services as well as development of related applications." CompTIA has been unwilling to associate an experience level with the i-Net+ exam (as it does for A+ and Network+); however, most industry observers understand it as recognizing someone with 24 to 36 months of relevant experience.

The industry leaders that CompTIA routinely assembles to create such exams helped define i-Net+, including the Association of Internet Professionals (AIP), EarthWeb, iGeneration, Inc., IBM, Intel, Microsoft, Novell, Prosofttraining.com (creators of the Certified Internet Webmaster, or CIW, program), and Wave Technologies, among others.

Becoming i-Net+ certified requires passing a single exam. The i-Net+ exam is comprised of 72 questions related to internetworking technologies, services, and issues. You must answer at least 53 correctly (a score of 73 percent) to pass. You are given an hour and a half to finish this test, which costs $125 for CompTIA members and $175 for nonmembers, while special incentives last.

The i-Net+ exam covers the following topics:

➤ *Business concepts*—Key legal issues, such as copyright, licensing, and trade-marks; globalization issues; push/pull technologies; and e-commerce

➤ *Internet basics*—Internet site functionality, caching services, URLs, and search indexes and engines

➤ *Internet clients*—Installing and configuring TCP/IP networking, MIME types, client support issues, working with patches and updates, plus managing cookies

➤ *Internet development*—Web-related programming technologies and interfaces, client-side and server-side programming languages, Web design and man-agement, development tools and strategies, multimedia, and Web site main-tenance and management

➤ *Internet security*—Fundamental security concepts and technologies, VPNs (virtual private networks), security monitoring, access security features, antivirus software, and network security requirements for the Internet, intranets, and extranets

➤ *Networking and infrastructure*—Internet infrastructure, Internet connectivity, TCP/IP protocols and services, domain names and DNS, remote access, troubleshooting IP networking, routing and interconnectivity devices, band-width types and issues, plus types and roles that various Internet servers play

For more information about this certification and the related exam, visit the i-Net+ home page at **www.comptia.org/certification/inetplus/inetplus.asp**, then click on the Objectives button. The exam code for the i-Net+ exam is IK0-001.

The i-Net+ exam is "broad" rather than "deep." It covers a big range of topics, but none of them in any great depth. The best way to prepare for this exam is through real-life Internet experience. The next best thing is to read widely on Internet topics.

CompTIA Testing

By now, you've read about both of the A+ tests and the Network+ and i-Net+ tests as well. You probably want to know what's involved in signing up for or taking such tests. Nothing could be easier to explain!

To sign up for any CompTIA exam, contact either Virtual University Enterprises (VUE) or Prometric:

➤ Reach VUE on its Web site at **www.vue.com/comptia/** or call 1-877-551-7587.

➤ To reach Prometric, call one of the following numbers for the relevant test:

> ➤ *A+* 1-800-776-4276

> ➤ *Network+* 1-888-895-6116

> ➤ *i-Net+* 1-877-803-6867

To sign up for a test, you must have a valid credit card or contact Prometric or VUE for mailing instructions to send the company a check or money order. You won't be able to register for a test until payment has been verified or your check has cleared.

To schedule an exam, call at least one day in advance. To cancel or reschedule an exam, you must call at least one day before the scheduled test time (or you may be charged, even if you don't show up to take the test).

When you wish to schedule a test, have the following information ready:

➤ Your name, organization, and mailing address.

➤ Your test ID, which is an identifier that only you can use. (In the United States, this is your social security number. If you live outside the United States, contact Prometric or VUE to ask what kind of identification you need when you take a CompTIA exam.)

➤ The name, number, and track of the exam you want to take:

> ➤ A+ Core exam (220-101)

> ➤ A+ DOS/Windows exam (220-102)

> ➤ Network+ exam (NK-N10-001)

> ➤ i-Net+ exam (IK0-001)

➤ A method of payment.

Once you sign up for a test, you'll be told when and where the test is scheduled. Try to arrive at least 15 minutes early. You must supply two forms of identification, one of which must be a photo ID.

All CompTIA exams are closed book. In fact, you can't take anything with you into the testing area; you'll be furnished with a blank sheet of paper and a pen. I suggest that you immediately write down whatever you've memorized for the test before you start the test. You'll have some time to compose yourself, to record this information, and even to take a sample orientation test before you begin the real thing. I suggest that you take the orientation exam; it will help you get more comfortable when you take the real test.

As soon as you complete your exam, the software tells you whether you've passed or failed. It also provides a report about your performance on various areas. Even if you fail the exam, I suggest you ask for—and keep—the test results that the test administrator can print for you. You can use these results to help you prepare to take the test again, if necessary. Alas, if you do need to take an exam again, you'll have to schedule another test with Prometric or VUE and pay the fee again.

How to Prepare for CompTIA Exams

At a minimum, you should use the following to prepare for the CompTIA tests:

➤ CompTIA provides pointers to plenty of training programs and study materials on its Web site under the Training Resources button.

➤ Because CompTIA publishes test outlines and objectives for all its tests, it recommends that you familiarize yourself thoroughly with these items before taking any test. Test outlines are accessible through the exam objectives Web pages mentioned earlier in this chapter.

In addition, you'll probably find any or all of the following materials useful in your search for expertise:

➤ *Study guides*—Numerous computer book publishers—including Certification Insider Press—offer A+, Network+, and i-Net+ certification–related titles. I've picked over this crop and found these titles to be informative and helpful for when you are preparing for these tests, but that doesn't mean you shouldn't check the other publishers out too.

➤ *Other publications*—You'll find plenty of other publications and resources if you take the time to look around on the Web or in your local bookstore; there's no shortage of materials available about A+, Network+, and i-Net+ test preparation.

This set of required and recommended materials represents a formidable collection of sources and resources for CompTIA exam topics and related information.

Need to Know More?

For convenience, I include the most important URLs mentioned so far in this chapter, along with pointers to a few other resources worth investigating for information about A+ certification, exams, training, and more:

 www.comptia.org Click on the Certification button on this page to access the home pages for A+, Network+, or i-Net+ certification information, which includes access to guides about the programs, test objectives, test-taking information, and more. This should be your first stop in any search for exam information.

 www.aplusexam.com The name of this site says it all—it's devoted entirely to helping its users take and pass the A+ exams. For $69, these folks will send you a CD-ROM that includes preparation materials, practice exams, and pointers to all kinds of useful stuff online.

 www.examcram.com This fully interactive web site provides the most up-to-date certification information plus access to practice exams, personal study pages, a free "Question of the Day" service, discussion groups, and more. It is designed specifically to complement the *Exam Cram* and *Exam Prep* study materials.

 www.gtspartner.com Global Training Solutions offers A+, Network+, and i-Net+ certification preparation programs worth investigating. It offers 15 days of materials to help individuals prepare for both A+ exams, plus a study kit for separate purchase, and provides 5-day prep courses for the Network+ and i-Net+ exams.

 www.mic-inc.com/Aplus/ Marcraft also offers A+ and Network+ certification preparation programs. It offers free practice tests as an enticement to visit its site; in addition, it provides a set of nearly 900 practice test questions for a relatively modest fee and a certification study kit for each topic.

 www.mindwork.com/aplusinfo.html Mindwork offers its own full-blown self-study materials and a quick prep guide for A+ certification for experienced PC technicians. Work on similar Network+ materials is currently under way.

Sun's Java Certifications

Terms you'll need to understand:

✓ Sun Certified Programmer for the Java Platform

✓ Sun Certified Developer for the Java Platform

✓ Sun Certified Enterprise Architect for Java 2 Platform, Enterprise Edition Technology

✓ Java Development Kit (JDK) 1.1 and 2

✓ Java 2

✓ Educational voucher ID

Techniques you'll need to master:

✓ Locating training and certification information on the Sun Educational Web site

✓ Deciding which of the Sun JDKs (1.1 or 2) you wish to concentrate on

✓ Obtaining descriptions and objectives for the relevant Certified Java Programmer, Certified Java Developer, and Certified Java Architect exams

✓ Identifying training and self-study options related to Java language certifications

Although Java is an extremely popular programming language and is used in many large, successful companies—including Sun, Novell, IBM, and even Microsoft—Sun still controls licensing for this language. That's why Sun is also the source for Java certification credentials at present. In fact, as of May 1999, Novell, IBM, Oracle, and other companies that use Java have all agreed to recognize Sun's Certified Java Programmer as the entry-point credential for this subject area.

Today, Sun offers three Java certification programs:

➤ *Sun Certified Programmer for the Java Platform*—Candidates who seek this credential must have a strong working knowledge of Java language concepts, keywords, terms, and capabilities. Applicants must pass one exam that tests their knowledge of the Java language and its proper use and invocation. This represents the first rung in Sun's Java certification ladder.

➤ *Sun Certified Developer for the Java Platform*—Candidates who seek this credential must first obtain the Certified Java Programmer credential for some valid Java Development Kit (JDK) (currently, JDK 1.1 and 2 are valid, and have corresponding tests available). Candidates must demonstrate their Java programming expertise by taking two tests: one to develop an application to Sun's specifications and the other to write an essay about the application they have written.

➤ *Sun Certified Enterprise Architect for Java 2 Platform, Enterprise Edition Technology*—Candidates for this certification must be able to understand system solutions design built around Java in both a business and a technical context. In addition, candidates must understand how to design, prototype, and deliver complex, multitiered applications using object-oriented approaches and be able to handle related deployment, development, and security concerns. Two exams and a programming assigment cover issues related to Java technology planning and design. The Certified Java Architect is Sun's elite Java Designer credential.

The ultimate source of information on Sun's Certified Java programs is the Sun Web site. Sun's certification home page is at **http://suned.sun.com/USA/certification/**. From there, you can access just about anything related to this program, its tests, and other requirements with a click of your mouse.

Java Certification Details

To begin, let's review the three Certified Java programs that Sun has to offer. In that process, you'll have a chance to review the tests that you must pass to obtain each credential, including an overview, objectives, and so on. You'll also learn how to sign up for the tests, track progress toward any of Sun's Certified Java programs, and keep tabs on late-breaking Java certification news from Sun.

The first of the three programs is called the Sun Certified Programmer for the Java Platform. Its goal is to verify an individual's basic knowledge of the Java programming language in the context of some particular Java development environment, which Sun calls a JDK. Currently, tests for two JDKs are available:

➤ *Version 1.1*—Not as universally supported by Web browsers, especially older ones, but growing in popularity; it's a later, more sophisticated release of the JDK.

➤ *Version 2*—Represents the latest and greatest implementation of the Java 2 platform; it's the one to bank on for future development because of its advanced features and functions.

To obtain credentials as a Certified Java Programmer, individuals must pass a single written exam. Each currently valid JDK has a separate test associated with it.

The second Java program is called the Sun Certified Developer for the Java Platform. Its goal is to verify an individual's ability to develop Java-based applications and systems, again in the context of some particular JDK. Thus, versions of the tests are available for the 1.1 JDK and the Java 2 JDK.

To obtain credentials as a Certified Java Developer, you must first obtain Certified Java Programmer credentials. Then, you must pass two additional tests. The first is called a performance-based test and requires you to implement a Java application to meet a set of specifications furnished by Sun; the second is an essay based on your work for the performance-based test.

The Sun Certified Enterprise Architect for Java 2 Platform, Enterprise Edition Technology is the third Java credential and applies only to the Java 2 JDK. The goal of this certification is to recognize a candidate's understanding of the Java 2 JDK's advanced features and functions, particularly focusing on creating multi-tiered, database-driven applications and services.

There are no prerequisites to becoming a Sun Certified Java Architect; however, candidates must pass two exams and a programming assignment covering the planning, design, deployment, and maintenance of complex distributed applications built to the Java 2 JDK. They must also understand the balancing of business needs and technology issues. The exams and design project are regarded as quite challenging because of the complexity of the material involved and the broad range of topics covered.

Table 7.1 summarizes the criteria for each of these three certifications.

In the sections that follow, you'll examine all three of the Certified Java programs in more detail and learn a little more about what's on the related exams. If you visit the URLs mentioned for each exam, in most cases you'll be able to jump straight to the nitty-gritty details about each one.

Table 7.1 Java certifications: Exams, questions, costs, time, and more.					
Certification	**JDK**	**Test ID**	**Questions**	**Cost**	**Time**
Java Programmer	1.1	310-022	60	$150	120 min.
Java Programmer	2.0	310-025	59	$150	120 min.
Java Developer performance test	1.1	N/A	N/A	$250	N/A
Java Developer essay test	1.1	310-024	5	$150	90 min.
Java Developer performance test	2.0	N/A	N/A	$250	N/A
Java Developer essay test	2.0	310-027	8	$150	120 min.
Java Architect multiple-choice test	2.0	310-051	48	$150	90 min.
Java Architect essay test	2.0	310-061	TBD	$150	TBD
Java Architect performance-based project	2.0	N/A	N/A	TBD	N/A

Although Web locations change over time, they're worth chasing down because Sun's Web site is the best source for Java certification information and requirements. The home page for Sun certification information is **http://suned.sun.com/USA/certification/**. From there, you can find all the details you might want quite easily.

Sun Certified Programmer for the Java Platform

As you've already learned, this program has one exam that covers basic knowledge of Java language terms and keywords, concepts, and techniques. It aims to identify those individuals who understand the Java programming language and its proper use. The topics covered in this exam may be broken down as follows:

➤ Java language fundamentals, such as statement types and syntax, legal and illegal use of language constructs, and so on

➤ The use of operators and assignment statements in Java, including operator precedence, type handling, and so on

➤ Declarations and access controls in Java, such as variables, arrays, classes, member methods, default constructors, and calling methods

➤ Flow control and exception handling, including nested conditionals; conditional statements; use of **break** and **continue** keywords; flow of control constructs such as **try, catch()**, and **finally**; and use of exception-handling statements and techniques

➤ Overloading, overriding, runtime type, and object orientation handling when working with objects, classes, methods, and variables

➤ Garbage collection, including behavior of the Java Virtual Machine's garbage collection facilities and points at which objects become eligible for collection as garbage

➤ Threads and thread handling, including creating, using, and removing threads; state handling of threads; use of thread messaging tools and techniques; and so on

➤ Use of standard Java packages, including **java.lang, java.awt**, and **java.io**

For more information about this test, visit the Java Programmer exam objectives pages located at **http://suned.sun.com/USA/certification/**. From there, click on the Certification For The Java Platform hyperlink. Choose Exam Objectives in the Sun Certified Programmer For The Java Platform drop-down box, then click on Go. Pick the Java platform JDK you wish to investigate. Likewise, choose the Sample Questions item in the drop-down box to see practice questions.

Sun Certified Developer for the Java Platform

For this certification, two tests are required beyond the Certified Java Programmer credential. The first is an unnumbered performance-based test, a programming assignment consisting of instructions and code that you must download from a special, password-controlled Web page on the Sun site. Then comes the numbered essay test. These two tests are distinct and will exercise different aspects of your knowledge of Java programming.

The objectives for the programming assignment are as follows:

➤ Write an application program in Java that incorporates these components:

    ➤ A user interface that meets stated requirements for both static and dynamic elements

    ➤ A network connection that uses specified protocols to connect to an information server to obtain data for display within the user interface

    ➤ A multithreaded, thread-safe network server that connects to a specified Java database

> ➤ A database created by extending the functionality of supplied code for which limited documentation is available

➤ Test the resulting application against a provided validation harness.

➤ List the significant design choices that were made during the implementation process and discuss their advantages and disadvantages.

➤ Briefly justify choices that were implemented by comparing design and implementation objectives with their corresponding advantages and disadvantages.

Constructing the application requires knowledge of the following Java technologies and components: TCP/IP networking, I/O streams, GUI construction using standard AWT components, the JDK 1.1 or 2.0 event model, object serialization, Javadoc, printing, packages, threads, and implementing interfaces.

The topics covered in the essay exam for the Certified Java Developer credential will vary, but normally the topics demonstrate similar levels of coverage and interrelationships, as shown in the following list:

➤ Briefly describe, in four sentences or less, two approaches to inform the caller of a method that the called method has failed its operation. One of these approaches should be the one that you implemented in your programming assignment.

➤ Briefly describe a total of no more than six advantages and disadvantages for each of the two approaches used to handle operations failures in a called method, in two sentences or less for each advantage or disadvantage.

➤ Briefly describe the approach you used in your assignment.

➤ Describe those specific design goals that informed your approach to the method that you selected in your submission.

For more information about test topics and sample questions for this exam, visit the Certified Java Developer exam objectives and sample questions pages at **http:/ /suned.sun.com/USA/certification/**. From there, click on the Certification For The Java Platform hyperlink. Choose Exam Objectives in the Sun Certified Developer For The Java Platform drop-down box, then click on Go. Pick the Java platform JDK you wish to investigate. Likewise, choose the Sample Questions item in the drop-down box to see practice questions.

Sun Certified Enterprise Architect for Java 2 Platform, Enterprise Edition Technology

Sun's Certified Enterprise Architect for Java 2 Platform, Enterprise Edition Technology certification requires that you complete three elements:

➤ First, you must pass a multiple-choice exam. The details for this exam are covered later in this section.

➤ Next, you must implement a certification database to a set of Sun-provided specifications. This database must be accessible to Sun evaluation personnel via the Internet, so you'll have to leave it live and running during the evaluation process.

➤ Finally, you must complete an essay test in which you answer questions related to the design and implementation decisions and techniques that you employed to build the certification database.

Completing the requirements for this certification can be a genuinely enriching experience, as these things go. They can also be grueling, time consuming, and require lots of preparation and effort!

Basically, the multiple-choice exam tests a candidate's skills in planning, designing, deploying, and maintaining complex distributed Java 2 Platform, Enterprise Edition (J2EE) applications across a wide range of topics and technologies. The exam covers the following:

➤ An understanding of a Java architect's role and duties, from the management of the development life cycle, to exploiting the advantages of a distributed object architecture, to the efficient use of Java's capabilities

➤ The design of a Java technology architecture: evaluating its suitability to particular problems and solutions, maximizing the trade-offs inherent in making use of Java solutions, using multitiered applications, and using servlets rather than CGI programs

➤ The integration of Java-based solutions with existing databases and applications, including using legacy databases or applications as a third application tier, and more

➤ The creation of new distributed, object-oriented Java-based applications, such as designing legacy application migration strategies, using Enterprise JavaBeans and publish/subscribe models, and using Java applets (client side) with legacy applications (server side)

➤ The design of secure Java technology architectures, including security requirements and design constraints, working over unsecured networks, and adding Java-based security components to new and existing multitiered applications

➤ The management of Java-based application performance, such as taking measurements and making relevant evaluations to optimize performance and the design of performance characteristics and capabilities in Java applications

➤ Fitting Java technology into production environments, including the development of "producible" applications, taking projects from the prototype or pilot stage into production, devising effective deployment and distribution strategies, and applying development strategies, object reusability, and project management techniques

Taking this exam is very much like going through a bachelor's curriculum in software engineering from planning and design through the deployment and maintenance phases.

The development project requires that you download Sun's specifications for an online, Internet-accessible certification database. After reading those specifications, you must create a design for the required system and then implement that design to meet Sun's stipulations as stated in the system specification. Most experts believe that the amount of work involved in building the required system takes somewhere between 40 and 100 hours, depending on each candidate's knowledge, skills, design choices, and implementation experience. Make sure that you give yourself enough time to do a good job on this project!

Once your application is available live on the Internet, candidates can take the final, unnumbered essay test, which explores their architecture, design, and implementation decisions in building the certification database. Here, you'll be asked to explore and explain your chosen software architecture, along with related design and implementation decisions, and to evaluate a set of trade-offs and compromises that you should have encountered in turning the specification into a running software system. Having done the work to create your implementation, this exam may require some thought and writing work, but is not necessarily a taxing experience.

Sun has recently revamped the Certified Java Architect exams. Keep an eye on the Web page at **http://suned.sun.com/USA/certification/javamain.html** for any late-breaking news about this certification. I've observed that newly hatched certifications can change in response to user feedback and experiences shortly after launch, so it's entirely possible that this program will be subject to some tuning and tweaking.

Java Certification Testing

By now, you've read about the test for Java Programmer certification, the two tests necessary for Certified Java Developer certification, and the three tests for Certified Java Architect certification. You probably want to know what's involved in signing up for or taking such tests. You can follow the same process for all the numbered Java certification tests—that is, for all tests other than the programming assignments for Certified Java Developer and Certified Java Architect, which you take through Sun Educational Services. For information on the programming tests, see the section later in this chapter titled "Registering for Programming Assignments." But don't worry! If you get confused, you can always call a Sun Educational Services Representative for help at 1-800-422-8020 or check the Sun Registration Web page at **http://suned.sun.com/USA/certification/ registration.html** for local phone numbers.

Registering for Numbered Java Certification Exams

To register for any of the numbered Java certification exams, you must first call Sun Educational Services to make arrangements for an educational voucher ID and to obtain the number for the nearest Prometric center. Only then can you call Prometric or register on its Web site to arrange a date and time for your test.

 You can always call Prometric at 1-800-755-EXAM or email **itech@ prometric.com** if you're outside North America, but you won't be able to sign up for a Sun test without first obtaining an educational voucher ID. The Prometric training registration Web site, **www.2test.com**, also handles Sun test sign-up. Additional registration details can be found at the Sun Registration Web page at **http://suned.sun.com/USA/ certification/registration.html**.

To sign up for a test with Sun, you have several choices. You can use a valid credit card, pay by purchase order if you have an established account with the company, or ask Sun Educational Services for mailing instructions to send a check or money order. You can register for a test only after payment is verified or your check has cleared.

Once you have an educational voucher ID, you must contact Prometric to schedule an exam. Call at least one day in advance. To cancel or reschedule an exam, you must call at least one day before the scheduled test time (or you may be charged, even if you don't show up to take the test).

When you wish to schedule a test, have the following information ready:

➤ Your name, organization, and mailing address

➤ The Sun educational voucher ID

➤ The name and number of the exam you wish to take

➤ A method of payment

Once you sign up for a test, you'll be informed as to when and where the test is scheduled. Try to arrive at least 15 minutes early. You must supply two forms of identification, one of which must be a photo ID. All Java certification exams are closed book. In fact, you can't take anything with you into the testing area. You'll be furnished with a blank sheet of paper and a pen. I suggest that you immediately write down whatever you've memorized for the test before you start the test. You'll have some time to compose yourself, to record this information, and even to take a sample orientation test before you begin the real thing. I suggest that you take the orientation exam; it will help you get more comfortable when you take the real test.

As soon as you complete your exam, the software tells you whether you've passed or failed. It also provides a report about your performance on various areas. Even if you fail the exam, I suggest you ask for—and keep—the test results that the test administrator can print for you. You can use these results to help you prepare to take the test again, if necessary. Alas, if you do need to take an exam again, you'll have to schedule another test and pay the fee again. Remember also that if you're pursuing Certified Java Developer or Certified Java Architect certification, after you complete the programming exercise part of the test through Sun Educational Services, you must contact Prometric to schedule the essay part of the test.

Registering for Programming Assignments

To sign up for the Certified Java Developer exam, you must first pass the Sun Certified Programmer for the Java Platform examination. There are no preliminary requirements for the Certified Java Architect certification. Next, call Sun Educational Services at 1-800-422-8020 or check the Sun Registration Web page at **http://suned.sun.com/USA/certification/registration.html** for local phone numbers so that Sun can help you identify your local Sun Educational Services office.

Next, you must call your local Sun Educational Services office and arrange for the $250 payment necessary to take the Certified Java Developer programming assignment (as of this writing, no pricing has been set for the Certified Java Architect programming assignment). Here again, a credit card will be your best option, but you can discuss alternative arrangements with your local representative (including payment by purchase order, if you or your company already have an account with Sun).

Once payment is received, you'll be granted access to a special Web page where you can download the instructions and code for your programming assignment.

You can take as long as you like to finish this assignment, but I recommend that you try to complete it within a month to keep yourself on track toward obtaining your certification.

How to Prepare for Java Certification Exams

At a minimum, you should obtain and study the following materials:

➤ Sun offers training courses and self-study materials to help you prepare for the various Java certification exams. Its JavaTutor on the Java Programming Language Library CD is a particularly worthwhile bit of self-study material (and may be ordered from Sun Educational Services). For more information about courses and self-study materials, go to the Training Options page at **http://suned.sun.com/HQ/methods/**.

➤ Because Sun publishes test outlines and objectives for all its exams, it recommends that you familiarize yourself thoroughly with these items prior to taking any test. Test outlines are accessible through the Java Certification home page for all certifications and all current JDKs.

In addition, you'll probably find any or all of the following materials useful in your search for Java expertise:

➤ *Study guides*—Most computer book publishers—including Certification Insider Press—offer Java certification–related titles or official documentation of the Java environment that can be helpful as you prepare for the Java certification tests.

➤ *Practice tests*—Numerous vendors offer practice tests for the multiple-choice tests associated with some of the Java certifications. Where applicable, locating and using such tests to help you prepare for an exam can be quite helpful. The Coriolis book *Java 2 Exam Prep* includes practice tests on its companion CD, and that book's author also offers free practice exams along with pointers to a variety of other resources on his Web page at **www.lanw.com/java/javacert/**.

➤ *Other publications*—You'll find plenty of other publications and resources if you take the time to look around on the Web or in your local bookstore, but there's no shortage of materials available about Java, if not directly on Java certification test preparation. A quick visit to our favorite online bookstore turned up over 200 titles in its "Programming Languages-Java" category.

This set of materials represents a useful collection of sources and resources to help you prepare for Java certification exam topics and related information.

Need to Know More?

 http://suned.sun.com/USA/certification/ This is the home page for all Sun certification information and includes ready access to information about the various Certified Java programs, including test objectives, sample questions, test-taking information, and much more.

 www.jars.com Jars is the Java archives online and a great source of information for just about anything Java related. The Java Resources hyperlink on its home page points to tons of Web sites, newsgroups, and mailing lists that cover the Java world admirably, including certification.

 There are numerous other members of the **comp.lang.java** Usenet newsgroup family. Here are some important ones:

➤ **comp.compilers.tools.javacc** Information about the standard Java compiler

➤ **comp.lang.java.databases** Information about Java and databases

➤ **comp.lang.java.gui** Information about Java-based user interfaces

➤ **comp.lang.java.machine** Information about the Java Virtual Machine

➤ **comp.lang.java.programmer** Programmer tools, tips, techniques, and more

➤ **comp.lang.java.security** Discussion of security-related Java issues

 http://javacert.com This is the Java Certification Exam Online study group, maintained by Ian Wojtowicz.

Chauncey's Certification Programs

Terms you'll need to understand:

✓ Associate Technology Specialist (ATS)

✓ Certified Technical Trainer (CTT)

✓ Educational Testing Service (ETS)

✓ National Science Foundation (NSF)

✓ NorthWest Center for Emerging Technologies (NWCET)

Techniques you'll need to master:

✓ Locating training and certification information on the Chauncey Web site

✓ Obtaining descriptions and objectives for specific Chauncey programs and exams

✓ Identifying self-study and training options related to specific Chauncey exams

✓ Viewing Chauncey program guidelines, application forms, and more on the Chauncey Web site

Alphabet Soup

The Chauncey Group International, Ltd. might well be one of the largest and most competent testing and certification organizations that you've probably never heard of. A subsidiary of the ETS (Educational Testing Service)—a company you likely have heard of before, as it produces the SAT (Scholastic Aptitude Test), the GRE (Graduate Record Exam), and other college and graduate entrance exams—Chauncey offers a number of interesting certification programs.

Chauncey offers two certifications that I cover in this chapter (among numerous other programs and association affiliations):

➤ *Certified Technical Trainer (CTT)*—CTT candidates are expected to have excellent teaching skills in some technical subject matter as defined by the International Board of Standards for Training, Performance, and Instruction (ibstpi). To become CTT certified, candidates must pass a computer-based exam and submit a videotape for an evaluation of their in-class training, management, and communications skills.

➤ *Associate Technology Specialist (ATS)*—ATS candidates must successfully pass a battery of tests developed in cooperation with the NorthWest Center for Emerging Technologies (NWCET). These exams are based on skill standards that NWCET developed for the U.S. National Science Foundation (NSF) as part of a national training initiative. All ATS candidates must take and pass one core skill exam to demonstrate basic technology and computing knowledge, as well as two exams in one of the eight "career clusters" associated with this certification. These career clusters range from databases to networking topics.

Note: The best source of information about Chauncey certification curricula is the company's home page at www.chauncey.com. This page provides links (and a pull-down menu) to just about everything related to Chauncey certification programs, exams, and requirements.

CTT Program

In addition to the IT certifications offered at companies such as Cisco, Microsoft, Sun, Novell, and others, each of those vendor programs also offers programs to certify instructors for associated official curriculum materials at "authorized" training centers. Microsoft offers a Microsoft Certified Trainer (MCT) credential, Novell offers a Certified Novell Instructor (CNI) credential, and numerous other programs also include specific instructor certification credentials.

Chauncey's CTT is possibly the greatest value in the certification marketplace and is accepted as a legitimate alternative to vendor-specific trainer certifications for many programs. Any CTT-certified trainer can work across multiple programs. In fact, it's nearly always less expensive to obtain CTT certification than to obtain just one vendor trainer certification, not to mention multiple trainer certifications. It's certainly difficult to find a better bang for your training dollar in today's IT training marketplace!

You have to make it past two exams to become CTT certified: a multiple-choice computer-based test that Prometric administers, and a video of instructional materials that you must prepare that demonstrates your teaching abilities for evaluation by Chauncey's training experts. Here are the details:

➤ The exam ID is 9S0-001 (Prometric) and costs $150. This test includes 105 questions, which you have up to 105 minutes to complete. To register for this exam, call Prometric at 1-800-727-8490.

➤ In addition, you are required to submit a 20-minute instructional video, according to Prometric's detailed instructions, with a completed application form and $150. The video is evaluated to determine whether it (and you) meet Chauncey's instructional demonstration requirements for the CTT. This part of the process is what Chauncey calls the "performance examination" because it requires you to perform on video.

The two required elements—that is, the computer-based exam and the video evaluation fee—add up to $300. In addition, you may choose to use a professional to prepare your video. The program does not require professional videos and many individuals have earned their certifications with videos that were prepared using home video cameras either on a standing tripod or operated by a colleague. If you choose to use a professional, it will cost around $200. The preparatory guides for the CTT exam are additional expenses if you decide to purchase them. Overall costs range from a minimum of $300 in test fees to over $500, based on your decisions.

If you want to obtain a multivendor training certification, start by viewing Chauncey's CTT Candidate Handbook of Information from **www.chauncey.com** (choose the Trainer Certification link, then the CTT Candidate Handbook of Information link). Reading this document requires Adobe Acrobat Reader version 3.0 or later. The CTT Candidate Handbook of Information provides a lot of useful information that will help you prepare for the CTT certification, including information you need to get started, not to mention useful tips and tricks that will improve your chances of a first-time passing experience. You can also call Chauncey's Customer Service number at 1-800-258-4914 for program information.

On page 47, the CTT Candidate Handbook of Information provides information about ordering *Instructor Competencies*, Volume 1, and a videotape called "Creating a Successful Videotape for the CTT Performance Examination." Volume 1 and the tape cost $43.90, plus shipping and handling charges, which is not only worth it but absolutely required if you expect to pass the CTT on your first try.

If you're wondering whether the CTT certification is really useful, here's a partial list of the vendors and organizations that accept the CTT credential in lieu of their own trainer certifications:

➤ Adobe

➤ AOL/Netscape

➤ Autodesk

➤ Lotus

➤ Microsoft

➤ Novell

➤ Oracle

➤ Sun

Some vendors (for example, Citrix) lower their train-the-trainer requirements for anyone who is already CTT certified.

ATS Program

ATS (Associate Technology Specialist) is an emerging certification program whose goal is to identify entry- to intermediate-level IT professionals across a number of key competencies. The exams available by Chauncey include the Core Skills exam, Web Development and Administration, Network Design and Administration, Programming/Software Engineering, Technical Writing, Technical Support, Digital Media, Database Development and Administration, and Enterprise Systems Analysis and Integration.

The broad outlines of the program include the following statements:

➤ All candidates must take the Core Skills exam that tests their basic computing knowledge and the extent of each candidate's familiarity with IT technologies, concepts, and principles. In addition, the Core Skills exam tests what employers are asking for, that is, employability skills. Such topics for the Core Skills exam include project management, communication, and analytical concepts.

➤ To meet an additional job skills requirement, ATS candidates must also take two additional exams in one of eight areas of IT expertise and knowledge:

  ➤ *Database*—Two exams covering database analysis, design, development, and implementation as well as database administration, security, and client services

➤ *Web*—Two exams covering Web site and Web application design, implementation, and management in simple and enterprise environments

➤ *Programming/Software Engineering*—Two exams covering software analysis, design, and development as well as implementation and deployment, including managing and testing releases

➤ *Technical Support*—Two exams on delivering technical support, including system operations troubleshooting and performance, monitoring and maintenance, and what's involved in keeping technical support operations up-to-date, including facilitation, customer service, migration, and upgrades

➤ *Digital Media*—Two exams covering multimedia developer job functions, including analysis, visual and functional design of multimedia applications, media production, acquisition, and implementation/testing

➤ *Enterprise Systems*—Two exams covering job functions for systems integrators, e-commerce specialists, and business analysts, such as defining strategic systems directions and high-level technology management, as well as ongoing tasks related to enterprise systems and integration issues, including defining customer requirements, determining business solutions, and implementing and monitoring such systems

➤ *Technical Writing*—Two exams covering document and electronic publishing specialist job functions, including analyzing project requirements, researching project content, and designing project documents, as well as (on the second test) developing and writing documents and publishing and packaging content for delivery to its consumers

➤ *Network*—Two exams covering the job functions of network technicians, administrators, and architects, including analyzing and designing networks, configuring and implementing networks, and testing networks as well as (on the second test) network monitoring and management and networking administration and maintenance tasks and routines

Each of the exams consists of 75 multiple choice questions and candidates are given 90 minutes to complete each exam. The ATS exams cost $50 each, and three exams are required to become certified. To register for an exam and to locate a test center near you, call Prometric at 1-877-636-6866.

Visit the ATS home page by selecting the Associate Technology Specialist link (or pull-down menu entry) at **www.chauncey.com** to check the status and availability of what promises to be a useful and valuable IT certification. On this page, you can investigate the core exam requirements, choose a particular career cluster, and investigate testing requirements. You can also call Chauncey's Customer Service number at 1-800-258-4914 for program information.

Chauncey Testing

Now that you've learned about these Chauncey certifications, you probably want to know more about registering for and taking one or more of the related exams. For ATS exam registration, call Prometric at 1-877-636-6866. The registration process differs for the computer-based and performance tests for the CTT.

You must first pass the computer-based CTT exam, then submit the videotaped performance exam with an application form to Chauncey. You must call Prometric at 1-800-727-8490 to register for the CTT computer-based exam (ID 9S0-001); it costs $150 to sign up.

To sign up for a computer-based Chauncey test, you must have a valid credit card or contact Prometric for mailing instructions to send the company a check or money order. You can register for a test only after payment has been verified or a check has cleared. When you're scheduling a test, have this information ready:

➤ Your name, organization, and mailing address.

➤ A unique identifier that only you may use. (In the United States, this is your social security number. If you live outside the United States, call Prometric to find out what kind of identification you need to provide when you take a Chauncey exam.)

➤ The name and number of the exam you wish to take (for example, CTT 9S0-001).

➤ A method of payment.

Be sure to bring two forms of signature ID, one of which must bear a photo, to the testing center. All Chauncey exams are closed book. In fact, you can't take anything with you into the testing area. You'll be furnished with a blank sheet of paper and a pen. I suggest that you immediately write down whatever you've memorized for the test before you begin. You'll have some time to compose yourself, to record this information, and even to take a sample orientation test before you begin the real thing. I strongly recommend taking the orientation exam; it will help make you more comfortable with the actual exam.

As soon as you complete a Chauncey exam, you are provided a printed score report that tells you whether you've passed or failed. It even provides detailed diagnostics information to indicate which areas you should study and which Chauncey training materials provide this information. Even if you fail a Chauncey exam, I suggest you keep the detailed test results. This tells you which areas you need to work on. If you happen to fail, you'll have to contact Prometric to schedule (and pay for) another test.

Submitting Your Videotape

Chauncey will process your videotape performance exam only after you pass the CTT computer-based exam. You must complete an official application form for the video and send it and the videotape to Chauncey along with payment—a check or money order for $150 or a completed Chauncey credit card form.

View the CTT Candidate Handbook of Information from **www.chauncey.com** (choose the Trainer Certification link, then the CTT Candidate Handbook of Information link) to get the application form, detailed payment instructions, and shipping address. Be prepared to wait four to eight weeks to receive notification of your pass/fail status for the video submission.

How to Prepare for Chauncey Exams

At a minimum, you should use the following materials to prepare for a Chauncey certification exam:

➤ Chauncey provides self-study materials to help you prepare for CTT certification exams. The CTT Candidate Handbook of Information includes an order form for necessary materials for the computer-based exam and a sample videotape that covers putting your own performance exam together and how to complete the required application form. Visit the CTT Candidate Handbook of Information at **www.chauncey.com** (choose the Trainer Certification link, then the CTT Candidate Handbook of Information link) for more information about study and preparation materials.

➤ Course Technology (**www.course.com/chauncey/**) has mapped the ATS exams to existing courseware. In addition, you can obtain information about the ATS test objectives by visiting **www.nwcet.org**.

➤ Keep your eyes on your favorite certification newsletter. Coriolis publishes a good one called *The Exam Cram Insider* at **www.examcram.com/insider/** that will keep you posted on Chauncey's programs.

In addition, you'll probably find any or all of the following materials useful in your search for Chauncey certification:

➤ *Study guides*—Numerous publishers, including McGraw-Hill, offer CTT certification–related titles of one kind or another. Ben Bergerson's *CTT All-in-One Certification Guide* (McGraw-Hill Professional Publishing, 2000) covers the CTT exam and preparing for the demonstration video in detail.

➤ *Other publications*—You'll find plenty of other publications and resources if you take the time to look around on the Web or in your local bookstore;

there's no shortage of materials available about CTT certification. I expect a similar situation to apply to the ATS program when it's formally launched for public participation.

The preceding set of materials represents a manageable collection of sources and resources for Chauncey exam topics and related information.

Need to Know More?

 www.chauncey.com This is the Chauncey Group's home page, which includes everything you need to know about the company's certification programs and affiliations. While at the Chauncey Web site, choose the Trainer Certification link, and then the CTT Candidate Handbook of Information link. This PDF contains specific information about the CTT computer-based and performance exams in addition to order forms for supplementary training materials and the application form for the performance exam. Make sure you read this file as you prepare for the CTT exam!

 For the latest information on ATS developments and other Chauncey certifications, review the *Inside the Chauncey Group* newsletter at **www.chauncey.com**. At the home page, click on the Publications button, then choose the Inside The Chauncey Group Newsletter link.

 Be sure to check out training-related publications, such as *Inside Technology Training* (available online at **www.ittrain.com**), for information about train-the-trainer programs such as Chauncey's CTT. This group also offers several excellent online newsletters; visit the TrainingSuperSite Newsletters Web site at **www.trainingsupersite.com/newsletters**.

Prosoft's Certified Internet Webmaster Program

Terms you'll need to understand:

- ✓ Certified Internet Webmaster (CIW) program
- ✓ CIW Professional
- ✓ Master CIW Administrator
- ✓ Master CIW Enterprise Developer
- ✓ Master CIW Designer
- ✓ Prosoft Linux Certified Administrator

Techniques you'll need to master:

- ✓ Locating training and certification information on the ProsoftTraining.com Web site
- ✓ Obtaining descriptions and objectives for specific Prosoft programs and exams
- ✓ Identifying self-study and training options related to specific Prosoft exams
- ✓ Downloading Prosoft program guidelines, application forms, and more

About Prosoft

The official name of the company behind the Certified Internet Webmaster (CIW) training program is ProsoftTraining.com. For brevity's sake, I'll call this outfit Prosoft throughout the rest of this chapter (partly at the company's request). However, should you want to visit Prosoft's Web site, look it up online, or research its offerings, you'll find the company's home page at **www.prosofttraining.com**.

Prosoft offers four different certifications under the umbrella of the CIW program, which include an entry-level CIW Professional certification and three master-level certifications, plus an additional credential called the Prosoft Certified Linux Administrator. Read on for an overview of these various credentials.

Note, as of this writing, Prosoft is developing a CIW Certified Instructor certification. Stay tuned to the company's Web site to learn when this credential will be available.

 The best source of information about Prosoft certification and courses appears on the certifications page at **www.prosofttraining.com/ products/certification.asp**. This page provides links (with pop-up explanations) to all of Prosoft's own certifications, plus i-Net+ and Network+ course offerings.

CIW Program

Basically, the Prosoft program uses an entry-level curriculum and exam called the CIW Foundations Track to test all students' knowledge of Internet basics. From there, a student can take any one of the CIW series exams to qualify for the CIW Professional designation. Finally, students can branch into three different tracks of Web activity—Web administrators, Web developers, and Web designers— each of which culminates in an advanced Master-level certification. Interestingly, you can either take the Prosoft Foundations exam to meet the CIW program's entry-level requirements or substitute CompTIA's i-Net+ exam instead. As with many other certification programs, you can take an official course to prepare for a test, or you can tackle any test head on, based on self-study and your own knowledge base. Starting from the Foundations exam, you can move into topical areas aimed at specific job roles for Web developers, designers, or administrators with increasing levels of expertise and specialization.

Here's how the various tracks work:

➤ Starting with Foundations, a candidate must pass any one of the CIW series exams to achieve CIW Professional status (two tests in all).

➤ Administrators continue on from Foundations into a track that starts with a Server Administrator course/test combination, then to an Internetworking Professional combination, and then to a Security Professional combination that culminates in certification as a Master CIW Administrator (four tests in all).

➤ Programmers continue on from Foundations to Web language course/test combinations on both Perl and JavaScript. From there, they tackle course/test combinations on Application Developer, Java Programming, Object-Oriented Analysis, Database Specialist, and Enterprise Developer topics. Completion of the series culminates in certification as a Master CIW Enterprise Developer (eight tests in all).

➤ Web designers continue on from Foundations to a Site Designer course/test combination, then to an E-Commerce Designer combination. This culminates in certification as a Master CIW Designer (three tests in all).

The Master CIW Certification tracks and requirements are depicted in Figure 9.1.

In the sections that follow, you'll learn more about the CIW Professional certification and how it maps into the three Master CIW tracks. Obtaining the Master CIW certifications requires only that you pass the sequence of exams shown in Figure 9.1; for that reason, I don't devote any additional coverage to these "aggregate certifications" except to use them to organize the underlying course/exam combinations. The Prosoft Linux Certified Administrator certification appears in the section by that same name that follows the various CIW component certifications and in the section "More about CIW and Other Web Certifications" later in this chapter.

 Many of the exams for the CIW certification tracks are not available until August 2000 or later. Keep your eye on the CIW Certification site at **www.ciwcertified.com/certifications/ciw_program.htm** for the latest exam information and release dates.

CIW Professional

To earn the CIW Professional certification, candidates must pass the CIW Foundations (1D0-410) exam and any CIW series exam. Students retain their CIW Professional designation until they pass all required exams for any of the three Master CIW certifications. The CIW Professional designation is commonly a step on the way to becoming a Master CIW Administrator, Master CIW Enterprise Developer, or a Master CIW Designer. Master CIW Administrator track students must complete all the exams that fall under this track to qualify for certification as a Master CIW Administrator. Taking courses is optional (and may occur in the classroom or online, as you choose), but all exams mentioned in the following list must be passed to qualify for this certification:

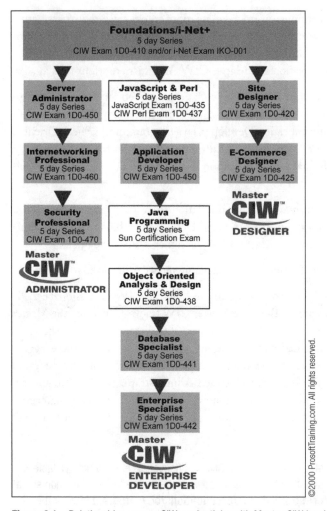

Figure 9.1 Relationships among CIW credentials, with Master CIW levels.

➤ *Server Administrator (five-day training class; Exam 1D0-450)*—This exam covers management, tuning, and deployment of corporate e-business solutions infrastructure elements. These include Web, FTP, and news and mail servers for midsize to large businesses.

➤ *Internetworking Professional (five-day training; Exam 1D0-460)*—This exam covers network architectures, infrastructure components, network performance, and enterprise TCP/IP networks.

➤ *Security Professional (five-day training; Exam 1D0-470)*—This exam covers security policy, security threats, countermeasures using firewall systems and intrusion detection tools, and deployment of e-business solutions, including transaction and payment security.

Completion of Exams 1D0-410 (Foundations) (or the i-Net+ exam), 1D0-450 (Server Administrator), 1D0-460 (Internetworking Professional), and 1D0-470 (Security Professional) results in certification as a Master CIW Administrator.

Master CIW Enterprise Developer Track

Students must complete all the exams that fall under this track to qualify for certification as a Master CIW Enterprise Developer. Taking courses is optional (and may occur in the classroom or online, as you choose), but all exams mentioned in the following list must be passed to qualify for this certification:

➤ *Web Languages (five-day training; Exams 1D0-435, 1D0-437)*—These exams cover the fundamentals of language design, syntax, elements, and programming for JavaScript (1D0-435) and Perl (1D0-437) to ensure basic proficiency in Web-related programming tasks.

➤ *Application Developer (five-day training; Exam 1D0-430)*—This exam covers client- and server-side Web applications using Rapid Application Development tools and related development environments and Web-based applications that include two- and three-tiered database programs.

➤ *Database Specialist (five-day training; Exam 1D0-441)*—This exam covers data-handling requirements, databases to match those needs, and Web-based data handling applications to expose, manage, and interact with those databases through the Web.

➤ *Enterprise Developer (five-day training; Exam 1D0-442)*—This exam covers multitiered database and legacy Web applications using Java, Java Application Program Interfaces (APIs), Java Database Connectivity (JDBC) solutions, middleware tools, and distributed object models that may include Common Object Request Broker Architecture/Object Request Broker (CORBA/ORB) and Internet Inter-ORB Protocol (IIOP).

Along the way to the Master CIW Enterprise Developer certification, Prosoft also requires completion of Sun's Java Programmer certification and requires an additional exam on Object-Oriented Analysis and Design (five-day training; Exam 1D0-438) for a total of seven exams (after completion of the Foundations exam or the i-Net+ exam).

Master CIW Designer Track

Students must complete all the exams that fall under this track to qualify for certification as a Master CIW Designer. Taking courses is optional (and may occur in the classroom or online, as you choose), but all exams mentioned in the following list must be passed to qualify for this certification:

➤ *Site Designer (five-day training; Exam 1D0-420)*—This exam covers established human factor principles to design, build, and maintain hypertext-based Web sites using standard Web authoring and scripting languages, content creation and management tools, and well-known digital media formats.

➤ *E-Commerce Designer (five-day training; Exam 1D0-425)*—This exam covers Web-related standards, technologies, and practices to support e-commerce applications. Also covered are relationships among cardholders, issuers, merchants, acquirers, payment gateways, and third parties through standard transaction models and APIs that include Secure Electronic Transactions (SETs), cryptography standards, Certificate Authorities, and services such as those provided by VeriSign and CyberCash.

Completion of the Foundations exam or the i-Net+ exam, plus 1D0-420 and 1D0-425, qualifies individuals for the Master CIW Designer certification.

More about CIW and Other Web Certifications

The CIW program has been endorsed by the Association of Internet Professionals (AIP) and the International Webmasters Association (IWA). Both these groups are nonprofit organizations of like-minded Web professionals. The CIW has not, however, been endorsed by another crucial body, the World Wide Web Consortium (W3C), which basically owns all the specifications for Web-related technologies. Likewise, another industry group, the Association of Web Professionals (whose online presence appears at **www.a-w-p.org**), has created its own certification program that embraces three named certifications:

➤ *Certified Web Technician*—Web technicians are responsible for implementing, operating, and maintaining Web sites. For more information on this certification, visit **www.a-w-p.org/skills-cwt.htm**.

➤ *Certified Web Designer*—Web designers are responsible for creating, designing, and architecting Web sites and for making appropriate use of Web-based technologies and applications. For more information on this certification, visit **www.a-w-p.org/skills-cwd.htm**.

➤ *Certified Web Manager*—Web managers are responsible for managing the staff, resources, and technologies involved in building, maintaining, and operating large-scale commercial Web sites. For more information on this certification, visit **www.a-w-p.org/skills-cwm.htm**.

Beyond the Web trade organizations, Novell's Certified Internet Professional (CIP) and iGeneration's (formerly HyCurve's) Certified Professional (iCP) certifications also resemble Prosoft's offerings. However, none of these vendor-sponsored programs has attracted the kind of following or participation that the CIW program enjoys. Consequently, CIW is generating more interest in the marketplace (and, of course, that's why it enjoys the lion's share of coverage in this book).

All four of these Web professional programs represent each company's attempts to match various standard curricula for Web certification, which helps to explain their similarities. For more information about Novell's CIP program, visit **www.netboss.com**. For more on iGeneration's iCP, visit **http://you.igeneration. com/certification/default.asp**.

So far, only the CIW seems to have generated sufficient market participation and momentum to be worth a chapter of its own in this book. However, I plan to keep an eye on this fast-moving, ever-changing market niche and will adjust this coverage as needed in future editions. Feel free to follow any of the other links I've provided so that you can visit these programs and judge them for yourself.

Perhaps most important, CIW courses are available through CompUSA, Executrain, New Horizons, Micro Center, and IBM training centers, among a large, comprehensive group of third parties. This means there's a nationwide (and emerging global) network of outlets where classroom CIW training is available. For a complete list of Prosoft's training partners, visit **www.ciwcertified.com/ registration/registration.htm**. Then click on the Select By Location link to find a training company near you that offers the course.

For a different approach, click on the Select By Course link on the same page, then choose a specific topic to produce a list of all the vendors and training companies that offer the course. It's an impressive collection by anyone's standards. Finally, online versions of courses are also available—as you'd expect from a company that offers Internet certifications—for much of their curriculum. A list of distance learning courses appears at **http://proflexsupport.prosofttraining.com/ v4browsers_ie.htm** (click on the Training Schedules link), although you may need to navigate to a similar page if you're not using Internet Explorer.

Prosoft Linux Certified Administrator

The Prosoft Linux Certified Administrator track is built around a five-day course designed to give IT professionals hands-on experience with installing and administering Unix systems. For this course, the overall emphasis is placed on unique features of Linux implementation. This track incorporates two days of Linux Fundamentals classroom coverage, along with three days of Linux System and Network Administration coverage.

The Prosoft Linux Certified Administrator track works best for individuals who are already working as system administrators and who are familiar with the ins and outs of this job role. This particular certification also works well for individuals already expert with other flavors of Unix who want to use Linux in a production environment.

Prosoft's LCO-610 Linux Certified Administrator certification exam is available worldwide through Prometric. To sign up for this exam, use the Find A Test Center locator at **www.2test.com** and select LINUX CERTIFICATION (PROSOFT) from the pull-down list. Call 1-877-795-6871 to register for this exam.

Other Linux certifications are covered in Chapter 10. Be sure to consider the Prosoft option if you wish to pursue Linux certification of any kind!

Prosoft Testing

Now that you've learned about these Prosoft certifications, you probably want to know more about registering for and taking one or more of the related exams. The registration process involves Prometric or Virtual University Enterprises (VUE) and is quite similar to other vendor programs that appear elsewhere in this book:

➤ *Prometric*—You can sign up for a test through the company's Web site (current exams only, no beta exams through the Web) at **www.2test.com,** or you can register by phone at 1-800-380-EXAM (in the United States or Canada).

➤ *VUE*—You can sign up for a test or get the phone numbers for local testing centers through the Web page at **www.vue.com/ciw/**.

To sign up for a test, you must possess a valid credit card or contact either company for mailing instructions to send them a check (in the United States). You can register for a test only when payment is verified or a check has cleared.

To schedule an exam, call or visit either of the Web pages that appear in the preceding list at least one day in advance. To cancel or reschedule an exam, you must call at least 12 hours before the scheduled test time or before close of business the preceding working day (or you may be charged, even if you don't show up to take the test). When you want to schedule a test, have the following information ready:

➤ Your name, organization, and mailing address.

➤ A unique identifier that only you may use. (In the United States, this is your social security number. If you live outside the United States, call Prometric or VUE to ask what kind of identification you need to provide when you take a Prosoft exam.)

➤ The name and number of the exam you wish to take.

➤ A method of payment.

Once you sign up for a test, you'll be informed as to when and where the test is scheduled. Try to arrive at least 15 minutes early. You must supply two forms of identification, one of which must be a photo ID.

All Prosoft exams are closed book. In fact, you won't be allowed to take anything with you into the testing area. You'll be furnished with a blank sheet of paper and a pen. I suggest that you immediately write down whatever you've memorized for the test before you actually begin to take the test. You'll have some time to compose yourself and to record this information.

As soon as you complete a Prosoft exam, the software tells you whether you've passed or failed. It even provides detailed diagnostics information to indicate which areas you should study and which Prosoft training materials provide this information. Even if you fail a Prosoft exam, I suggest you ask for—and keep—the detailed test results that the test administrator can print for you. This tells you which areas you need to work on. If you happen to fail, you'll have to contact Prometric or VUE to schedule (and pay for) another test.

How to Prepare for Prosoft Exams

At a minimum, you should use the following materials to prepare for a Prosoft certification exam:

➤ Prosoft provides self-study materials to help you prepare for CIW certification exams, whether you take your courses in the classroom or via distance learning. Be sure to consult these materials as you prepare for your tests.

➤ At present, there isn't much available by way of ancillary materials from publishers, be it in the form of study guides, exam crams, practice tests, and so on. However, I happen to know that several publishers are planning to support the CIW program with such materials, so you should keep your eye on the marketplace for news about such things.

Sometime in the near future, you'll probably find any or all of the following materials useful in your search for CIW certification:

➤ *Study guides*—Several publishers, including Coriolis and IDG Books, plan to offer CIW certification-related titles of one kind or another.

➤ *Other publications*—You'll find other publications and resources if you take the time to look around on the Web or in your local bookstore, especially in online newsletters (such as Coriolis's *Exam Cram Insider* newsletter, available at **www.examcram.com/insider/** or from magazines such as *Certification Magazine* at **www.certmag.com** or *Professional Certification Magazine* at **www.procertmag.com**).

The preceding set of materials should soon comprise a usable collection of sources and resources for CIW exam topics and related information.

Need to Know More?

 www.ciwcertified.com This is Prosoft's home page for all things related to the CIW program. Partners, students, and instructors can use this page to locate the CIW information they need.

 www.ciwcertified.com/catalog/catalog.htm Visit this Web page to download the complete CIW course catalog; this Web page also lists which courses must be completed to qualify for the various Master CIW certifications.

 www.examcram.com/insider/ This is Coriolis's *Exam Cram Insider* newsletter home page and is a great place to keep tabs on certification topics of all kinds, including recent developments with the CIW program.

 www.certmag.com This is MediaTec's quarterly certification-focused *Certification Magazine* and is another great place to keep tabs on certification topics of all kinds, including information about the CIW program.

 www.procertmag.com This is the home page for *Professional Certification Magazine*, a quarterly magazine that covers certification and career issues. It's also a good place to visit when looking for late-breaking certification news and program changes.

 Be sure to check out training-related publications, such as *Inside Technology Training* (available online at **www.ittrain.com**) for information about Prosoft's CIW program. This group also offers several excellent online newsletters; visit the TrainingSuperSite Newsletters Web page at **www.trainingsupersite.com/newsletters/**.

Linux Certifications

Terms you'll need to understand:

✓ Red Hat Certified Engineer (RHCE)

✓ Red Hat Certified Examiner (RHCX)

✓ Train-the-Trainer (T3)

✓ Linux Professional Institute (LPI)

✓ LPIC Level 1, Level 2, and Level 3 certifications

✓ Sair Linux and GNU Certified Professional (LCP)

✓ Sair Linux and GNU Certified Administrator (LCA)

✓ Sair Linux and GNU Certified Engineer (LCE)

✓ Master Sair Linux and GNU Certified Engineer (MLCE)

Techniques you'll need to master:

✓ Locating training and certification information on the various Linux certification Web sites

✓ Obtaining descriptions and objectives for specific Linux programs and exams

✓ Identifying self-study and training options related to specific Linux exams

✓ Keeping up with the shifting Linux certification landscape

About Linux and Certifications

Linux is an Open Source implementation of the Unix operating system, started by computer guru Linus Torvalds in the early 1990s. Today, there are over 100 various implementations of Linux available. Some versions are free for the down-loading, others are available at low cost, and still other Linux implementations are sold as full-fledged commercial products with technical support and every-thing.

Linux has become a market phenomenon as it gains momentum and increased private and commercial use. Linux also functions as something of a poster child for the "ABM" (Anyone But Microsoft) movement in that many buyers who wish to avoid running Microsoft operating systems tend to gravitate to Linux.

In this chapter, I can't cover every Linux certification there is, but I do cover three Linux certification programs that have captured significant interest and atten-tion. Because I have three programs to cover, the same format you've seen in earlier chapters in this book is triplicated (except for the "Need to Know More?" section at the end of the chapter, which consolidates Web pointers and other program information for all three programs in one location).

The three Linux certification programs I cover include the following:

➤ Red Hat Inc.'s Red Hat Certified Engineer (RHCE) and related programs

➤ The Linux Professional Institute's LPI Program

➤ The Software Architecture Implementation and Realization group (Sair), which has teamed up with Prometric to create a program called the Sair Linux and GNU certification program

In the sections that follow, you'll find information about all three of these pro-grams in the order in which they appear in the preceding list.

Red Hat Linux Certification

Red Hat Inc. sells a commercial version of Linux to the marketplace. In the wake of the biggest Linux market share for any such vendor and an extremely success-ful Initial Public Offering in 1999, Red Hat is a major player in the Linux soft-ware world. Thus, its Red Hat Certified Engineer program has garnered significant interest and widespread adoption and support as well. Here, you'll learn about this certification program and what it has to offer.

Alphabet Soup

➤ *Red Hat Certified Engineer (RHCE)*—Red Hat's primary Linux certification, this identifies individuals who can design, install, configure, maintain, and troubleshoot systems and networks built around Red Hat's Linux implementation.

➤ *Red Hat Certified Examiner (RHCX)*—This is Red Hat's train-the-trainer (T3) course. Individuals who wish to teach courses and administer the RHCE exam from the Red Hat curriculum must take this course (and pass the RHCE exam as well).

➤ *Red Hat Developer Training*—This program provides training for developers who wish to write software for the Red Hat Linux environment and includes one track for kernel and device driver developers and another track for application and GUI programmers. At present, there is no certification associated with this training program, and these courses are available only at Red Hat's Portland, Oregon, facility, which is why this topic gets no further coverage in this chapter. Visit **www.redhat.com/services/training/developer.html** for more information on this program.

➤ *Red Hat Certification Central*—This Web site is available only to RHCEs and provides private access to technical information, proof of certification, and other premier services. Located at **www.redhat.com/services/rhce_form.html**, this site is accessible only to individuals who hold a valid RHCE certificate (and PIN number).

The best source of information about Red Hat certification and courses appears on the company's training and certification pages at **www. redhat.com/services/training/training.html**. This page provides links to all of Red Hat's various certifications, plus related training courses and materials.

RHCE and RHCX Programs

The Red Hat Certified Engineer credential is actually the summit of a certification ladder. Red Hat defines a complete curriculum of courses that provides training for these job roles:

➤ *Red Hat User*—Prepares users to understand and work with Linux systems, including command line processes and desktop productivity functions. Requires completion of a single course, RH033: Introduction to Red Hat Linux I, II. This course lasts four days, costs $1,998, and is offered at three Red Hat locations in the United States and through Global Knowledge, a Red Hat

Certified Training Partner. Visit **www.redhat.com/services/training/training_rh033.html** for more information on this course. There is no Red Hat certification associated with this job role.

➤ *Red Hat Operator*—Prepares IT professionals to install, configure, and network Linux workstations and servers in the workplace. Requires completion of two courses, RH133: Red Hat Linux System Administration I, II and RH253: Red Hat Linux Networking and Security Admin. Each of these two classes takes four days; RH133 costs $2,098, and RH253 costs $2,198. Both are offered at three Red Hat locations in the United States and through Global Knowledge. Visit **www.redhat.com/services/training/training_overview.html** for pointers to both of these courses. There is no Red Hat certification associated with this job role.

➤ *Red Hat Certified Engineer (RHCE)*—Prepares experienced Unix administrators, developers, or networking professionals to become completely familiar with Red Hat Linux architecture, components, customization, and capabilities. Although this certification involves only a single course and/or exam (individuals may sign up for a course/exam combination or may simply take the exam without the course), the RHCE is a serious test of one's knowledge and ability in working with Unix in general and with Red Hat Linux in particular.

The course/exam combination is called RH300: Red Hat Certified Engineer Course. It takes five days to complete (four days for the course, one day for the exam) and costs $2,498. The exam-only version is called RH302: RHCE Certification Lab Exam, takes one day to complete, and costs $749.

RHCE candidates are strongly advised to complete the Red Hat prerequisites—all the courses involved for the Red Hat User and Red Hat Operator job roles, plus training in LAN/WAN fundamentals—before attempting the RHCE course and/or exam. For more information about the RHCE prerequisites, visit **www.redhat.com/services/training/training_prereq.html**. Likewise, candidates are also strongly advised to use the published RHCE exam objectives to guide their study and preparation for the exam. For more information about these objectives, visit **www.redhat.com/services/training/training_course.html**.

The Red Hat Certified Examiner credential aims to identify IT instructors who can teach the RH300 and RH302 classes and administer the associated RHCE laboratory exam. Thus, the associated course focuses as much on the configuration, setup, and delivery of the lab exam as it does on the material delivered in the four days of class that may optionally precede that exam.

Obtaining the RHCX credential requires that individuals be RHCE certified, then take an additional course, RH310: Red Hat Certified Examiner (RHCX) T3 Course. This course lasts three days and costs $1,549. It is delivered only at

Red Hat's Durham, North Carolina, facility. Only individuals who obtain the RHCX credential may teach the RHCE courses at a Red Hat or Red Hat Certified Training Partner facility. For more information about this course, related requirements, and a sign-up schedule, visit **www.redhat.com/services/training/training_rh310.html.**

Red Hat RHCE Testing

Now that you've learned about the RHCE, you probably want to know more about registering for the written and laboratory exams. The registration process involves either Red Hat itself or one of its Red Hat Certified Training Partners (currently, this includes only Global Knowledge and IBM Global Services, but Red Hat is working to certify other third-party training companies as well).

To sign up for the RHCE exam, you must currently contact either Red Hat, Global Knowledge, or IBM Global Services. If you can pay by credit card, you can handle everything you need to sign up for an exam with a single phone call or through a Web site. If you want to pay by check, you must contact one of the companies for mailing instructions. Likewise, you can make arrangements with one of the companies to establish credit and use a company purchase order to schedule the exam or the course/exam combination. Please note that you can register for a course or an exam only when payment is verified, when a billing relationship exists (for handling purchase orders), or when your check has cleared.

To schedule an exam, call or visit one of the vendors as far in advance as possible (there are only limited opportunities to sign up for RH300 and RH302, so plan ahead). To cancel or reschedule an exam, you must agree to Red Hat's cancellation policies. Red Hat's cancellation policies require forfeiture of part of the sign-up fee unless at least 11 working days' notice is given—that is, it costs 80 percent of the total fee to cancel two working days or less before the course or exam and 50 percent to cancel between 3 and 10 working days before the course or exam. With 11 working days' notice or more, you get a complete refund of the fees (or can reschedule without penalty).

To sign up for a Red Hat course and/or exam, visit the Red Hat Registration Web page at **www.redhat.com/services/training/training_reg.html.** Here, you'll find contact names, Web sign-up pages, email addresses, and phone numbers to register at U.S., U.K., Germany, and Asia Pacific locations. To sign up for RHCE training and/or exams at Global Knowledge, consult the company's Web page at **http://db.globalknowledge.com/catalog/registerlist.asp.** To sign up for RHCE training and/or exams at IBM Global Services, consult the company's Web page at **www-3.ibm.com/services/learning/spotlight/linux.html.** Should either of these URLs not work, double-check the partner listings on the Red Hat Certification page at **www.redhat.com/services/training/training.html.**

All Red Hat exams are closed book. In fact, you won't be allowed to take anything with you into the testing area. You'll be furnished with a blank sheet of paper and a pen. I suggest that you immediately write down whatever you've memorized for the test before you actually begin to take the test. You'll have some time to compose yourself and to record this information.

When you complete a Red Hat exam, you'll have to wait for the instructor to compile a score for your test.

How to Prepare for Red Hat Exams

At a minimum, you should use the following materials to prepare for a Red Hat certification exam:

➤ Red Hat provides comprehensive statements of its prerequisites for the RHCE and also offers a complete outline of its own RHCE training course. Be sure to consult these materials to help you prepare for your exam.

➤ If you do take the RHCE classroom training, be sure to consult your student manuals as well. These offer comprehensive coverage of the topics that will appear on the exam and supply a great preparation tool.

➤ You'll also find lots of options from third parties to help you prepare for the RHCE exam. A quick visit to an online bookstore, with a search on "RHCE," turns up over half a dozen entries. As time goes by, the number of such options will only increase.

Thus, you should find any or all of the following materials useful in your search for RHCE certification:

➤ *Exam Cram and Prep*—Coriolis offers an *RHCE Linux Exam Cram*, by Kara Pritchard, for the RHCE (1999). Also, Dee-Ann LeBlanc's *General Linux I Exam Prep* includes coverage of the RHCE as well as other Linux certifications.

➤ *Study guides*—Several publishers, including Osborne/McGraw-Hill and Sybex Books, among others, offer RHCE certification-related titles of one kind or another.

➤ *Other publications*—You'll find plenty of other publications and resources if you take the time to look around on the Web or in your local bookstore; there's no shortage of materials available about Linux certification in general and RHCE in particular, especially in online newsletters (such as Coriolis's *Exam Cram Insider*, available at **www.coriolis.com/eci/**) or from magazines such as *Certification Magazine* at **www.certmag.com** or the *Linux Gazette* at **www.linuxgazette.com**.

The preceding set of materials should soon comprise a usable collection of sources and resources for Red Hat exam topics and related information. Next: On to the LPIC Program!

The LPIC Program

LPIC stands for "Linux Professional Institute Certification." The Linux Professional Institute (LPI) is the brainchild of Unix expert and author Dan York, who has worked tirelessly since 1998 to get LPI and its various certifications off the ground. The LPIC program is a vendor-neutral Linux certification program that offers evidence of general Linux skills and knowledge.

The LPIC program is designed as a three-level certification program for Linux professionals at the operator, administrator, and advanced specialist levels. For an excellent overview of the motivation for the LPIC program, read Dan York's article on Linux certification in the *Linux Gazette* at **www.linuxgazette.com/issue33/york.html**.

No Alphabet Soup, for Once!

The LPIC program is broken into three numbered levels, as follows:

➤ *LPIC Level 1*—This is a base-level Linux operator certification in which individuals must develop a level of knowledge and competency that's roughly equivalent to the RHCE prerequisites. This means the ability to install, configure, network, maintain, and troubleshoot Linux systems for use as workstations or servers, without necessarily knowing all the kernel-level or architecture details of the system or all its advanced capabilities.

To obtain LPIC Level 1 certification, candidates must pass two exams: 101: General Linux, Part 1 and 102: General Linux, Part 2. The 101 exam covers fundamental system administration activities that are common to all Linux versions. The 102 exam covers basic installation, configuration, operations, shells and scripting, and X Windows, plus networking fundamentals and services and basic system security.

➤ *LPIC Level 2*—This is an intermediate-level Linux certification in which individuals must demonstrate a level of knowledge and competency that's roughly equivalent to the RHCE. This includes advanced Linux administration topics and tools, plus Linux monitoring, optimization, and tuning for a variety of performance and security goals. The Level 2 certification is still under development; items mentioned in the next paragraph may change by the time this certification becomes publicly available.

To obtain LPIC Level 2 certification, candidates must pass two exams: 201: Advanced Administration and 202: Linux Optimization. The 201 exam covers general system administration activities that include problem detection, tracking and resolution skills, construction of advanced shell scripts using sh and sed, and advanced coverage of internetworking topics, with a strong emphasis on IP protocols and services. The 202 exam covers how to monitor, track, and tune Linux systems; manage the Linux boot sequence; how to determine whether and when the Linux kernel should be upgraded and how to create a custom Linux kernel; and how to work with programming libraries, upgrades, and bug fixes.

Stay tuned to the LPI Web site at **www.lpi.org/c-process.html** for more information about LPIC Level 2.

➤ *LPIC Level 3*—This is an advanced-level Linux certification in which individuals must demonstrate a deep and thorough knowledge of the Linux kernel and one or more subsystems. It's also a level of certification with some responsibility for managing or coordinating the activities of others, planning system rollouts and deployments, managing budgets, and interacting with organizational managers to set and meet IT implementation requirements. The Level 3 certification is still under development; items mentioned in the next paragraph may change by the time this certification becomes publicly available.

To obtain LPIC Level 3 certification, candidates must pass any two exams from a broad slate of possibilities. Current exam possibilities include the following:

➤ *321 Windows Integration*—Working with Linux and Windows 2000, NT, 9x, and so on.

➤ *322 Internet Server*—Using Linux to support list servers, news servers, FTP, HTTP, DNS, ISP, NFS, and possibly Perl scripting as well.

➤ *323 Database Server*—Using Linux to support a database engine, with related application and Web-based services.

➤ *324 Security, Firewalls, Encryption*—Using Linux to establish a secure network perimeter, with appropriate monitoring, intrusion detection, security controls, and authentication services.

➤ *325 Kernel Internals and Device Drivers*—Developing software for the Linux environment, including kernel-level services and device drivers (a working knowledge of the C programming language may be required).

➤ *32x Additional Electives*—As additional electives are developed, they will fall into the number range of 326 to 329.

Stay tuned to the LPI Web site at **www.lpi.org/c-process.html** for more information about LPIC Level 3.

As I write this material, only exams for LPIC Level 1 are available, but exams for both Level 2 and Level 3 are promised for delivery in the next year. Check **www.lpi.org/p-index.html** (the LPI exam objectives page) to see which exams are currently available as you read this material. (Hint: The only objectives you'll find there are for exams that you can actually take!)

LPI Testing

Now that you've learned about the LPI certifications, you probably want to know more about registering for and taking the exams. The registration process involves Virtual University Enterprises (VUE), which is currently the sole testing outlet for LPI exams. All LPI exams cost $100 each (at least, the ones that are currently available; there's no telling if the more advanced exams will cost the same or more).

To take an LPI exam, you must first create a VUE user account at **www.vue.com/ contact/obtainLogin.html**. After that, you can register for any LPI exam. This involves locating a test center where you want to take an exam, scheduling that exam, and making payment. You can handle all these activities at **www.vue.com/ linux/linuxexam.html**. In fact, VUE provides a great set of instructions called "How to Register for an Exam" at **www.vue.com/linux/howtoregister.html**. Consult these for detailed information on all the ins and outs of exam registration.

 If you already have a relationship with VUE for other certification programs, such as MCSE or CNE, you can use the same account number and contact information you used before. However, you must call VUE and request that they activate your other account for LPI exams. The necessary phone numbers appear at **www.vue.com/ contact/loginRequestNumbers.html**.

All LPI exams are closed book. In fact, you won't be allowed to take anything with you into the testing area. You'll be furnished with a blank sheet of paper and a pen. I suggest that you immediately write down whatever you've memorized for the test before you actually begin to take the test. You'll have some time to compose yourself and to record this information.

When you complete an LPI exam, you obtain immediate feedback on your score from VUE's automatic scoring system. Ask your test center administrator to print you a copy of your test results so that you can refer to them later, should you need to.

How to Prepare for LPI Exams

At a minimum, you should use the following materials to prepare for an LPI certification exam:

➤ LPI provides comprehensive statements of its objectives and requirements for all LPI exams and also offers sets of practice questions for such exams. Be sure to consult these materials to help you prepare for your exams; you'll find them at **www.lpi.org/p-index.html**.

➤ LPI itself offers no training, nor does it endorse any such training from third parties. You can, however, find a comprehensive list of such third parties at the Linux Training Resources Web page at **http://training.linsight.com**.

➤ LPI itself offers neither study guides nor cram materials, but you'll find several options from third parties to help you prepare for LPI exams. A quick visit to an online bookstore, with a search on "LPI," turns up multiple entries. Many computer publishers have LPI certification books under way, so your options should improve with time.

Thus, you should find any or all of the following materials useful in your search for LPI certification:

➤ *Exam Prep*—Dee-Ann LeBlanc's *General Linux I Exam Prep* includes coverage of the LPI Level 1 exams as well as other Linux certifications.

➤ *Study guides*—Several publishers, including New Riders Publishing and IDG Books Worldwide, among others, offer LPI certification-related titles of one kind or another.

➤ *Other publications*—You'll find plenty of other publications and resources if you take the time to look around on the Web or in your local bookstore, but there's no shortage of materials available about Linux certification in general and LPI in particular, especially in online newsletters (such as Coriolis's *Exam Cram Insider*, available at **www.examcram.com/insider/**) or from magazines such as *Certification Magazine* at **www.certmag.com** or the *Linux Gazette* at **www.linuxgazette.com**.

The preceding set of materials should soon comprise a usable collection of sources and resources for LPI exam topics and related information. Next: On to the Sair program!

The Sair Linux and GNU Certification Program

Sair is a wholly owned subsidiary of the international training company Wave Technologies. Prior to its acquisition in early 2000, Sair was recognized as a leading purveyor of Unix training, exams, and consulting. Sair uses Prometric as its testing outlet, which gives it global reach for its Linux and GNU certification exams. The Sair Linux and GNU certification program is vendor neutral and offers evidence of general Linux knowledge and skills.

The Sair Linux and GNU certification program is a three-tiered program. Each level corresponds to some named certification. Here, you'll learn more about this certification program and its related credentials.

Note: GNU stands for "GNU is Not Unix," which makes it a self-referential or recursive acronym. Broadly speaking, GNU represents an important body of "copyleft" code and utilities that many versions of Unix, including Linux, treat as part of the overall operating environment. Thus, it makes sense for the certification to mention this important body of work by name!

Alphabet Soup

Let's start by reviewing the general cognomen for individuals who pursue Linux certification from Sair, then examine the three certifications and their acronyms for each of the program's three levels:

➤ *Linux Certified Professional (LCP)*—Any person who passes the Sair Linux Install and Configuration test or the System Administration test at any of the three certification levels attains LCP status. It's the basic entry-level Sair Linux and GNU certification, much like the MCP is for Microsoft.

➤ *Linux Certified Administrator (LCA)*—The official title for this certification is Sair Linux and GNU Certified Administrator, abbreviated LCA. This is the entry-level certification for the program that identifies individuals who can function at the power-user level and can perform adequately as help desk staff members for Linux topics or as entry-level Linux administrators.

➤ *Linux Certified Engineer (LCE)*—The official title for this certification is Sair Linux and GNU Certified Engineer, abbreviated LCE. This is the intermediate-level certification for the program that identifies individuals who can function as everyday Linux administrators and can handle simple design, installation, configuration, maintenance, and troubleshooting topics.

➤ *Master LCE (MLCE)*—The official title for this certification is Master Sair Linux and GNU Certified Engineer, abbreviated MLCE. This is the topmost level of certification in this program and identifies individuals who have attained deep knowledge and understanding of the inner workings of Linux and its associated GNU tools. Such individuals can function as senior Linux administrators and specialists and can handle complex design, installation, automation, configurations, maintenance, and troubleshooting topics.

Each certification, with the exception of LCP, requires passing four exams and is claimed to be the equivalent of 128 hours worth of classroom training.

Basic Sair Certification Requirements

The various Sair Linux and GNU certifications have been designed to cover the same ground at increasing levels of coverage and complexity, so obtaining any Sair certification is contingent on passing four similar exams:

➤ *Installation and Configuration-Level ? (Test 3X0-?01)*—For each level of certification, this exam covers issues related to installation and configuration of Linux and GNU tools.

➤ *System Administration-Level ? (Test 3X0-?02)*—For each level of certification, this exam covers issues related to managing, troubleshooting, upgrading, and maintaining Linux systems and GNU tools.

➤ *Networking-Level? (Test 3X0-?03)*—For each level of certification, this exam covers issues related to installing, configuring, managing, and troubleshooting Linux networking protocols and services, plus related GNU tools and system utilities.

➤ *Security, Privacy and Ethics-Level ? (Test 3X0-?04)*—For each level of certification, this exam addresses security topics, plus coverage of privacy and ethics matters for Linux systems.

Only the level number (1, 2, or 3, corresponding to LCA, LCE, and MLCE, respectively) changes for each specific certification. Thus, the LCA Installation and Configuration exam is named Installation and Configuration-Level 1, and its exam ID is 3X0-101; likewise, the same topic for MCLE would be Installation and Configuration-Level 3 and 3X0-301, respectively.

As I write this, only Level 1 exams are available. Level 2 and 3 exams should be available within the next year. For current status, check the list of available exams at the Prometric Web site at **www.2test.com**. (Hint: Any exam you can sign up and pay for is one you can take! Right now, that means only 3X0-101, 3X0-102, 3X0-103, and 3X0-104.)

Sair Linux and GNU Testing

Now that you've learned about the Sair certifications, you probably want to know more about registering to take their exams. The registration process involves Prometric, which is currently the sole testing outlet for Sair exams. All currently available Sair exams cost $99 each (there's no telling if the more advanced exams will cost the same or more).

To sign up for a Sair exam online, you must first create a Prometric user account at **www.2test.com**. After that, you can register for any Sair exam. This involves locating a test center where you want to take an exam, scheduling that exam, and making payment. You can handle all these activities at **www.2test.com** as well. By phone, you must call 1-888-895-6717 to register for a Sair exam.

 If you already have a relationship with Prometric for other certification programs, such as MCSE or CNE, you can use the same online account name and password you've used before at **www.2test.com**. Just make sure you pick the Linux (Sair, Linux & GNU) entry from the pulldown menu when you select the type of exam for which you wish to register.

To sign up for a test, you must possess a valid credit card or contact Prometric for mailing instructions to send them a check (in the United States). You can register for a test only when payment is verified or a check has cleared.

To schedule an exam, call or visit the **www.2test.com** Web page at least one day in advance. To cancel or reschedule an exam, you must call at least 48 hours before the scheduled test time or before close of business two working days beforehand (or you may be charged, even if you don't show up to take the test).

When you want to schedule a test, have the following information ready:

➤ Your name, organization, and mailing address

➤ The name and number of the exam you wish to take

➤ A method of payment

Once you sign up for a test, you'll be informed as to when and where the test is scheduled. Try to arrive at least 15 minutes early. You must supply two forms of identification, one of which must be a photo ID.

All Sair exams are closed book. In fact, you won't be allowed to take anything with you into the testing area. You'll be furnished with a blank sheet of paper and a pen. I suggest that you immediately write down whatever you've memorized for the test before you actually begin to take the test. You'll have some time to compose yourself and to record this information.

When you complete a Sair exam, you obtain immediate feedback on your score from Prometric's automatic scoring system. Ask your test center administrator to print you a copy of your test results so that you can refer to them later, should you need to.

How to Prepare for Sair Exams

At a minimum, you should use the following materials to prepare for a Sair certification exam:

➤ Sair provides comprehensive statements of its objectives and requirements for all its exams and also offers sets of practice questions for such exams. Be sure to consult these materials to help you prepare for your exams; you can find them through the road map at **www.sairinc.com/roadmap.php3**. (Hint: Click on any exam for which you want objectives.) Sair also offers a set of support materials that includes detailed objectives by topic and a set of background references for further reading; visit **www.sairinc.com/support.php3** for those details.

➤ Sair itself offers no training, but it does authorize third parties to act as SLG-ACEs (Sair Linux GNU-Accredited Centers for Education). For a list of such third parties, click on the Training Centers button on the Sair home page at **www.sairinc.com**.

➤ Sair itself offers neither study guides nor cram materials, but you'll find several options from third parties to help you prepare for their exams. Sair has established an official Sair Linux and GNU imprint with John Wiley & Sons. Many computer publishers have Sair certification books under way, so your options should improve with time.

Thus, you should find any or all of the following materials useful in your search for LPI certification:

➤ *Exam Prep*—Dee-Ann LeBlanc's outstanding *General Linux I Exam Prep* includes coverage of the Sair Level 1 exams as well as other Linux certifications.

➤ *Study guides*—Several publishers, including John Wiley & Sons and IDG Books Worldwide, among others, offer Sair certification–related titles of one kind or another.

➤ *Other publications*—You'll find plenty of other publications and resources if you take the time to look around on the Web or in your local bookstore, but there's no shortage of materials available about Linux certification in general and Sair in particular, especially in online newsletters (such as Coriolis's excellent *Exam Cram Insider*, available at **www.examcram.com/insider**) or from magazines such as *Certification Magazine* at **www.certmag.com** or the *Linux Gazette* at **www.linuxgazette.com**.

The preceding set of materials should soon comprise a usable collection of sources and resources for Sair exam topics and related information. Next: a concluding note on the value of the certifications covered in this chapter.

What's Linux Certification Worth?

Astute readers will already have noticed that, of the three programs covered in this chapter, the RHCE is by far the most mature and well developed. Because Red Hat certification works best for sites that use their product and the other two programs are still in the rollout phase, this quite naturally raises the question that heads this section.

I could answer this question in many ways (not all of them serious). However, taking the question seriously means answering it in terms of today's marketplace, then speculating on where that marketplace will be tomorrow. Today, a Linux certification is more of a vanity certification than a "must-have" credential. Given that such certification matters most in the workplace, Linux's relatively low market share means that you see very few job postings or classified ads that call for Linux certification by name. Thus, the answer to the question, if posed today, is either "not much" (taking a purely statistical view based on market share) or "whatever you can make it worth" (taking the attitude that obtaining any certification shows hustle and dedication, but realizing that you're going to have to explain to many employers why that certification has tangible value).

In the future, the answer to this question goes no way but upward. That is, with increasing use of Linux in the workplace and with increasing interest in this operating system and related technology, Linux not only is a good certification to have, but might even emerge as the "next big thing" in the IT certification world. One thing's for sure: Only time will tell how big a winner a Linux certification can be!

When it comes to selecting which of the three certifications you should back, hopefully the choice of RHCE versus the other two is pretty easy to make. That is, if you can make a reasonably long-standing commitment to Red Hat's Linux implementation, it's a good choice; if not, either of the vendor-neutral certifications is bound to cover more options than a vendor-specific one. On the other hand, deciding between LPI and Sair means watching which way the market will go, and there's not enough information yet to pick one of these options over the other. At present, because each side has its Level 1 certification complete, there's no clear advantage to either party.

Need to Know More?

 www.redhat.com/services/training/training.html This is the home page for Red Hat's training and certification offerings and thus points to all the various resources related to the RHCE and RHCX mentioned in this chapter.

 http://db.globalknowledge.com/catalog/certlisting.asp?code=RHCE This is Global Knowledge's RHCE information page. In addition to pointers to the RH300 and RH302 course/exam combo and exam-only offering, this page includes information about other courses that individuals might want to consider to meet Red Hat's demanding prerequisites requirements.

 www.linuxgazette.com This is the home page for *Linux Gazette* magazine, a useful source of information for those interested in Linux topics in general and in Linux certification topics in particular.

 www.lpi.org/c-index.html Although there's lots of useful information all over the LPI site, the certification index page brings together most of the stuff you'll want to access on a regular basis, including information about the LPI certification process and pointers to exam objectives, exam preparation tips, and information on how to register for exams.

 www.vue.com/linux/linuxexam.html If you pursue LPI certification, you'll be taking your exams from VUE. This page covers everything you need to know about signing up, scheduling, paying for, and taking such exams.

 http://training.linsight.com Linsight is a clearinghouse for Linux certification and related training information. It's a good resource to help you locate Linux training in your area.

 www.sairinc.com This is the home page for Sair Linux and GNU certification information; the navigation buttons at the top of this page should help you locate whatever you seek (if not, try the search engine—it seems to work pretty well).

 www.2test.com This is the home page for Prometric's online test registration. If you're pursuing Sair Linux and GNU certification, you'll want to bookmark this page!

Learning about Other Certifications

Although the formal portion of this book is finished, I feel obliged to leave you with some additional bits of information. For one, I think it's important to acknowledge that the certification programs I've covered in this book don't begin to encompass the vast array of offerings or certifications that are available to people interested in such things. That's why I include a section here called "Other Certifications," which mentions some of the many certifications not covered elsewhere in this book.

Likewise, I include another section called "Making It All Make Sense," wherein I give you the chance to see how your interests, abilities, and experience stack up against the various certifications I've covered. For what it's worth, you can also use this same information to evaluate your potential relationship with other certifications, whether mentioned in this chapter or not.

This chapter concludes with a brief section titled "Trends in the Certification Game," where I report and comment on some interesting new developments in cross-vendor certifications.

Other Certifications

To begin, I'll mention a few additional certifications that you might find interesting, assuming that you've found what I've already covered to be interesting as well. After that, I'll follow up with a list of briefly annotated pointers to other certifications that you can chase down on your own, if what you see appeals to you.

I'd like to single out a general certification-oriented Web site for praise. The Institute for Network Professionals offers its own vendor-neutral certification called the Certified Network Professional (CNP) that's worth investigating in its own right. However, what hooked me was this group's Certifications page, which lists just about every known IT certification, with pointers to the related Web sites. Be sure to check out this incredible resource at **www.inpnet.org/html/ certifications.htm**.

Starting from its origin at Bay Networks, Nortel Networks offers a comprehensive consultant certification program, including credentials related to the company's products but also related to specific job functions that include network designers, network architects, and network support professionals. For more information, visit the company's Networks Certification Program page at **www.nortelnetworks. com/servsup/certification/** to investigate its training and certification options.

The computer security field is bursting with activity right now, with more vendor and vendor-neutral certifications popping up than you might know what to do with. Among the many possible alternatives in this hot, hot, hot certification space, check out the following:

➤ Check Point Software Technologies has a plethora of security-related certifications that you can explore through **www.checkpoint.com/services/ overview.html**.

➤ The International Information Systems Security Certification Consortium (ISC)² offers a vendor-neutral security certification called the Certified Information Systems Security Professional (CISSP). Learn more about this fascinating computer security credential at **www.isc2.org**.

➤ Internet Security Systems at **www.iss.net** offers a variety of security-related courses and is in the process of designing a set of security certifications for its products (and those of third parties). Stay tuned to its Web site for more details.

➤ Learning Tree International, a well-known training company, offers its vendor-neutral System and Network Security Certified Professional program, among other certifications. View it at **www.learningtree.com/us/cert/progs/ 680.htm**.

➤ Prosoft offers a CIW Security Professional track as part of its CIW Professional credential. Flip back to Chapter 9 in this book for more information about this particular program. It's another good vendor-neutral security certification.

➤ SAP offers a certification program that promises high earnings potential to those who can withstand its rigorous certification process. SAP Certified R/3 Consultants or Certified Technical Consultants can pretty much name their terms and their prices in today's blazing SAP consulting marketplace (not to mention opportunities for permanent jobs). In fact, SAP is so good at bringing companies and workers together that its online job postings refer to positions at partner and affiliate companies, plus in-house listings. Candidates should be prepared to pay around $1,000 just to take the exam. If you also take the preparatory classes at the SAP Partner Academy, you'll pay $10,800 or more. Visit **www.sap.com** for more information about its certifications.

 Other ERP/MRP software companies, such as J.D. Edwards and Baan, also have good training and certification programs. Although not as hot as SAP's programs, they do offer great career development and advancement potential. Get ready to spend some serious money—as certifications go—on training and exams.

Here's a brief list of URLs that provide information about other certifications that might be worth a look:

➤ *www.helpdesk2000.net/certification/index.html*—Help desk jobs are emerging as a standard entry point into an IT career. For that reason, help desk certifications are becoming increasingly prevalent. Help Desk 2000 is a division of Support Technologies, Inc., which was founded in response to requests from help desk professionals for education on best practices and methodologies. This led to the creation of a Help Desk certification program that includes five distinct certifications:

➤ Certified Help Desk Director (CHDD)

➤ Certified Help Desk Manager (CHDM)

➤ Certified Field Support Technician (CFST)

➤ Certified Help Desk Professional (CHDP)

➤ Help Desk 2000 Certified Instructor (CI)

The uptake of this program in the marketplace has been quite positive, and for those looking for a perfect entry-level IT certification, this is a great place to start!

➤ *http://certification.miningco.com*—About.com offers an outstanding collection of pointers to vendor and other technical certification programs. This is a great place to start any exploration of certification options, especially for programs that I didn't cover in detail in this book.

➤ *www.compaq.com/training/aseinfo.html*—Compaq offers a certification called the Accredited Systems Engineer (ASE); visit the URL for more information. Be sure to check out the company's DEC- and Tandem-related certifications as well.

➤ *http://app-01.www.ibm.com/support/Education_Training.shtml*—IBM offers more than a dozen certification programs. It provides certifications on all its major product lines as well as for each of its large subsidiaries (most notably, Lotus Development Corporation and Tivoli Systems). Visit this URL and then click on any of the listings that include "Certification" in their names to learn more about each of these various programs.

➤ *www.3com.com/support/mns/*—3Com, the networking products and services giant, offers a Master of Network Sciences certification, which you can read about here. As vendor certifications go, this one is broader and more thorough than you might expect.

Making It All Make Sense

Given that I've covered certifications for everything from entry-level PC technicians (A+) to extremely senior internetworking gurus (CCIE)—and many points between—you might find yourself wondering, "How does all this apply to me?"

Unfortunately, there are no simple answers to this question, but you can determine what's relevant to your interests and your career possibilities if you take the time to answer a few simple questions:

➤ *Does this certification match any of my prior knowledge or experience?*

If the answer is "Yes," chances are good that you can jump into the related program with minimum difficulty and without having to immerse yourself in the background knowledge necessary to master the subject matter. The better the fit between a certification and your prior experience and knowledge base, the easier that certification will be for you to obtain.

➤ *Does this certification seriously engage my interest or enthusiasm?*

Without some motivation, going through the motions of obtaining a certification can be tedious and even overwhelming. Whether or not you already have the necessary background experience and knowledge, without interest and enthusiasm, you'll have to work harder than you might like to obtain any certification you pursue.

➤ *Do the products, technologies, and knowledge related to this certification fit my current workplace? Do they fit my plans for a future workplace?*

If the answers to both of these questions are "No," you'll probably want to pass on this one, unless you collect certifications the way others collect stamps or rocks. Because of the time and expense involved in obtaining certification—and the importance of hands-on experimentation and experience—chasing a certification on a topic when you don't have access to the hardware or software involved can be very frustrating.

➤ *Am I ready to spend evenings, weekends, and vacations chasing this credential?*

Even entry-level certifications, such as the A+, take weeks, if not months, to prepare for and pass. Major certifications, such as the CCIE or the MCSE+I, can take more than a year to complete. This means spending all your spare time during that interval learning, studying, and practicing for the test(s) rather than watching a ball game or talking on the phone. Are you really ready to make this sacrifice? If not, don't waste your money chasing something you won't finish.

➤ *By itself, is the certification enough to get me the job I want?*

On the various certification-related mailing lists, I see young people asking whether a certification is better than, or a reasonable substitute for, a college degree. The overwhelming response from people working in the field is, "Stay in school!" Most large companies, and many small ones, won't even consider hiring someone as a technical employee without a college degree and some work experience, no matter how many certifications the candidate has. Don't go thinking that certification is enough to get you into a high-paying job if you don't have some education and experience to go with it. If you don't have the education, you'd better have more experience, or vice versa, but you must have at least one of these essentials in addition to a certification to get the job.

➤ *Can I afford to fail? Can I afford to pass?*

Even your humble author has failed a couple of certification exams, and he writes books about this stuff. If you're financing your certification on a shoestring, what happens if that shoestring breaks? Clearly, chasing a CCIE when you don't have a couple of thousand dollars to spare for preparing could be a big mistake. If you have to retake a test that costs $1,000, can you really afford it? Even if you pass, can you really afford it? Be realistic about what you pursue—you can start out with an A+ for under $300, move up to an MCP for about the same amount, and then chase an MCSE for about $600 more, if you do things the inexpensive way. You might want to consider designing a ladder of certifications for yourself to climb, rung by rung, based on the complexity and expense of each rung. If you can land a better-paying job at each step along the way, you can afford the increasing expense of climbing to the next rung. If not, stop and catch your breath, then reformulate your goals.

Above all, you want to be comfortable chasing whatever certification you pursue. If you're not the programmer type, don't even think about the Certified Java credentials. Likewise, if you don't aspire to run a large, complex internetwork or to work at a leading-edge ISP or communications company, the CCIE probably isn't for you. Try to fit your interests, your obsessions, your strengths, and your budget to these certifications; you'll succeed, no matter what you do.

Trends in the Certification Game

In 1998, Novell announced that it would accept CompTIA's Network+ exam (NK-N10-001) in lieu of the company's own Networking Technologies exam (50-632). In 1999, Prosoft indicated that it would accept CompTIA's i-Net+ exam in lieu of its own Foundations exam for the CIW certification. I think this is the start of a major trend in certification whereby you'll see more vendor-neutral certifications such as Network+ (and A+ or i-Net+ for that matter) take over from vendor-specific exams or certifications (such as the Novell Networking Technologies exam).

In fact, Microsoft has long been willing to permit CNEs to skip its Networking Essentials exam because CNEs had to pass Novell's Networking Technologies exam to obtain the CNE in the first place. Unfortunately, Microsoft's revised Windows 2000 MCSE no longer includes an entry-level networking exam but does include two networking-related exams—a core exam 70-216, Implementing and Administering a Microsoft Windows 2000 Network Infrastructure, and a potential core exam 70-221, Designing a Microsoft Windows 2000 Network Infrastructure—that take networking knowledge requirements to a new level for MCSEs. It pretty much rules out their acceptance of Network+, however. Rats!

Keep your eyes peeled on the trade magazines—especially focused certification and training magazines such as *Microsoft Certified Professional Magazine* (**www.mcpmag.com**) and *Inside Technology Training* (**www.ittrain.com**)—for more information on the fascinating phenomenon of cross-certification. I think you'll see more of this kind of thing happening in the certification marketplace in the months and years ahead.

Other emerging certification trends certainly include the following:

➤ *More (and hopefully better or, at least, more focused) certifications*—The recent proliferation of security certifications shows that where vendors and industry organizations realize there's a demand for knowledge and expertise, certification programs will be quick to emerge.

➤ *More difficult (and hopefully more meaningful) certifications*—Microsoft has made a near-religious issue of its attempts to strengthen and improve the value of its MCSE certification with the changes it's introducing for its Windows 2000 credentials. From limiting beta exams to invitation only, to beefing up the "interface driving" portions of its exams, to doing everything it can to make its exams relevant to real-world job skills, Microsoft is leading the way to a new and improved set of certifications. Likewise, other vendors watch Microsoft's programs with a gimlet eye to make sure that the value of the credentials stays strong and positive. This may be what's behind Cisco's drive to 2.0 versions of its credentials, even though it also has a lot of newly acquired technology to keep up with.

As you ponder your certifications of choice and the marketplace they occupy, I wish you luck and the joys of experience and learning. In Chapter 12, I turn my focus to explaining how to plan your certification strategies and in Chapter 13 to the best study methods for certification exams. Enjoy!

Planning Your Certifications

For many people—especially those starting out or starting over with an IT career—one certification simply isn't enough. Whether you're a brand-spanking newbie or a grizzled veteran, it probably makes sense to consider your certifiability across a number of topical areas or vendor-specific programs as you create your own sequence of certifications (which I'll call a "custom certification ladder," if you don't mind).

Here's what I want to accomplish in this chapter:

➤ I will explain how you might rate any arbitrary certification, according to a number of criteria that include average time to completion, number of exams, average level of difficulty, self-study options available, and total expense. This isn't exactly the same as understanding a certification from the inside out, but it provides a workable, if "rough and ready," way to compare certifications to one another. This will create a kind of recipe to let you rate any certification program that might catch your eye.

➤ Next, I will provide a set of rankings for the certifications covered in Chapters 2 through 10 in this book. This should help you compare how the various certifications fit together and the order in which you might approach them.

➤ Finally, I will provide a set of ideal descriptions of job candidates for the four most likely positions that involve certifications. By reading these over and comparing them with your own knowledge base, you decide where you might want to start your certification adventures and where they might wind up.

This chapter concludes with a "Favorite Certification Ladders" section, in which I report on the most common certification sequences that IT professionals appear to be following. This should give you an opportunity to stack up the results of your own investigations and assessments against the combinations that seem to occur most frequently in the IT community.

Rating Certifications

Assuming that you've read the material in the rest of this book, I'll start by mentioning what most experts and IT professionals consider to be the most important criteria when rating IT certifications. As each criterion is introduced, it will be defined and explained. Each criterion falls into some range of values, which I'll also explore and explain. Finally, I'll explain how to map a criterion's position in its value range into some kind of ranking value. For example, given that certifications can take from one month to two years to complete, we could use the number of months as a ranking value, or we could divide the number of months by 2.4 (to map 24 months into a 10-point scale).

At the end of the ranking exercise, simply add the ranking values for all criteria to calculate a ranking score for the certification. Then compare ranking values to decide how certifications compare to one another. Table 12.1 provides this type of ranking for the certifications covered in Chapters 2 through 10 and should give you a good idea of how to apply this recipe to other certifications.

There is some room for fudge factors here. Mapping all ranges into the same scale for each criterion gives all criteria equal weight. Mapping some ranges into bigger scales gives their associated criteria greater weight because we add values to calculate a certification's overall ranking. Thus, I'll explain the weighting that my formula gives to various criteria so that you'll understand how to change the ranking characteristics. If you decide you don't like my approach, you can create your own!

Choosing Certification Ranking Criteria

Throughout this book, I've explained some of the most important criteria related to the various certifications that I covered. Nevertheless, there are other factors that should be considered as well. That's why you'll find some information in this chapter that isn't mentioned in the program overviews in Chapters 2 through 10.

The criteria that I'll use to rank these certifications include the following:

➤ *Career level*—This criterion assigns one of four values to a certification, based on how it's positioned for candidates: entry level or beginner gets a value of 2, intermediate or novice gets a value of 4, advanced or senior level gets a value of 6, and expert or specialist level gets a value of 8. Thus, the A+ certification would be worth 2 on this scale, and the CCIE certification would be worth 8.

➤ *Average time to completion*—This criterion lists the average of the fastest known time to completion and the longest reasonable time to completion for the certification, unless the certification itself includes a time requirement. For example, the fastest MCSE 4.0 completion that I've ever heard about was one month; a long but not unreasonable completion time is 24 months (two years). Thus, I set the average at 12 months. On the other hand, you must take the first and second A+ exams within 90 days of each other. Allowing some time to gear up for the first test, I arbitrarily set the average completion time for the A+ at three months. Thankfully, this squares up nicely against an analysis of average completion times in the "real world!"

➤ *Number of exams*—This criterion includes the number of exams that candidates must pass to obtain their certification. It does not take into account the average number of tries to pass an exam.

➤ *Cost of exams*—This criterion adds up the cost for all exams that candidates must pass to obtain their certification. As with the preceding criterion, it does not take into account the average number of tries to pass any exam.

➤ *Experience requirement*—Some certifications are entirely amenable to book or classroom learning, whereas others are unapproachable without real-world, hands-on experience with the tools and technologies that such certifications cover. Here, I'll rank their requirement as low (2 points), medium (4 points), high (6 points), or extremely high (8 points). For this criterion, I'd rate the Windows 2000 MCSE as high and the CCIE as extremely high.

➤ *Income potential*—Some certifications are pretty common or don't add much additional income potential to their holders. I'll rank their potential as low (2 points), medium (4 points), high (6 points), or extremely high (8 points). For this criterion, I'd rate the Windows 2000 MCSE as medium and the Oracle Application Developer as extremely high. Some values are higher than 8 for "special cases," such as the CCIE (14 points).

Although there are undoubtedly more criteria that we could use to rank certifications, these six produce values that are useful enough to make our comparisons interesting. For example, I could easily define another cost metric that uses the average cost for Web-based training because so many certification programs offer that kind of education today. As it turns out, this particular ranking adds little value to the existing data because it stays in line with the values for self-study cost and classroom cost. In the next section, you'll find Table 12.1, which ranks the various certifications that appear in Chapters 2 through 10 according to these criteria.

Certification Ranking Table

Table 12.1 ranks a total of 49 certifications, taken from Chapters 2 through 10. To save space, I've shortened the longer certification monikers (I associate all nonobvious abbreviations with chapter numbers in the Notes column; this should help you figure out what they mean). I've also distinguished between dual versions for some certifications, such as the MCSE for Windows NT 4.0, which appears as MCSE4.0, and the one for Windows 2000, which appears as MCSE2K.

Here are definitions for the various column headings:

➤ *Name*—Provides a moniker for a certification. That moniker will be associated with a chapter number in parentheses in the Notes column for those that aren't obvious.

➤ *Level*—Defines a job ranking for a certification as entry level (2), intermediate (4), advanced (6), or expert (8).

➤ *Time*—Defines the average time to completion of the certification in months.

➤ *# Exams*—Itemizes the number of exams required to complete the certification.

➤ *Cost*—Itemizes the total cost for the exams that must be paid for to complete the certification. I divide this number by 100 to scale it to the other ranking values.

➤ *Experience*—Defines the amount of hands-on experience required to attain this certification. Valid values are low (2), medium (4), high (6), and extremely high (8).

➤ *$$$*—Defines the income potential for holders of this certification. Valid values are low (2), medium (4), high (6), and extremely high (8). You'll see some values higher than that for "special cases," such as the CCIE (which gets a 14!).

➤ *Rank*—Sums the total of all ranking values for the current certification.

➤ *Note*—Points to a numbered footnote or chapter that might document assumptions, expand a moniker, or provide additional information. For example, Microsoft offers Exam 70-240 at no cost to qualified candidates to replace three constituent exams; nevertheless, I count the total number of exams required for a Windows 2000 MCSE as 7, even though using 70-240 lowers that number to 4.

One final note: To facilitate easy lookup, all certification monikers are listed in alphabetical order.

When Real Candidates Meet Ideal Requirements

Based on recent industry statistics, as many as 5 million individuals worldwide are at some stage in an IT certification process where they haven't yet completed

Table 12.1			Relative rankings for IT certifications.					
Name	Level	Time	# Exams	Cost	Experience	$$$	Rank	Note
A+	2	3	2	2.56	4	2	15.56	1
ATS	2	6	3	1.50	2	2	16.50	
CCDA	4	3	1	1.00	4	4	17.00	
CCDP	6	12	4	4.00	6	6	38.00	2
CCIE	8	24	2	12.0	8	14	68.00	3
CCNA	4	3	1	1.00	4	4	17.00	
CCNP	6	12	4	4.00	6	6	38.00	4
CDE	6	6	3	4.00	6	6	31.00	5
CIW Prof	4	6	2	2.50	4	4	22.50	(Chap. 9)
CNA	2	3	1	1.00	4	2	13.00	
CNE	6	14	7	7.00	6	4	44.00	6
CNI	8	6	2	15.00	8	6	45.00	7
CTT	6	3	2	5.65	6	6	28.65	8
i-Net+	4	3	1	1.85	4	4	17.85	9
JavaArch	6	6	3	5.50	6	6	32.50	(Chap. 7)
JavaDev	4	4	2	4.00	4	6	24.00	(Chap. 7)
JavaProg	4	4	1	1.50	4	6	20.50	(Chap. 7)
LCA	4	8	4	3.96	4	4	27.96	
LCE	6	8	4	3.96	6	4	31.96	
LCP	2	3	1	1.00	4	2	13.00	
LPIC L1	4	6	2	2.00	4	4	22.00	(Chap. 10)
LPIC L2	6	6	2	2.00	6	4	26.00	10 (Chap. 10)
LPIC L3	8	6	2	2.00	8	6	32.00	10 (Chap. 10)
MCDBA	6	10	5	5.00	6	6	38.00	
MCIWAd	6	12	4	5.00	6	6	39.00	(Chap. 9)
MCIWDes	6	9	3	3.75	6	6	33.75	(Chap. 9)
MCIWEnt	8	18	8	10.00	6	6	56.00	(Chap. 9)
MCNE	8	18	6	6.00	6	6	50.00	6
MCP	2	2	1	1.00	2	2	10.00	
MCP+I	4	6	3	3.00	4	2	22.00	
MCP+SB	6	4	2	2.00	4	6	24.00	
MCSD	6	10	4	4.00	6	6	36.00	

(continued)

Table 12.1 Relative rankings for IT certifications *(continued)*.

Name	Level	Time	# Exams	Cost	Experience	$$$	Rank	Note
MCSE2K	6	14	7	7.00	6	4	44.00	
MCSE4.0	6	12	6	6.00	6	4	40.00	
MCSE+I	6	18	9	9.00	6	4	52.00	
MCT	8	6	2	15.00	8	8	47.00	11
MLCE	8	12	4	3.96	8	8	43.96	
MOUS P/C	2	1	1	0.60	2	2	8.60	12
MOUS Exp	4	4	1	0.60	4	2	15.60	13
MOUS Mstr	4	8	5	3.00	4	4	28.00	14
Network+	4	3	1	1.75	4	4	17.75	9
OCP-AD	8	15	5	6.25	8	8	50.25	
OCP-DBA	6	12	5	6.25	6	8	43.25	6
OCP-DBO	4	3	1	1.25	4	6	19.25	
OCP-Fin	6	9	3	3.75	6	8	35.75	
OCP-Java	6	15	5	6.75	6	8	46.75	
ProLnx	6	6	1	1.25	6	4	24.25	(Chap. 9)
RHCE	6	6	1	7.49	6	4	30.49	
RHCX	8	6	1	15.49	8	4	42.49	15

1 Used the higher test cost for both exams at once for non-CompTIA members to set the cost value.

2 Chose the four-exam track for CCDA with associated exam costs for calculating values. Prerequisite certifications not included in exam cost calculation.

3 Gave the CCIE the highest "employment value" ($$$) rating of all certifications mentioned here.

4 Chose the four-exam track for CCNP with associated exam costs for calculating values. CCNA prerequisite not included in exam cost calculation.

5 Guesstimated the cost of the Novell practicum (CDE lab exam) at $200; pricing information not available.

6 Used the highest possible number of exams to tabulate exam count and costs.

7 Used the cost of the Novell "train-the-trainer" class to calculate cost, as it's required in lieu of a CTT or other T3 status.

8 Exam cost includes estimated dollar amount for video preparation.

9 Used the exam pricing for non-CompTIA members to calculate exam costs.

10 Exams not yet available, so neither is pricing; assumed that costs would be the same as for Level 1 exams.

11 Used the cost of exams and other preparation costs, including the Microsoft Trainer Kit.

12 This row covers both the MOUS Proficient certification for Office 97 topics and the MOUS Core certification for Office 2000 topics.

13 This row covers the MOUS Expert certification for both Office 97 and Office 2000 topics.

14 This row covers the Master MOUS certification for both Office 97 and Office 2000 topics.

15 Used the cost of the T3 course as the exam cost, because the course is required in lieu of an exam.

all the requirements for a certification (add to that between 10 and 12 million individuals who already have at least one certification, and you've got quite a crowd). I'm pretty sure that somewhere between double and four times that number are probably considering whether they should obtain some kind of IT certification. That's a huge audience!

The reason I included these descriptions in this book is to help you evaluate your readiness to tackle an IT position that involves a technical certification of some kind by comparing what you know against what employers fondly hope that ideal candidates know. Going through this exercise should also help you figure out what you need to learn to prepare yourself for the exams that any IT certification inevitably requires.

IT Professionals in the Real World

Although there is nearly an infinite number of potential job roles for IT professionals in the workplace, I'm going to stick to those four job roles that my research tells me are the most likely to employ certified individuals. As you ponder your own options, if your goals don't match at least one of these roles, don't lose heart—you can still learn more about your area of interest after reading them over and comparing what you already know to what employers think you need to know.

In the list that follows, I describe these four job roles with an ideal job candidate for each one. Because so few of us are ideal, it should come as no surprise that few real candidates can stand up to a perfect, paper ideal. Although the requirements for any of these roles may seem formidable, they are by no means impossible to meet. However, you should be keenly aware that it takes time, involves some expense, and requires hard work to get through any certification process.

As you consider any particular job role, remember that these are the most heavily populated job roles that employ certified individuals. In plain English, this means that lots of people already occupy these roles. By extension, because others have walked these paths ahead of you, you should be able to reach your certification goals as well. It's not like you're a brave pioneer, going where no IT professional has gone before. If others can do it (and, in fact, have done it), so can you!

Four Fabulous Job Roles Where Certification Counts

These descriptions of job roles are based on three years of emails from readers, IT industry and certification surveys, a thorough and ongoing review of most major IT certification programs (that's what drives this whole book, in fact), and some interesting discussions with other certification gurus at recent trade shows:

➤ *PC Technician*—PC Technicians handle basic technical support for IT infrastructures or provide help desk functions and services. They cover everything from standard hardware and commodity software to supporting custom in-house applications and services. The most common certification for PC Technicians is the A+ from CompTIA.

➤ *Network Administrator*—Network Administrators support IT infrastructures by installing, configuring, and managing desktop and server machines. They are also usually responsible for installing, configuring, and maintaining common network services, including file, print, fax, and Internet access. More senior network administrators may also manage custom or enterprise-level applications and services, including accounting systems, Enterprise Resource Planning (ERP) systems, and database environments. Here, common certifications include credentials such as Microsoft's MCSE or Novell's CNE and MCNE.

➤ *Internetworking Professional*—Internetworking professionals manage complex network infrastructures that are most usually TCP/IP based, plus related routing, name services, security structures, and more. Whether an organization connects to the Internet, operates its own intranet, or is part of an extranet, internetworking professionals make these complex collections of wide and local area networks work. Here, individuals with credentials such as Cisco's CCNA, CCNP, and CCIE are at home (as are other internetworking and security specialists).

➤ *Programmer*—Programmers create in-house systems, help make Web sites interactive, and customize and deploy complex software such as database or ERP systems. In short, programmers take the software building blocks that make up most modern IT environments, put those pieces together, and tailor them to suit the unique information processing needs in modern organizations. Here, programs such as the MCSD, Sun's Java credentials, and Oracle or CIW developer certifications come into play.

Ideal Job Candidates Look Like This

For each of the four job roles outlined in the preceding section, I next provide a list of ideal characteristics. Remember—these are ideal candidates, and only a chosen few real candidates will be able to match all the characteristics covered.

An Ideal PC Technician

➤ Understands PC hardware, including motherboards, CPUs, RAM, interface cards, hard disks and various removable media, keyboards, mice, and display devices, including installation, troubleshooting, and repair.

➤ Understands device drivers, including how to locate, download, install, troubleshoot, and replace them. Also understands how drivers work with software, including DMA and IRQs, and how to detect and resolve hardware conflicts.

➤ Understands PC operating systems, including DOS, multiple versions of Windows (3.x, 9x, NT, and Windows 2000), along with familiarity with Linux, MacOS, and other typical desktop operating systems. Knows how to install, configure, patch, upgrade, and troubleshoot operating system software and services.

➤ Understands PC applications, including common productivity applications, email, graphics, Web browsers, and other everyday software components. Is able to install, configure, upgrade, and install such software.

➤ Possesses usable customer support skills, including listening, replicating problems, providing solutions, and strong people skills.

An Ideal Network Administrator

➤ Understands basic principles of networking, including cabling, NICs, and networking hardware of all kinds.

➤ Understands common networking protocols, including TCP/IP, IPX/SPX, NetBEUI, NetBIOS, AppleTalk, and other protocols as needed.

➤ Understands one or more network operating systems (NetWare, Linux/Unix, Windows NT, or Windows 2000). Knows how to design, configure, install, maintain, and troubleshoot server and desktop installations.

➤ Understands key network services, including name and directory services, file and print services, distributed applications, email, news, HTTP, DNS (and possibly WINS), DHCP, plus other services as required. Knows how to install, configure, maintain, update, and troubleshoot such services.

➤ Interacts intelligently with ISPs or long-haul communications providers and works with VPNs, encryption, authentication, and security services to establish safe, usable connections with the Internet and external service providers.

➤ Works with users to provide appropriate network services, technical training, technical support, capacity planning, and needs analysis to make sure that applications and services delivered meet user and organizational requirements.

An Ideal Internetworking Professional

➤ Understands networking thoroughly, including cabling, NICs, routers, gateways, switches, hubs, and other local and wide area networking hardware and connections. Must know how to install, configure, upgrade, maintain, and troubleshoot all networking and internetworking elements.

➤ Understands how to specify, procure, install, configure, maintain, and troubleshoot remote network services for access to service providers, private networks, VPNs, and other internetwork connections. Must understand technologies from POTS to ATM, including ISDN; X.25; frame relay; T1, T3, and so on; E1, E3, and so on; cable modems; and more. Must be able to manage ISPs and long-haul communications providers, including specification, procurement, installation, configuration, maintenance, updates, and troubleshooting.

➤ Understands key internetworking services, including directory and name services, DNS (possibly also WINS), and DHCP and how these services interact with switches, routers, and other key elements of internetworking infrastructure.

➤ Understands routing protocols, services, and management, including interior and exterior routing protocols, RIP, OSPF, EGP, BGP, and other routing protocols and services as required.

➤ Understands network security and integrity principles, practices, and services, including such things as authentication, security hardware, Kerberos v5, PKI, intrusion detection systems, and more. Knows how to specify, procure, install, configure, maintain, upgrade, and troubleshoot related hardware and software elements.

➤ Works with users to provide appropriate network services, technical training, technical support, capacity planning, and needs analysis to make sure that applications and services delivered meet user and organizational requirements.

An Ideal Programmer

➤ Thoroughly understands one or more high-level programming languages, such as Java, Python, Visual Basic, C++, C, and so on. Able to architect, design, implement, test, debug, troubleshoot, and maintain simple and complex systems.

➤ Thoroughly understands one or more scripting languages, such as JavaScript, Perl, WSH, Unix shells, sed, awk, and so on. Able to automate routine tasks using such languages, and perform arbitrary tasks to manipulate files, parse text input, and translate data among multiple forms and formats.

➤ Understands modern programming principles, including object-oriented design, distributed programming techniques, client/server software design, implementation, testing, debugging, and maintenance.

➤ Understands principles and practices for production software development, including version control, code libraries, source control systems, documentation, code reviews, testing tools and methodology, plus software release management.

➤ Understands principles behind interactive Web pages and Web-based applications, including one or more of JavaServer Pages, Java servlets, Active Server Pages, ActiveX controls, and more.

Careful review of each of these "wish lists" for ideal candidates shows that there's at least a bachelor's degree lurking in these requirements (if not a master's degree for the internetworking professional and programmer lists). Although it's undeniably important to know what the various acronyms stand for and how they relate to a particular job function, only a very select few will be able to meet all requirements for any particular role! Gives you something meaty to aim for, though.

Favorite Certification Ladders

Frankly, there are so many ways to slice and dice this information that it's almost scary. I've chosen to present these certification ladders in terms of the same job roles I introduced in the preceding section. That's because these roles seem to fit directly into the most commonly climbed certification ladders better than anything else.

If you combine these ladders with the rankings from the first major section of this chapter and the ideal candidate descriptions from the preceding section, you should be able to decide where to start your own certification ladder. You should also be able to figure out how to climb that ladder's rungs in whatever way works best for you.

Here, then, are the top four job role-related certification ladders, based on our earlier descriptions of the job roles they match:

➤ *PC Technician*—A+ remains the most popular entry-level certification and can be enough to help you get your foot in the door for an entry-level help desk or technical support position. The next rung could include one of the ancillary help desk certifications mentioned in Chapter 11. From there, it's wise to specialize in a desktop operating system, which probably means obtaining an MCP for Windows 98 (70-098), Windows NT Workstation (70-073), or Windows 2000 Professional (70-210). After that, an MCSE or a CNE may make sense if you want to advance to the next most popular certification ladder, Network Administrator.

➤ *Network Administrator (Microsoft flavor)*—Start with A+, Network+, then get an MCSE. For Windows NT 4.0 MCSEs, the 70-059 TCP/IP exam and the 70-087 IIS 4.0 remain the most common electives. For Windows 2000 MCSEs, I recommend taking 70-221: Network Infrastructure as your "Designing" core exam, plus two electives with networking applications or relevance (for example, 70-080: IEAK 5.0 and 70-088: Proxy Server 2.0 fit this admonition, although it's possible that 70-088 may be retired in the next year or so). Numerically speaking, this is the most commonly chosen certification ladder with multiple rungs. After this, you might choose to advance to the Internetworking Professional ladder if you want to keep climbing.

➤ *Network Administrator (Novell flavor)*—Start with A+, Network+, then get a CNE (and optionally an MCNE). Unless you know that you'll be working with an older version of NetWare, follow the NetWare 5 track. If your NetWare network uses TCP/IP, select the BorderManager exam (50-642) as an elective. If pursuing the MCNE, take whichever of these exams you can count as electives: TCP/IP (50-145), Web Server Management (50-710), or BorderManager Enterprise (50-650).

➤ *Internetworking Professional*—Start with A+, Network+, and on to i-Net+. Next, begin climbing the Cisco ladder (detours for relevant Microsoft or Novell exams may be worth taking to qualify you for jobs that require network administration as well as internetworking tasks). Start with the CCNA, continue to the CCNP, and go all the way for the CCIE if you can take the heat! Pick the Routing and Switching track, unless you have compelling reasons to take the WAN Switching or Specialties tracks (this will require a specific and focused job target to justify).

➤ *Programmer (Microsoft flavor)*—Start with some basic programming training, be it self-study of a popular Microsoft programming language such as Visual Basic, C++, or FoxPro, or classroom study of one or more of the same topics. Get an MCSD, with a focus on your programming language of choice (statistics say that this means Visual Basic, C++, and FoxPro, in order of popularity). Take additional MCP classes as your interests dictate; this could also mean obtaining an MCDBA if you decide to pursue database programming as a specialty and use Microsoft's SQL Server. Where other databases are in use, pursue those certifications instead, if applicable. For Web-related development topics, peruse the MCSD curriculum carefully—there are developer courses and operator courses for technologies such as Site Server. Make sure that you take the right ones!

➤ *Programmer (Java flavor)*—Start with some basic programming training and some exposure to object-oriented design concepts, tools, and techniques. Here again, self-study, classroom, or online training options are widely available. Take the Sun Java Programmer exam for your JDK of choice (we recommend the Java 2 JDK because it has the longest run still ahead of it). If you want to climb the Sun Java certification ladder, take the Sun Java Developer exams next (and you can go on to the Sun Java Architect certification from there if you want). For other Java certifications—such as Netscape, IBM, Novell, and so on—take on the intermediate certification next and decide whether you want to stop there or keep going.

By this time, you've probably noticed that although I said I was going to cover four job role ladders, I've actually documented six. That's because two of those ladders—namely, Network Administrator and Programmer—come in two flavors each. It still adds up to four job role ladders.

When it comes to picking a common certification ladder or custom-crafting one of your own, let your working circumstances and ambitions be your guides to the rungs you choose and how you order them. Remember that hands-on experience is a key ingredient to earning any certification and that workplace exposure to the products and technologies in which you seek certification is the best way to get that experience. That way, you won't find yourself chasing a Cisco certification when there's no Cisco hardware or software around for you to play with. Should that ever happen to you, you'll need to do one of two things:

➤ Find a new place to get your experience where there is some Cisco stuff to play with.

➤ Choose a different certification—hopefully, one for which there is some relevant hardware or software for you to play with in the workplace (or at other locations where you can spend time and effort learning what you need to know).

Although it can be hard to remember in the heat of pursuit, the application of a little common sense when choosing or building your own certification ladder can help ease the climb tremendously. Don't forget to take a break every now and then, compare your plans to the reality that surrounds you, and make whatever adjustments might be necessary. Go ahead, you can do it!

Certification Study Tips and Techniques

In this final chapter of the book, I provide numerous suggestions about how you should approach studying for your certification exams. These suggestions are meant to build on one another and will deliver the best results if used in combination. Nevertheless, you should feel free to pick and choose among them. Although I strongly urge you to try them all, use only those that work for you. Each of these tips or techniques is discussed in its own section.

Outlining from Objectives

No matter what kind of IT certification you may choose to pursue, you'll want to start with related exam objectives and work your way through from start to finish. The idea of "outlining from objectives" applies at each step along the way:

➤ Begin your studies by reviewing the objectives, making sure that you understand what they mean, and what topics, concepts, and technologies they cover.

➤ As you read your way through self-study materials or through online or classroom training, make a point of relating the elements you're learning about to specific exam objectives. Many forms of study material—particularly study guides and practice exams—make a point of establishing this relationship for you. However, if you get in the habit of doing this for yourself, you can annotate a set of exam objectives with related information and use this to guide your review just before you take an exam!

➤ As you take practice exams, make a note of the questions that relate to specific objectives. When you review, you can skip the ones you know well and concentrate on the questions you're less sure of. This is one of the best ways I know of to review for an exam.

➤ After you go through your study materials and practice exams, look over your annotated objectives. Is there anything that you can't relate to the materials you've already checked? If so, you'd better look around for more materials so that you can figure out what you're supposed to know regarding such "mystery objectives."

By organizing your studies and practice around the objectives, you'll keep a clear eye on your final goal: passing the exam. Because you can make sure you've covered everything as you study, you're far less likely to be surprised (it can still happen because vendors and organizations add new questions to their exams on a regular basis).

Join a Support Group

There are two kinds of groups that you can join (or form) to help improve your odds at passing certification exams. One of these kinds of groups may already exist, but you may have to form the other kind. The first kind is a local branch of a user group related to the vendor or organization that sponsors your chosen certification. The second kind is an ad hoc group, which I call a "study group," that results when you bring a group of individuals together to share notes and experiences, answer questions, and debate a set of exam objectives.

User groups exist for many of the certifications I cover in this book. By using your favorite search engine with a search string such as "user group and Windows NT" or "user group and NetWare or Novell," you can turn up pointers to local, national, and international user groups. Most such groups have local chapters in most major metropolitan areas and regional chapters in less heavily populated areas. Many such groups operate ongoing certification review study sessions and discussions, and some even offer classes (I've taught such classes for free at the Central Texas LAN Association, or CTLA, in Austin, Texas).

Likewise, joining a user group can boost your buying power. It's not unusual for such groups to negotiate discounts on study guides, official press materials, practice exams, and even on the software or systems that you might need to get ready for a certification exam. In addition, many user groups offer free access to test labs and training sessions to their members (and annual membership fees seldom exceed more than a couple hundred dollars; this is another good way to get some hands-on experience while preparing for your exams).

Local study groups are more ad hoc and require you to identify or assemble a group of people who share a common focus on the same certification exam. At user's groups, such assemblies are often called Special Interest Groups (SIGs). When they occur outside an organizational umbrella, you can call them whatever you want to.

Here are some ways that you can identify or form a study group:

➤ Use email to identify other students in your area who are studying for the same exam. Start a conversation on that topic and try to identify who's really serious about prepping for that exam.

➤ Post a notice at a local community college, four-year college, or university to solicit interest in forming a study group. Academic institutions are full of students, and they spend lots of time prepping for exams anyway. Why not recruit a certification study group from the same organization?

➤ Ask around at local training centers, computer stores, and vendor-sponsored seminars. (Hint: A Microsoft seminar on Windows 2000 is a great place to prospect for potential study group members.)

By now, you've probably got the idea that there are lots of ways to find other people like you who not only want to tackle some particular exam, but also believe that there's safety—and value—in numbers.

One final note: By working in a group, you can agree on a common set of study materials and practice exams. Then you can divide up the exam objectives and assign individuals to cover specific subtopics or areas. Everyone can share the results, but no one has to spend as much time outlining the objectives.

Practice Makes Perfect

When it comes to preparing yourself for an exam encounter, nothing beats a good practice exam. By putting yourself into the exam situation and tackling questions designed to get you ready for the real thing, you gain two profound advantages:

➤ You desensitize yourself to the anxieties that taking exams can create.

➤ You give yourself the opportunity to check what you've been learning against a set of questions designed to stretch your knowledge to its limit.

The first item helps you concentrate on what you're reading and what you know when you do finally get into the hot seat at a testing center. The second item forces you to apply your knowledge to specific scenarios, problems, issues, and factual questions. You need to be able to do all this to do well on any certification exam.

There are oodles and scads of vendors who offer practice tests on certification subjects of all kinds. They can be purchased on CD-ROM, diskette, or downloaded from the vendor's Web site. They vary in format, from simplistic tests comprised of a list of questions and a list of answers to tests that accurately simulate the testing experience. Of course, this variance is also evident in the price.

My advice is shop around. By doing a simple Internet search, you will turn up plenty of sites you can turn to for practice, many of which cover multiple topics and offer great value. Below are just a few sites to get your exploring started:

➤ *http://certification.miningco.com/compute/certification/*—This site from the About.com Network offers online practice tests for A+, Cisco, Microsoft, Oracle, Prosoft, Novell, and Sun.

➤ *http://www.certportal.com/*—Here you will find free online tests to help prepare the aspiring MCSE, MCSD, CCIE, CCNA, CNE, and others.

➤ *http://gocertify.earthweb.com/*—Visit this site for a list of practice tests resources. You will also find articles, FAQs, quizzes, and downloads to help you prepare to pass.

I'd be remiss if I left this topic without mentioning the folks at **www.examcram. com**. They have a great certification-oriented Web site and offer access to all kinds of valuable information, but their daily email delivery of a free "Question of the Day" from tons of exams from the Microsoft, Novell, CompTIA, Linux, Cisco, Oracle, and Sun certification programs makes them a killer source for great practice questions for anyone who's pursuing an IT certification. Be sure to check them out when you're looking for questions to practice on. The price is entirely right!

Investigate Training Options

Although self-study certainly is cheaper than classroom or online training, sometimes you will find yourself stumped by subject matter. When that happens, access to an instructor is hard to beat. Also, some people simply learn better in a structured classroom environment than they do on their own.

That's why I strongly recommend that you investigate online and in-class training offerings for any certification you pursue. You may ultimately decide against buying either kind of training, but you'll still benefit from this exercise anyway. That's because many online, classroom, and general-purpose training companies offer valuable certification information on their Web sites as incentives for students to spend money with them. A quick market survey will also give you a pretty good idea of what's available in the training marketplace and how much your various options will cost. Expect to spend anywhere from $200 to $500 a day for in-class training (it seldom costs more, but it does happen) and anywhere from nothing to $300 a day for online training.

If you ever find yourself completely befuddled by a certification subject and you have to pass the exam to get your certificate, consider taking some training to help you over the hump. Instructors can respond to your questions and can often restate information in terms you can understand when the training or reading materials don't tell you what you need to know. This can happen quite spontaneously in the classroom, but don't discount the value of online training. Most online training companies offer chat rooms to interact with students, hold regular online "office hours" with instructors, and provide email support to their students. Either live or online, you can get additional help and interaction when you go the training route.

Another benefit that certification training can deliver is access to a different set of materials. Most in-class or online training classes include printed student handbooks or work from textbooks of one kind or another. This information not only will help you follow along in class, but provides another source of review (and objectives outlining) as you prepare to take your exams.

Pump the Experts

Access to instructors is rightfully touted as one of the best benefits of certification training because it gives you the opportunity to ask an expert just about anything you want to—as long as it's relevant to the topic at hand. Many instructors provide their email addresses to their students and can continue to function as technical resources long after a class is over.

Other places to go trolling for expertise include user group meetings (where vendor, organization, or third-party experts often appear as featured speakers) and through certification- or training-oriented mailing lists, newsletters, newsgroups, and Web sites. I myself answer an average of 150 questions a week, arising from newsletter columns, Web site articles, and so on. Numerous other certification experts are also available through the same channels.

Publishers like to make their authors available at online bookstores and even through their own Web sites to participate in topical chats. If you keep your eyes on your favorite book Web sites for publishers such as Coriolis, IDG, Sybex, New Riders, and others, you'll get the occasional opportunity to ask someone who's written a book on your topic of interest some questions. You have to be able to type reasonably well to chat effectively online, but hey, the help is free—and often quite valuable. Give it a try!

Call on Your Community

As this and other certification-oriented books readily attest (believe me, you don't even want to count all the URLs and other online pointers in this book, unless you plan to visit them all), the online world is a treasure trove of information. This world is ready to give you some real pearls of wisdom and experience—in most cases, all you have to do is ask for them! Of course, knowing who (and where) to ask for help can be tricky at times, but if you ask those "virtual neighbors" who have the right knowledge base for help or support, it will usually be forthcoming.

For any given area of certification, there are four kinds of online sources or resources that will be worth investigating for access to an active community of involved users and, thus, for access to the information, advice, opinions, and experience they can bring to bear on your problems or questions. These four kinds of resources are as follows:

➤ *Mailing lists*—No matter what the certification topic may be, it's likely that you can find multiple mailing lists that cover that topic. To find them, check around vendor Web sites, use your favorite search engine (a search string such as "MCSE and mailing list" works pretty well), ask your study or user's groups, and keep your eyes open while you're online. These things are everywhere, and they are completely geared to a question-and-answer kind of dialogue. In many cases, you can get answers to technical or certification questions faster on a busy mailing list than from a vendor technical support operation!

➤ *Newsletters*—Most of the certification experts—such as Coriolis and MCP Magazine—email regular newsletters to opt-in readers. So do lots of vendors—for example, Sunbelt Software is a purveyor of Windows software, but they also send terrific weekly MCSE and Windows Administration newsletters.

Some of these newsletters are weekly, others semimonthly, and others monthly. These can be great sources of pointers to all kinds of information and will often post email addresses where you can send your questions. What's more, because newsletters are always looking for newsworthy items and try to help their readers find the "good stuff" for certifications, they often include pointers to the best mailing lists, newsgroups, and Web sites in their topic areas.

To learn more about some of the specific newsletters I've mentioned, visit these URLs:

➤ www.examcram.com/insider/

➤ www.mcpmag.com

➤ www.sunbelt-software.com

➤ *Newsgroups*—Newsgroups normally belong to the Usenet hierarchy, which includes over 70,000 newsgroups today. In that case, you can ask your ISP to furnish an electronic list of the newsgroups that it carries and search that file for vendor or organization names or certification acronyms.

Other newsgroups outside the Usenet hierarchy are private, supplied by newsfeeds from some vendor or organization. These are usually short enough to scan for items of interest. For example, Microsoft operates a newsfeed at **msnews.microsoft.com** (to sign up, enter this name as the root server in your newsreader or **news://msnews.microsoft.com** in your Web browser). Newsgroups of interest in its list of newsgroups include keywords such as "cert," "MCSE," and "exam." You can also search archived Usenet discussions for certification information at **www.deja.com**.

➤ *Web sites*—Web sites come in so many forms that I'll cut to the chase and say that here I'm talking about Web sites where certification is an active topic of interest and discussion and where you can ask questions and get answers to certification or technical questions. This rules out a lot of Web sites but leaves in many training and certification sites. Don't forget to check out vendor Web sites where those vendors offer training, technical support, certification products or services, and the like. Many of these will help you find answers to your questions or at least help you find other resources online where you can get them answered.

Some of my favorite certification-related Web sites include the following:

➤ *Exam Cram*—**www.examcram.com**

➤ *Information Technology Training*—**www.ittrain.com**

➤ *Institute for Network Professionals*—**www.inpnet.org**

If you can't find anything that you can use at these sites, don't worry; there are thousands more to choose from!

Go to the Source

Whenever you're chasing information about certification programs, don't forget to go to the source—that is, to the Web site for the vendor or organization that sponsors the certification. In addition to the official line on the certification program, a surprising number of these sites act as clearinghouses for third-party information, particularly when vendors create official partnerships for things such as training, practice exams, study guides, and other ancillary certification-related materials.

Before you go looking for certification information anywhere else (and you'll probably want to do that), make sure that you investigate the sponsor's certification pages with great attention and care. In most cases, you'll find most of what you need to get started on a certification, and in some cases, you can find everything you'll need.

Here's a list of the kinds of things that you should be able to investigate at any sponsor's certification site (you may not be able to find all these things, but you should be able to find most of them):

➤ *Program description*—Begin by reading the sponsor's description of its certification program or programs. Try to find answers for questions such as these: What does the program certify? What kind of people are qualified? How can you participate? Make sure that you get the big picture.

➤ *Certification description*—Next, attack the sponsor's description of the certification that you wish to pursue. Make sure that you understand how many exams might be involved, what order they're best taken in, how much exams cost, and the other basic items I've tried to cover in this book. The information at the Web site is likely to be right if what you find in this book differs from what you find at the site (they can update the Web content whenever they want, whereas once this book is in print, it never changes again).

➤ *Exam information and objectives*—As you dig into any certification, you'll need to understand the topics and coverage related to the exams you must pass to obtain that credential. Make sure that you locate the exam objectives and use them as you study and practice for the real thing. Make sure that the exam you're tackling isn't about to be retired and that you're working on a certification that isn't about to retire.

➤ *Current news and events*—Things change all the time in the IT industry; that's why certification programs are always in flux. Be sure to check the sponsor's news stories, program updates, and other reporting on recent changes, additions, and retirements in the certification area. This kind of information will help you create a plan of attack for any certification and can help you decide when your plans must change.

➤ *Exam status and retirements*—Because exams are so important to certification, they usually get their own news area where beta exams are announced, changes to current exams are documented, and retirements for aging exams are disclosed. As you form your certification strategy, be sure to locate and consider this information as you develop your plan of attack. Note also that reading beta exam announcements is a great way to get a preview of coming certification attractions, even if you have no intention of ever taking a beta exam!

➤ *Pointers to resources*—Certification sponsors often provide pointers to all kinds of resources related to their certification programs on their Web sites. Such resources can include things such as detailed discussions of prerequisites for certifications, recommended reading lists to prepare for certifications or individual exams, free sample practice exams, white papers and training materials, and much more. Although you can't find all these things on too many certification Web sites, all of them are potentially valuable. Thus, if you find only some, your efforts will still be rewarded.

➤ *Partnerships for training, exams, publications*—Certifications spawn partnerships like salmon on a run up their home stretch of river. Investigating such partnerships on the sponsor's Web site is a great way to find out about training courses in the classroom, online, or on CD (CD-based training may sometimes be called CBT, or computer-based training). It's also a great way to find out who the best practice test vendors might be and where to get such exams.

Also, many certification programs spawn official presses (such as Microsoft Press, Novell Press, Cisco Press, and so on). Sponsors are always glad to let you know about such programs because they usually get a cut of the proceeds when you buy their books. Particularly for less popular certification programs, such relationships can be a real boon because they help to ensure that documentation on the program, exams, and training materials will be more widely available.

While you're investigating these partnerships, don't forget to visit the partner Web sites. In many cases, you'll discover that these vendors offer Web site links, newsletters, or mailing lists where you can take advantage of some of the community spirit and support I mentioned earlier in this chapter.

➤ *Taking exams*—Because so many certification sponsors use third-party companies such as Prometric or Virtual University Enterprises (VUE) to administer their exams, you'll want to check the sponsor's Web site to figure out where to go to sign up for the exams. This will probably take you to the third-party Web site at **www.2test.com** (Prometric) or **www.vue.com** (VUE) where you can get the straight scoop on how to sign up for exams, how to pay for them, how to locate a testing center, and when you can take whatever specific exam for which you have prepared.

Appendix
Job Prospecting for the
Newly Certified

In this appendix, I provide information about hiring likelihood related to various certification programs. Much of this information was elicited from technical recruiters whom I interviewed for a magazine story on the value of certification to recruiters. I also outline their rankings of certification programs (and the certifications they contain). I also address some of the most common questions I get from readers having to do with the relative value of experience versus certification and that of a college education versus a technical certification.

How Technical Recruiters See the World

Before I share the results of my research with technical recruiters, I feel compelled to explain what technical recruiters really do (in my humble opinion) and when they can be most helpful to job candidates. I mean this exposition to be completely straightforward and honest, so I must apologize in advance if I do the able and excellent technical recruiters in this world any disservice by the observations I've made on their roles in bringing employers together with potential employees.

To begin, it's important to understand that technical recruiters are a lot like real estate agents. That is, the amount of money they earn depends directly on the size of the "sale" they make. For technical recruiters, the bigger the salary of a person they place with a company, the bigger their payment for making that placement. In most cases, technical recruiters receive a percentage of the placed person's annual salary, which may be as low as 15 to 20 percent or as high as 50 percent. For someone earning $100,000 a year, that's a lot of money, either way. For someone earning $40,000 a year, it's the difference between $6,000 to $8,000 and $20,000. From this story, it's important to draw some morals. Here's a list of points to ponder:

➤ *Moral Number 1*—Technical recruiters tend to concentrate on more senior-level positions, typically at and over the $50,000 per year level.

➤ *Moral Number 2*—Technical recruiters do not tend to place many entry-level people, nor do they often get called to fill entry-level positions. In this climate of extremely low unemployment, this is changing somewhat, but it's still a good rule to keep in mind.

➤ *Moral Number 3*—Expensive, senior talent is worth more to an organization than inexpensive, junior talent. Many companies that think nothing of paying big bucks to fill a key position will balk at spending under $10,000 to fill an entry- or junior-level position.

By far, the readers who've asked me whether they should consult a technical recruiter are entering the IT marketplace for the first time or at a fairly junior level. Each and every time they ask, I have to gently explain the economics of technical recruiting and why it's unlikely that a technical recruiter will be able to help them out.

That's not to say that there's no hope for those on the more junior side of the IT employment spectrum. Just because recruiters—who, like real estate agents, make money off sales (placements) and listings—make more money from more senior people doesn't mean that they're entirely unwilling to help. It just means that they're unlikely to have found you your current job. But it's okay (in fact, it's a good idea) to acquaint yourself with these professionals because both you and they know that the job you're looking for now is unlikely to be the job you keep for life. When you do cross the line between junior and senior positions, your acquaintances in technical recruiting circles may become your new best friends.

Beyond technical recruiters, don't overlook the importance of job posting sites and more automated ways to interact with placement professionals. That's why sites such as **www.dice.com**, **www.computerwork.com**, and **www.jobanimal.com** have a place in any reasonable job search. However, if you look closely at these sites, you'll see that even they favor intermediate- to senior-level positions simply because of the phobia against handling entry-level jobs that appears pervasive in the recruiting industry.

It's wise to include these sites as targets for your résumés, but it's not smart to count on any one of them to come through with a job, particularly if you're looking for an entry-level position. Job placement Web sites do have some other advantages, however—they are often great sources for career advice, résumé-writing clinics, job-hunting tips, and other bits of related wisdom. Even if they don't find you a job, they can still be useful sites to visit!

Enough about this side of the recruiting industry. Let's talk next about what I learned from them regarding their attitudes toward certification and how they rank certifications.

How Technical Recruiters See Certifications

When asked about certifications, technical recruiters inevitably say that they're nice to have but that they don't tell the whole story about any candidate. In their follow-ups to this apparently inevitable remark, over 80 percent of the recruiters I talked to went on to make the same two remarks:

➤ Given a choice between a certification and job experience, recruiters believe that employers will choose experience every time.

➤ More experience is clearly better than more certifications.

When pushed to the limit, recruiters will concede that when two or more candidates have basically the same experience and educational background, employers will tend to prefer those individuals who are certified. However, as soon as you create scenarios for them to ponder where certification is weighed against experience, they'll go straight for the experience and leave the certifications behind.

Should you, a devoted chaser of IT certifications, be worried about this? I don't think so, simply because you yourself should recognize that when two candidates present themselves, and one has a certification and less experience and the other has no certification but significantly more experience, employers will opt for the experienced candidate as long as that experience is germane to the tasks at hand. It's always been that way, in every field, inside and outside IT. It's really no big deal.

Does this mean that you should forgo certification and get some experience instead? Not necessarily, especially if you want to learn the tools, technologies, concepts, and skills that certification can teach you. Don't forget that although obtaining a certification can't substitute for experience, it does involve learning, demonstrates a certain amount of motivation and follow-through, and shows that you're serious enough about the subject matter to get an official stamp of approval.

Does the relatively greater value of experience mean that certification has no value at all? Absolutely not, especially if you want to work in an environment where the certification sponsor's products, tools, or technologies are in everyday use. Certification is no magic bullet, and it's certainly no guarantee of employment in most cases (although there are some exceptions, as you'll see later in this section), but it does make a difference, especially when you have it and someone else (with similar experience or lack thereof) does not!

When faced with a list of nine popular certification programs, recruiters from 11 recruiting firms rated them in a predictable order, as follows:

1. Cisco

2. Oracle

3. Sun Java

4. Red Hat Linux

5. LPI Linux

6. Sair Linux

7. Microsoft

8. Novell

9. CompTIA

Many recruiters did not know the difference between Linux certifications but tended to rank them as a category above Microsoft, Novell, and CompTIA. I had to eliminate Prosoft CIW from the list because a large majority of recruiters (77 percent) had never heard of this program.

Before you're tempted to make much of these rankings and reorient your certification priorities, remember Moral Number 1. These rankings clearly reflect which positions make the most money and which are therefore most likely to involve the services of technical recruiters.

In fact, I performed the same exercise with a list of technical certifications that included CCIE, MCSE, MCNE, several Oracle certifications, all Sun Java certifications, the RHCE, and the CompTIA certifications, and the results stacked up in exactly the same order by earnings potential of the positions involved. If earnings makes the difference to you, take heed of these results. However, if the number of available positions, degree of experience required, and effort involved in obtaining the certification make a difference, don't let these rankings sway your inclinations too much.

Education, Experience, and Certification

In this final section of this appendix, I address the two questions I'm asked most frequently by readers in one form or another (although I can't claim to represent these questions exactly for all readers, as stated, they do capture the most pressing concerns in the reader base):

1. Is an IT certification worth more than a college degree to employers?

2. What's more important to employers: an IT certification or experience working with the products?

Let me tackle these questions in order and share the results of some recent research with you as well as my opinions on these subjects. Before I respond to these questions, I feel compelled to state some of my own biases on these topics so that you'll be able to understand the context in which my answers appear:

➤ I think that IT certifications represent a great way to show interest and initiative in technical subject areas.

➤ I think that ongoing education and study is part of working in the IT profession.

➤ I think that there's a big difference between a general education, such as getting a college degree, and obtaining an IT certification.

➤ Many certifications do not test for real-world skills and abilities, so the value of certification versus experience is often one-sided in favor of experience.

All this said, let me now go on to address these two questions:

1. Is an IT certification worth more than a college degree to employers? (The most common variant of this question is, Should I get my degree or get an IT certification instead?)

To a very small extent, the answer to this question is "That depends on the certification." For extremely high-level and demanding certifications, such as Cisco's CCIE or the high-end consulting certifications from companies such as SAP, JD Edwards, or Software AG, the learning and preparation effort required to get the certification is pretty comparable to the learning and effort required to get a college degree. That said, many such certifications do expire with time; once obtained, a college degree may go out of date, but the college or university will not take it away from you and tell you to come back to earn another one!

For just about any other kind of IT certification, I believe that a college degree (particularly a bachelor's or a more advanced degree) is worth more to employers than an IT certification. My research in talking to a group of more than 100 IT employers across a broad spectrum of industries tells me that they think so, too. Here again, this doesn't mean that certification has no value; it just puts its relative value against a college degree in perspective for most IT certifications (parents everywhere who've paid for college can now heave a huge sigh of relief).

If you find yourself asking this question and are forced to choose between one or the other, I recommend that you choose the degree (but you could always take it in an IT-related subject to better prepare yourself for your chosen field of effort). Another explanation for the importance of a degree, distilled from my interviews with employers, is that obtaining a degree is as much about demonstrating general learning skills and developing good study habits as it is about mastering any particular subject matter. Especially in technical fields, most experts and educators agree that personal knowledge bases must be refreshed every 5 to 10 years. Employers look at college degrees and related honors or academic achievements as evidence that an individual can learn new material as needed as well as evidence of knowledge of whatever subject matter they've studied.

However, even with a degree in computer science or MIS, you may still want to pursue IT certification also. That's why an increasing number of colleges and universities are offering—and in some cases requiring—IT certifications from Novell, Microsoft, Cisco, and so on to the students in such programs. That's because a college degree only demonstrates general familiarity with some subject matter or field of study, whereas most IT certifications are strongly focused in some particular field of study or on some particular vendor's products and technologies. In the final analysis, both a college degree and one or more technical certifications in areas relevant to job activities and performance create the most desirable combination for most employers.

2. What's more important to employers: an IT certification or experience working with the products? (One telltale variant of this question comes out as, "I've got a certification but no experience, and I can't find a job. What should I do?" I'll answer this question along with my discussion of the experience versus certification issue next.)

Although this may come as a shock to many individuals who regard certifications as the key to improved employment and a bigger paycheck, every one of the more than 100 employers I talked to, and every one of the 18 or so technical recruiting firms that I interviewed, responded to this question by saying, "We always prefer relevant experience to technical certification." However, before you give up hope and decide not to pursue the IT certification you've been considering, let me quickly add some of the important ways that certification does make a difference to both employers and recruiters:

➤ Both audiences (employers and recruiters) that I interviewed agreed that certification matters most for entry-level positions and for junior-level positions in general. The attitude here might be summarized as follows: "If I have to choose between two candidates who have similar backgrounds or degrees, and one is certified while the other is not, I will tend to choose the certified individual."

➤ For more senior-level positions, experience is much more important to these audiences than is certification. Most of the people I interviewed said that for positions paying more than $75,000 a year, they are far more interested in a person's track record and their level of direct, hands-on experience and ability in dealing with the tools and technologies they must manage than they are in the certifications that such an individual may or may not hold.

All this said, there is a significant minority (about 25 percent) of such organizations where they require their IT staff, both junior and senior, to obtain and maintain current technical certifications, not just to enter but also to stay in their jobs. The thinking here appears to be that a current technical certification, on the order of an

MCSE, CNE, or CCNP, is evidence that these individuals are current in their fields of expertise and up-to-date on new and emerging technologies.

Finally, for those who've obtained a technical certification and still can't get a job, let me explain that "any experience is good experience." If you look around your community, you'll quickly learn that many churches, charities, school systems, and not-for-profit organizations welcome volunteers, even for IT-related positions and activities. You can probably find one of these organizations in your area that would welcome any kind of help they can get with their IT operations. This is a great way not only to get some valuable experience—and a letter of recommendation to go with it—but also to do some good for your community while improving your employment opportunities at the same time. It's great to help others while at the same time helping yourself!

Another option to consider is an internship at a company as opposed to a salaried position. Internships provide a way for companies and prospective employees to try each other out and for employees to get a taste for what the work is like— albeit at a significantly lower rate of pay than the real thing. When you see that paycheck, just repeat the experience mantra "any experience is good experience."

I hope I've addressed your most common concerns and issues about finding a job with your certification. If not, please feel free to email me at **ed.tittel@examcram.com** with your comments, criticisms, or questions. Just don't be surprised if you give me some ideas that show up in the next edition of this book!

Note: The material in the final section of this appendix originally appeared in a modified form as a column for the May 13, 2000, issue of Sunbelt Software's W2KNews email newsletter. Reproduced by permission.

Glossary

. . . .

A+

The name given to the exam created by the Computing Technology Industry Association (CompTIA) that is designed to certify individuals who are competent PC technicians and whose knowledge covers hardware and software products, principles, and technologies from many vendors.

AATP (Authorized Academic Training Program)

A Microsoft term referring to an institution of higher learning (usually a community college, four-year college, or university) that offers the official Microsoft training curriculum under a special license to academic institutions. This program has been discontinued, but you may still see occasional mention of this acronym.

Active Server Page

An HTML page containing VBScript or JScript that displays dynamic Web page content; Microsoft's alternative to JavaServer Pages.

ActiveX

A Microsoft Windows-only technology, based on OLE (Object Linking and Embedding) technology, that competes with Java as the language of choice for Web content.

adaptive tests

Tests that recognize when a test taker misses a question and pose simpler questions on the same topic, then ask gradually more difficult questions on that topic until the test taker's expertise (or lack thereof) in the category is established.

AFSMI (Association for Services Managers International)

A worldwide professional organization devoted to the areas of technical support and IT services management that cooperated with the Computing Technology Industry Association (CompTIA) to help develop its certification tests (that arrangement has since been dissolved). For more information, visit the AFSMI Web site at **www.afsmi.org** or contact the company at 1-941-275-7887. Also known as AFSM International.

AOL (America Online)

The world's largest Internet Service Provider.

AppleTalk

Apple Computer's local area network architecture for Macintosh computer systems.

ATM (Asynchronous Transfer Mode)

A networking architecture based on B-ISDN (Broadband Integrated Services Digital Network) in which data is transferred in small, fixed-size packets at rates up to 622Mbps.

ATS (Associate Technology Specialist)

The Chauncey Group's credential for entry- to intermediate-level IT professionals. ATS covers a range of skills and requires candidates to pass one core exam along with two exams in one of eight career clusters.

awk

An input-processing and pattern-matching language that scans one or more input files for lines that match any of a set of patterns specified in a set of directives. All input files are read in whatever order is stipulated; if no input filenames are provided, awk reads data from the standard input as defined for the local runtime environment.

BGP (Border Gateway Protocol)

A modern exterior routing protocol for TCP/IP networks that provides a way for routers at the edges of their respective routing domains to exchange messages and information.

BGP is widely used on the Internet and is described in RFCs 1266 and 1269, among others.

BorderManager

A software application that provides a secure connection to the Internet from Novell NetWare networks.

C++

A widely used object-oriented programming language created by Bjarne Stroustrup, based on C.

cable modem

A device that uses cable television lines to send and receive Internet data.

capacity planning

In the IT/business arena, a process in which a company's computer resources are evaluated against the company's goals, from which a plan is developed to meet IT and business requirements against budgets and timing constraints.

CCDA (Cisco Certified Design Associate)

Cisco's entry-level design credential, which requires individuals to be able to design and deploy simple routed and switched networks as well as configure, operate, and maintain them. To obtain this certification, applicants must pass a single exam.

CCDP (Cisco Certified Design Professional)

Cisco's middle-tier design credential, which requires individuals to be able to design and deploy complex routed LANs and WANs, plus switched LANs and LANE environments. Likewise, individuals must be able to configure, operate, and maintain such networks and connections. To obtain this certification, applicants must first obtain Cisco Certified Network Associate (CCNA) certification for all tracks, a Cisco Certified Design Associate (CCDA) certification for the Routing and Switching track, and a Cisco Certified Network Professional (CCNP) certification for the WAN Switching track, and then pass either two or four exams, depending on which exam track they elect.

CCIE (Cisco Certified Internetwork Expert)

The top-tier operational Cisco certification, aimed at individuals who have advanced technical skills and knowledge and who know how to configure networks for optimum performance. They must also understand how to maintain complex, far-flung, multivendor networks. Applicants must pass two exams for this certification: a written exam and a laboratory evaluation.

CCNA (Cisco Certified Network Associate)

Cisco's entry-level operational certification, aimed at individuals who must manage simple routed LANs or WANs, small ISPs, or smaller switched LAN or LANE environments. Applicants must pass one exam to obtain this certification.

CCNP (Cisco Certified Network Professional)

Cisco's middle-tier operational certification, aimed at individuals who must install, configure, operate, and

troubleshoot complex routed LANs, routed WANs, switched LAN networks, or Dial Access Services. Applicants must first obtain Cisco Certified Network Associate (CCNA) certification and then take either two or four additional exams, depending on which test option they elect.

CDE (Certified Directory Engineer)

A Novell certification that identifies exceptionally qualified professionals with directory knowledge for the IT sector. Applicants must hold a primary IT certification—for example, CNE, CCNP, CCIE, Compaq ASE, or MCSE—and be able to use Novell Directory Services (NDS) and associate directory technologies in the management of operating systems, applications, enterprise-level installations, and directory solutions used in business environments. This certification requires passing two written core exams and a laboratory exam.

CDIA (Certified Document Imaging Architech)

CompTIA certification. Applicants must demonstrate skill in planning, defining, and specifying every feature of document imaging systems.

certification ladder

The progression from entry-level to senior-level certifications.

Certified Java Architect

Sun's elite Java Designer credential for individuals who demonstrate their expertise in planning, designing, deploying, and maintaining complex distributed Java applications.

Applicants must demonstrate an understanding of systems design in both business and technical environments. There is a multiple-choice and an essay exam for this certification, along with a programming assignment.

Certified Java Developer

A Java certification in which individuals must pass an essay exam in addition to creating a full-blown Java application based on specifications from Sun.

Certified Java Programmer

A Java certification in which individuals must take a written test aimed at a specific Java Development Kit (JDK).

Chauncey

The testing and certification organization, a subsidiary of the Educational Testing Service (ETS), that offers occupational and educational certification programs, including CTT (Certified Technical Trainer) and ATS (Associate Technology Specialist).

Cisco

The market leader in routing and swithcing hardware. Cisco certifcation is among the most difficult of all vendor-based certifications.

CIW (Certified Internet Webmaster)

The credential offered by Prosofttraining.com that includes an entry-level CIW Professional certification in addition to three different certifications.

CNA (Certified Novell Administrator)

Novell's entry-level certification. Obtaining a CNA requires passing

any one of five tests: basic administration for three versions of NetWare (5, 4.11/intraNetWare, or 3.12) or for two versions of GroupWise (5 or 4).

CNE (Certified Novell Engineer)

The most sought-after Novell certification. CNEs specialize in a particular version of NetWare (presently 3.x, 4.x, or 5) and must pass five or six required tests (depending on the track) and one elective test to qualify.

CNI (Certified Novell Instructor)

Novell's instructor certification. CNIs must meet both an instructional requirement and training and examination requirements for whatever Novell courses they may wish to teach.

CompTIA (Computing Technology Industry Association)

An organization that includes most major PC hardware and software manufacturers. This organization offers several certifications: A+, Network+, i-Net+, and CDIA.

CPU (central processing unit)

The basic printed circuit board or chip that supplies fundamental computer functions; the "brain" of the computer.

CTEC (Certified Technical Education Center)

A location where you can take a Microsoft Official Curriculum course taught by Microsoft Certified Trainers.

CTT (Certified Technical Trainer)

Chauncey Group's trainer credential for which applicants must demonstrate strong teaching skills. The certification requires both a multiple-choice exam and a 20-minute videotape substantiating the candidate's teaching ability.

DBA (database administrator)

A generic term for the job description of those individuals who must create and maintain databases. Also makes up part of the name for Oracle's Certified Database Administrator (DBA) track.

DBO (database operator)

Oracle's entry-level Oracle8 certification, for which students must pass only a single exam.

DHCP (Dynamic Host Configuration Protocol)

A network service that provides for the automatic assignment of IP (Internet Protocol) addresses to workstations logging on to a TCP/IP network and the setting of subnet masks.

DMA (direct memory access)

A method of transferring data between the memory components of devices (for example, hard drive to controller to RAM) while bypassing the CPU.

DNS (Domain Name System)

A massively distributed name database technology based on TCP/IP that's used across the global Internet to resolve domain names (such as **www.microsoft.com**) into the numeric IP addresses (such as 207.46.130.45) which is used to direct transmissions between senders and receivers on the Internet.

E1/E3

The European cousins of T1/T3 lines; EX lines were devised by the ITU-T (Telecommunication Standardization Sector of the International Telecommunications Union). An E1 line supports signals at 2.048Mbps (32 channels at 64Kbps). An E3 line is the equivalent of 16 CEPT (Conference of European Postal and Telecommunications Administrations) E1 data channels, with a maximum bandwidth of 34.368Mbps.

EGP (Exterior Gateway Protocol)

An exterior routing protocol for TCP/IP networks that provides a way for routers at the edges of their respective routing domains to exchange messages and information. EGP is now outmoded and has been replaced by the Border Gateway Protocol (BGP). EGP is described in RFC 1093.

Enterprise Resource Planning (ERP)

A special-purpose software environment, such as those available from SAP, Baan, JD Edwards, and other similar companies, that permits organizations to use financial, human resources, and other data resources to analyze current organization trends and behavior and to plan future business or strategic activities.

FoxPro

Also called Microsoft Visual FoxPro, an Xbase development system for building Windows database applications; one of the three programming languages accepted as part of the Microsoft MCSD developer certification.

frame relay

A digital network packet-switching protocol that most commonly is used over T1 and T3 lines.

GNU

GNU stands for "GNU is Not Unix." Broadly speaking, GNU represents an important body of "copyleft" (programmers can freely use and modify the code as long as they make it available to the public under the same licensing condition) code and utilities that many versions of Unix, including Linux, treat as part of the overall operating environment.

HTTP (Hypertext Transfer Protocol)

The protocol or set of rules used for Web-based communications (that is, to connect to Web servers and transfer HTML pages).

IBM (International Business Machines Corporation)

The largest computer company in the world, IBM offers a broad range of certification programs, including those from its subsidiaries, such as Lotus Development Corporation and Tivoli Systems, Inc.

IEAK (Internet Explorer Administration Kit)

A set of software tools for customizing and distributing Internet Explorer in a networked environment.

ILT (Instructor-Led Training)

Oracle Education's comprehensive set of classroom courses for exam preparation and general training. Ultimately, the Oracle exams are derived from classroom experience

with students, and Oracle indicates that ILT classes will always cover all the material necessary to take and pass the related test.

i-Net+

A vendor-neutral credential for Internet and Web professionals offered by CompTIA.

internetwork

A network made up of multiple physical networks (local and wide area networks).

IPX/SPX (Internet Packet Exchange/ Sequenced Packet Exchange)

An important Novell NetWare network protocol. IPX is in layer 3 of the OSI (Open System Interconnection) Model; SPX is in layer 4.

IRQ (interrupt request)

One of 16 specific signal lines in a PC that exist between a computer's CPU and bus slots. An IRQ signals the CPU when a peripheral event process has started or stopped.

ISDN (Integrated Services Digital Network)

A digital communication standard for sending data, voice, and video at a maximum bandwidth of 128Kbps. PRI ISDN has voice and data transfer rates of up to 1.544Mbps.

ISP (Internet Service Provider)

A business that gives you access to the Internet, usually for a monthly fee.

Java

A compact, powerful, platform-independent, object-oriented programming language developed at Sun

Microsystems, widely used for Web-based and distributed applications.

JavaServer Pages
An HTML page containing Java code that works with Java servlets to display dynamic Web page content.

JDK (Java Development Kit)
Sun's software tool set for creating Java applications. Current versions are 1.1 and 2.

Kerberos v5
A networked user authentication system developed at the Massachusetts Institute of Technology as part of Project Athena; now used as the authentication mechanism on many Unix and Windows 2000 networks, among others.

laboratory evaluation
The second test for the Cisco Certified Internetwork Expert (CCIE) certification. Applicants are subjected to a variety of simulated situations to test their hands-on abilities and diagnostic skills. They must implement a network or a communications environment from scratch, reconfigure existing environments, and troubleshoot multiple environments that have been deliberately misconnected, misconfigured, or otherwise messed with.

LCA (Linux Certified Administrator)
Officially, the Sair Linux and GNU Certified Administrator. An entry-level certification that identifies individuals who are Linux power users and can provide assistance as help desk staff members for Linux topics or as entry-level Linux administrators.

LCE (Linux Certified Engineer)
Officially, the Sair Linux and GNU Certified Engineer. An intermediate-level certification that identifies individuals who can perform everyday Linux administrator duties and can design, install, configure, maintain, and troubleshoot Linux sytems.

LCP (Linux Certified Professional)
Any person who passes the Sair Linux Install and Configuration test or the System Administration test at any of the three certification levels attains LCP status. It's the basic entry-level Sair Linux and GNU certification, much like the MCP is for Microsoft.

Linux
A free, open-source operating system created by computer science student Linux Torvalds in 1993. Linux is quickly becoming the operating system of choice by ISPs.

long-haul communications provider
A communications company whose business involves transporting digital voice and data traffic over long distances. Such communications can involve land lines or terrestrial communications or may require broadcast to satellites for relay around the world.

LPIC (Linux Professional Institute Certification) Level 1
The Linux Professional Institute's entry-level Linux operator certification. Certificants must have knowledge of

the installation, configuration, networking, maintenance, and troubleshooting of workstations or servers running Linux. Two exams are required.

LPIC (Linux Professional Institute Certification) Level 2

The Linux Professional Institute's intermediate-level Linux certification. Individuals must demonstrate a level of knowledge and competency that's roughly equivalent to the RHCE. Two exams are required but will not be available until the second half of 2000.

LPIC (Linux Professional Institute Certification) Level 3

The Linux Professional Institute's advanced-level Linux certification. Individuals must demonstrate a deep and thorough knowledge of the Linux kernel and one or more subsystems and meet IT management requirements. This certification is still under development.

MacOS

Originally referring to Apple's System 7 operating system, MacOS now commonly refers to all versions of Apple's operating systems.

MBT (Media-Based Training)

Oracle's term for self-paced, computer-based training materials. There's a substantial overlap between MBTs available from Oracle and the various certification exams, but sometimes it's necessary to complete two MBTs to adequately prepare for an examination.

MCDBA (Microsoft Certified Database Administrator)

An intermediate-level Microsoft certification that works for individuals pursuing either the MCSE or the MCSD tracks, this certification requires passing four or five tests, depending on the track. It aims to certify database professionals who work on Windows networks with SQL Server and database applications or services.

MCNE (Master CNE)

Novell's most elite certification, which designates recipients as certified specialists in one of seven areas of expertise. The requirements vary from specialty to specialty but involve anywhere from four to six tests beyond CNE certification.

MCP (Microsoft Certified Professional)

A Microsoft certification that certifies anyone who's qualified for any Microsoft certification credential. It encompasses more than 60 exams at present. Passing almost any exam (except Exam 70-058: Networking Essentials or any of the Office-related exams) qualifies an individual as an MCP. This is a stepping-stone to the much-vaunted Microsoft Certified Systems Engineer (MCSE) credential, which requires passing six or seven tests.

MCP+I (MCP + Internet)

A Microsoft certification that certifies Microsoft Certified Professionals (MCPs) who prove their Internet expertise and who qualify to plan security, installation, and configuration of server products; implement server extensions; and manage server resources. Three core exams are required to pass.

MCP+SB (MCP + Site Building)

A Microsoft certification that certifies individuals who can design, build, and maintain corporate Web sites. It requires that individuals first become Microsoft Certified Professionals (MCPs), then pass any two from a pool of three tests.

MCSD (Microsoft Certified Solution Developer)

A Microsoft certification aimed at developers rather than systems or network managers. Candidates for this certification prove their abilities to build Web-based, distributed, or e-commerce applications. Knowledge of solution architectures, application development strategies and techniques, and development tools is required of all candidates, who must pass three core exams and one elective exam to qualify.

MCSE (Microsoft Certified Systems Engineer)

A Microsoft certification that certifies individuals who prove their expertise with desktop and server operating systems, networking components, and Microsoft BackOffice products. To qualify, candidates must pass six or seven exams—four or five core exams and two electives.

MCSE+I (MCSE + Internet)

A Microsoft certification that certifies individuals who prove their expertise in using Microsoft products and technologies in Internet or intranet environments. Candidates must first become Microsoft Certified Systems Engineers (MCSEs), then pass three Internet core exams and two Internet-specific electives.

MCT (Microsoft Certified Trainer)

A Microsoft certification that identifies individuals who are qualified to teach elements of the Microsoft Official Curriculum (MOC). Individuals obtain MCT credentials on a topic-by-topic basis by passing the related MCP exam and meeting classroom teaching skills requirements. MCTs must also maintain current certification as an MCSE to qualify to teach Microsoft courses.

Microsoft

Currently the market leader in operating system technology and productivity applications. Microsoft offers the most varied selection of all vendor-based certifications.

Microsoft exam IDs

The numbers assigned to specific Microsoft certification tests. For example, the exam ID for the TCP/IP test is 70-059.

MLCE (Master LCE)

Officially, the Master Sair Linux and GNU Certified Engineer. This is the highest level of certification in this program. Certificants can function as senior Linux administrators and specialists and can handle complex design, installation, automation, configurations, maintenance, and troubleshooting of Linux.

MOC (Microsoft Official Curriculum)

Elements of the collection of official courseware developed by Microsoft for use in-house and at Microsoft-authorized training facilities, such as CTECs and AATPs.

MOUS (Microsoft Office User Specialist)

The certification is at the bottom of the Microsoft certification hierarchy. This program recognizes three levels of certification: a Proficient (or Core) Specialist for Word and Excel, Expert Specialist, and Master for those who are experts in all Office components.

needs analysis

In the IT arena, a review of a company's computing and networking needs from which budgets, procurement, deployment schedules, and long-range IT goals are determined. *See also* **capacity planning**, a key element of needs analysis.

NetBEUI (NetBIOS Extended User Interface)

A network protocols suite developed to transport NetBIOS (Network Basic Input/Output System) information over a network.

NetBIOS (Network Basic Input/Output System)

A DOS and Windows network interface that is required for communications over a NetWare network running NetBEUI, TCP/IP, or IPX/SPX systems.

Netscape

A company acquired by America Online in 1998 that provides the popular Web browser Netscape Navigator.

NetWare

A popular network operating system developed by Novell. The versions available are 3.x, 4.x, and 5.

network administrator

The individual responsible for the maintenance of a company's network.

Network+

An exam from the CompTIA that aims to provide vendor-neutral credentials for network technicians (who seldom work in single-vendor environments, in any case).

NIC (network interface card)

An adapter board that plugs into a computer's motherboard to which the network cabling is attached, and that allows the computer to communicate on the network.

Novell

The networking software giant that offers some of the most respected technical certifications available.

object-oriented design

The process of creating an application or system based on objects (program modules) from a model.

OCP (Oracle Certified Professional)

A catch-all term that identifies anyone who obtains an Oracle certification, either as a database administrator (DBA) or as an Oracle application developer.

Office User Specialist

See **MOUS (Microsoft Office User Specialist)**.

OLA (Oracle Learning Architecture)

Oracle's term for its Web-based training materials. Although these are largely self-paced and entirely computer based, OLA training also includes the opportunity to interact with an instructor via email or online chat facilities. Thus, it strikes a balance between the ILT (Instructor-Led Training) and MBT (Media-Based Training) approaches.

Oracle

The leading relational database vendor in today's marketplace. Oracle's database products are used in many corporations and organizations around the world.

Oracle Certified Application Developer track

An Oracle certification that focuses on preparing database professionals to use Oracle's Developer/2000 Releases 1 and 2 tools and technologies to build state-of-the-art, database-driven applications. It requires you to pass five tests.

Oracle Certified Database Administrator track

One of the tracks for Oracle Certified Professionals (OCPs). Obtaining this credential requires passing four or five tests. *See also* **DBA**.

Oracle Certified Financial Applications Consultant

An IT professional credential for applicants who demonstrate ability in installing, maintaining, and configuring financial applications in an Oracle environment. Applicants must pass three exams: two core exams and one elective exam that covers either Order Procurement or Fulfillment.

Oracle Certified Java Developer

An Oracle certification that recognizes those Web developers who master using Oracle8i to create e-commerce, information delivery, and other Internet-related applications. There are three levels of certification that require up to five exams, including performance-based and essay exams, depending on which level you decide to pursue.

Oracle8 Certified Database Operator track

One of the tracks for Oracle Certified Professionals (OCPs). Obtaining this credential requires passing a single test. *See also* **DBO**.

OSPF (Open Shortest Path First)

An interior routing protocol based on a spanning tree routing algorithm for TCP/IP protocols developed by Dr. Radia Perlman and described in RFCs 1246 and 2329, among others.

Perl (Practical Extraction and Reporting Language)

A programming language developed by Larry Wall. Perl may either be interpreted at runtime or compiled into binary executables and is highly regarded for its powerful string-handling and pattern-matching facilities. Perl is widely used for CGI programming and other Web-related applications.

PKI (Public Key Infrastructure)

A set of protocols for exchanging information about digital certificates.

PKI defines a mechanism whereby two parties can turn to a trusted third party, called a certificate authority, to obtain proof of each other's identities. PKI is described in RFC 2510, among others.

POTS (plain old telephone service)

The ordinary analog telephone system that most homes use.

program tests

Tests that use traditional multiple-choice questions, graphical exhibits, and simulations. They follow a regular, predictable sequence of questions drawn at random by category from a database of potential questions. Everyone sees the same number of questions and gets an equal amount of time to finish.

Prosoft

A moniker for Prosofttraining.com, a company that offers the CIW (Certified Internet WebMaster) certification, among other vendor-neutral certifications and IT training opportunities.

Prosoft Certified Linux Administrator

The credential conferred on an individual who completes the requirements for basic Linux knowledge and Linux system and network administration. This is a vendor-neutral Linux certification.

Python

An interpreted, interactive, object-oriented programming language that combines an understandable and readable syntax with powerful built-in commands and operators.

RAM (random access memory)

A group of memory chips that comprise a computer's main workspace. Each byte of memory may be accessed "randomly" by its address rather than sequentially.

RFC (Request For Comments)

A document that describes standards for a publicly available technology; an official Internet Engineering Task Force (IETF) specifications document.

RHCE (Red Hat Certified Engineer)

Linux credential for experienced systems administrators who demonstrate their abilities in installing, configuring, and maintaining Red Hat Linux and related services.

RHCX (Red Hat Certified Examiner)

Red Hat's train-the-trainer credential; required for individuals who wish to teach RHCE courses and administer the laboratory exam.

RIP (Routing Information Protocol)

A simple distance vector-based interior routing protocol used on TCP/IP networks. The current version of RIP in use on the Internet is RIPv2, which is described in RFC 1923.

Sair

A wholly owned subsidiary of the international training company Wave Technologies. Before it was acquired in early 2000, Sair was recognized as a leading source of Unix training, exams, and consulting.

sed (stream editor)

Originally implemented as a built-in Unix facility, sed is a powerful stream editor that includes various pattern-matching and substitution facilities, which explains why it's so often used to automate processing of text and command files.

SQL (Structured Query Language)

A specialized language for obtaining information from databases that allows multiple users on a network to access the same data.

Sun

A Sun Microsystems subsidiary that produces the JDKs (Java Development Kits) along with other resources for programming developers and IT professionals.

system administrator

Generally, anyone who is responsible for managing and maintaining a computer system, usually a network server of some type. *See also* **network administrator.**

T1/T3

Dedicated phone connections that support data transfer rates of 1.544Mbps and 45Mbps, respectively. The lines consist of multiple 64Kbps channels: a T1 delivers 24 64Kbps channels; a T3 line consists of 672 voice channels.

TCP/IP (Transmission Control Protocol/Internet Protocol)

An adaptable protocol developed by ARPA (Advanced Research Projects Agency) that connects dissimilar computers into complex collections of networks, such as the Internet.

TechNet

A monthly CD subscription available from Microsoft that includes all the

Windows NT BackOffice Resource Kits and their product documentation, the Microsoft Knowledge Base, white papers, training materials, service packs, interim release patches, supplemental driver software released since the last major version for most Microsoft programs and all Microsoft operating systems, and more. Available online at **www.microsoft.com/technet/**.

Unix

One of the earliest multitasking, multiuser operating systems that is still one of the most popular in use today. Most Web servers run on Unix.

Visual Basic

Microsoft's alternative to the Basic programming language, used mainly to create client front-ends for Windows applications.

VPN (virtual private network)

A wide area network connected by wires provided by a public communications carrier (for example, the Internet) that works like a private network.

WINS (Windows Internet Name Service)

A Microsoft Windows network service that resolves NetBIOS names to IP addresses.

WSH (Windows Scripting Host)

A built-in script interpreter found in Windows 98, Windows NT, and Windows 2000. It provides a moderately powerful and useful script processing facility for multiple Windows operating systems.

X Windows
A Unix and Linux GUI (graphical
user interface) developed at the
Massachusetts Institute of Technology.

X.25
The international CCITT (Consulta-
tive Committee for International
Telegraphy and Telephony) standard
for wide area packet-switched
communications.

Index

W